CHARMING SMALL HOTEL GUIDES

VENICE
LAKES &
MOUNTAINS

GW00545864

CHARMING SMALL HOTEL GUIDES

VENICE
LAKES &
MOUNTAINS

VENICE & THE LAGOON ISLANDS,
VENETO, LOMBARDIA, TRENTINO-ALTO
ADIGE AND FRIULI-VENEZIA GIULIA

EDITED BY

Fiona Duncan & Leonie Glass

DUNCAN PETERSEN

This new expanded 2006 edition conceived, designed and produced by
Duncan Petersen Publishing Ltd,
31 Ceylon Road, London W14 0PY
E-mail: dp@macunlimited.net
Website: http://www.charmingsmallhotels.co.uk

3rd edition

Editorial Director Andrew Duncan
Editors Fiona Duncan & Leonie Glass
Contributors Richard Collins, Emily Fitzroy, Diana Johnson,
Rose Monson, George Pownall, Michaela Scibilia, Nicky Swallow
Production Editor Helen Warren
Maps by Encompass Graphics
Photography by Rory Gill

Sales representation and distribution in the U.K. and Ireland by
Portfolio Books Limited
Unit 5, Perivale Industrial Park
Horsenden Lane South
Greenford, UB6 7RL
Tel: 0208 997 9000 Fax: 0208 997 9097
E-mail: sales@portfoliobooks.com

A CIP catalogue record for this book is available
from the British Library

ISBN 1-903301-42-4

DTP by Duncan Petersen Publishing Ltd
Printed by Printer Portugesa, Portugal

Contents

INTRODUCTION

IN THIS INTRODUCTORY SECTION

Welcome to this new edition of *Charming Small Hotel Guides Venice, Lakes and Mountains.* Recently, we introduced some big changes which have made the guide more popular than ever with our readers - see below.

Not only that, but this guide remains unique: the only English-language colour accommodation guide to Venice.

• *Every hotel has been given a colour photograph and a full page of its own.*

• *The maps have been upgraded.*

• *The layout has been changed in order to take you more quickly to essential information.*

• *The area covered has been enlarged to take in more of the lakes and mountains inland.*

• *A restaurants section.*

We believe that these are real improvements, rather than change for its own sake. In all other respects, the guide remains true to the values and qualities that make it unique (see opposite), and which have won it so many devoted readers. This is its fourth new edition (including the first edition) since it was first published in 1998. It has sold hundreds of thousands of copies in the U.K., U.S.A. and in five European languages.

WHY ARE WE UNIQUE?

This is the only independently-inspected (no hotel pays for an entry) English-language accommodation guide that:

- has colour photographs for every entry;

- concentrates on places that have real charm and character;

- is highly selective;

- is particularly fussy about size. Most hotels have fewer than 20 bedrooms; if there are more, the hotel must have the feel of a much smaller place. We have found that a genuinely warm welcome is much more likely to be found in a small hotel;

- gives proper emphasis to the description, and doesn't use irritating symbols;

- is produced by a small, non-bureaucratic company with a dedicated team of like-minded inspectors.

See also *'So what exactly do we look for?'*, page 8.

So what exactly do we look for? –
Our selection criteria

• A peaceful, attractive setting. Obviously, we make allowances for entries in urban areas.

• A building that is handsome, interesting or historic; or at least with real character.

• Adequate space, but on a human scale. We don't go for places that rely too much on grandeur, or with pretensions that could be intimidating.

• Good taste and imagination in the interior decoration. We reject standardized, chain hotel fixtures, fittings and decorations.

• Bedrooms that look like real bedrooms, not hotel rooms, individually decorated.

• Furnishings and other facilities that are comfortable and well maintained. We like to see interesting antique furniture that is there to be used, not simply revered.

• Proprietors and staff who are dedicated and thoughtful, offering a personal welcome, but who aren't intrusive or overly effusive. *The guest needs to feel like an individual.*

• Interesting food. In Venice, it's increasingly the norm for food to be above average. There are few entries in this guide where the food is not of a high standard.

• A sympathetic atmosphere; an absence of loud people showing off their money; or the 'corporate feel'.

Villa Abbazia, Follina

A FATTER GUIDE, BUT JUST AS SELECTIVE

In order to accommodate most entries with a whole-page description and colour photograph, we've had to print more pages. *But we have maintained our integrity by keeping the selection to around 200 entries.*

Over the years, the number of charming small hotels in Venice and the surrounding area has increased steadily – not dramatically. We don't believe that there are presently many more than about 200 truly charming small hotels in Venice, and that, if we included more, we would undermine what we're trying to do: produce a guide which is all about places that are more than just a bed for the night. Every time we consider a new hotel, we ask ourselves whether it has that extra special something, regardless of category and facilities, that makes it worth seeking out.

TYPES OF ACCOMMODATION IN THIS GUIDE

Despite its title, the guide does not confine itself to places called hotels or places that behave like hotels. On the contrary, we actively look for places that offer a home-from-home feel (see page 10). We include small- and medium-sized hotels; plenty of traditional Italian guesthouses (*pensioni*) – some offering just bed and breakfast, some offering food at other times of day, too; restaurants with rooms; *agriturismi*, which are usually bed-and-breakfasts on farms or working rural estates; and some self-catering apartments, in town and country houses, provided they offer something special.

NO FEAR OR FAVOUR

To us, taking a payment for appearing in a guide seems to defeat the object of producing a guide. If money has changed hands, you can't write the whole truth about a hotel, and the selection cannot be nearly so interesting. This self-evident truth seems to us to be proved at least in part by the fact that pay guides are so keen to present the illusion of independence: few admit on the cover that they take payments for an entry, only doing so in small print on the inside.

Not many people realize that on the shelves of bookshops there are many more hotel guides that accept payments for entries than there are independent guides. This guide is one of the few that do not accept any money for an entry.

Castell Rundegg, Merano

HOME FROM HOME

Perhaps the most beguiling characteristic of the best places to stay in this guide is the feeling they give of being in a private home – but without the everyday cares and chores of running one. To get this formula right requires a special sort of professionalism: the proprietor has to strike the balance between being relaxed and giving attentive service. Those who experience this 'feel' often turn their backs on all other forms of accommodation – however luxurious.

VENICE, LAKES AND MOUNTAINS FOR THE TRAVELLER

Venice hardly needs any introduction, famed as it is throughout the world as a city of incomparable beauty, romance and artistic wealth. Built on mudbanks which extend into the tidal waters of the Adriatic where East meets West, Venice was once a great maritime power ruled by its doges, and a place of plot, intrigue and decadence. A city of water and of light, with an atmosphere which is at once fascinating and disturbing, its fragile fabric of canals and palazzi, churches, alleyways and campi has somehow survived the threats of both flood and mass tourism, and remarkably little has changed throughout the centuries. Nowhere in Venice will you see an ugly sight; even the Macdonalds near the Rialto is just about bearable. At any time of the year you can escape the crowds of tourists who throng Piazza San Marco, the Rialto and the main thoroughfare between the two by simply slipping into the backstreets where there is always a church, a canal, a café to divert you; the best time to visit, however, is in spring and early summer or autumn, when the crowds are thinner and the weather can be lovely. There can often be long spells of warm weather and blue skies in March, while June can be wet and overcast.

Stretching inland from Venice in a great arc as far as the Austrian border to the north and the shores of Lake Garda to the west is the province of Veneto. While the landscape of the vast Veneto Plain which fans out behind Venice is largely industrialized and pancake flat (save for the green Euganean Hills and Berici Mountains), it is full of interest. The great cities of Padua, Treviso, Vicenza and Verona are time-consuming enough, but then there are the villas of Palladio and other attractions such as the charming little towns of Asolo and Montagnana. To the west of Venice, the Plain edges into the province of Friuli-Venezia Giulia, curving round the coastline towards Trieste and the border with Slovenia and, to the north, reaching into the high Alps and the border with Austria.

The presence of the mountains gives this guide a rich flavour and makes the range of accommodation contained in it, from Venetian palazzo to Tyrolean chalet, wonderfully varied. The mainly mountainous province of Trentino-Alto Adige, which stretches north from Lake Garda, feels a million miles away from Venice. As the mountains rise towards the Austrian border, so the distinction between the two countries becomes blurred. Here in this northernmost region of Italy, also known as Southern Tyrol, you will find that the people are German-speaking (all the place names have both German and Italian translations) and that they share the same culture and traditions as their neighbours over the border. The hospitality is warm, the scenery is breathtakingly beautiful, often with the jagged peaks of the Dolomites serving as a dramatic backdrop. In winter you can ski and in summer you can walk. It would be hard to imagine a more delightful and varied holiday than to start in the Southern Tyrol, descend to the serene shores of Lake Garda (in this guide we include the western shore which falls into the province of Lombardia), then cut across the Veneto Plain taking in Verona, Vicenza, Padua, and finally reach the greatest glory of all, Venice itself. You will not lack for lovely places to stay along the way, and with this guide you can plan the perfect trip.

CHOOSING YOUR ROOM

In Venice, you can enormously enhance the quality of your accommodation by securing a good room. Many of the hotels in this guide have rooms which are similar in both price and quality, but others, whilst remaining the same in price, are much more varied in quality. You can quite easily find yourself paying the same rate for a dull box as for a light and airy space with a balcony overlooking a canal, and unless you specifically ask (and make your booking in plenty of time) you are not likely to secure one of the few good rooms. Hoteliers have told us of guests who, on their return visit, ask for the room they had before, not realizing that there are far better ones to be had at the same price. Where appropriate, therefore, we have taken pains to point out which are the rooms you should try for first; in a few cases, we have advised not choosing that hotel at all unless you can secure a particular room. We have not always mentioned room numbers, as these are prone to change.

HOTELS, VILLAS, LOCANDE, AGRITURISMO

The range of accommodation on offer in Venice and North-East Italy should be enough to satisfy all tastes and most pockets, with a variety of names almost as numerous as those describing types of pasta. 'Hotel' is common enough, but so is its Italian equivalent 'albergo'. 'Villa' can apply either to a town or country hotel and is used by proprietors with some latitude: occasionally one wonders why a nondescript town house or farmhouse should be called a villa while a more elegant building restricts itself to albergo. 'Palazzo' and 'pensione' generally refer to urban accommodation while 'agriturismo' means farmhouse bed-and-breakfast, or indeed, self-catering apartments. 'Residence', 'relais', 'locanda', 'castello' and 'fattoria' are also found.

The variety that one finds under these various names is extraordinary, from world-ranking luxury hotels to relatively simple guest houses.

TOURIST INFORMATION

The tourist information offices for each province are listed with the relevant maps on pages 15–31. Most cities and a few popular towns also have their own tourist offices offering information on local travel, museums, galleries and festivals.

We list on page 12 Italy's official public holidays when banks and shops are shut and levels of public transport reduced. In North-East Italy, like the rest of the country, each town has its own local holiday, usually the feast day of the patron saint, often celebrated with a fair or fireworks. Venice, of course, stages its annual pre-Lent Carnival and many other events unique to the city, most famous of which are the Biennale, the world's largest contemporary art exhibition which takes place from June to September in odd-numbered years, and the International Film Festival, held on the Lido in early September every year.

New Year's Day (Capodanno) Jan 1; Epiphany (Epifania) Jan 6; Good Friday (Venerdì Santo); Easter Sunday (Pasqua); Easter Monday (Pasquetta); Liberation Day (Liberazione) April 25; May Day (Festa del Lavoro) May 1; Assumption of the Virgin (Ferragosto) Aug 15; All Saints' Day (Ognissanti) Nov 1; Immaculate Conception (Immacolata Concezione) Dec 8; Christmas Day (Natale) Dec 25; St Stephen's Day (Santo Stefano) Dec 26.

FLIGHTS

The principal airport for the region is Venice Marco Polo, and there are also small airports at Treviso and Verona which receive limited flights from abroad. Car hire is available at all three.

PET LIKES

These are some of the things that stand out for us in many of the hotels in which we stayed. Maybe they will strike you too.

- Wonderful old buildings, sympathetically restored – palazzi in Venice, classical villas in the Veneto, castles in the foothills of the Alps, Tyrolean chalets in the mountains
- Hotels in superb positions with glorious views
- Murano glass chandeliers (pretty ones)
- Venetian marble floors (when strewn with rugs)
- Silk damask furnishing fabric (when not overdone)
- 'Buffet' breakfasts with fruit, cheese, cold meats and yogurts
- Spotlessly clean bedrooms and bathrooms – especially high quality in the mountain hotels
- Good quality linen and comfortable pillows

PET HATES

If Venetian hoteliers have a fault, it is that they are happy for their hotels to coast along rather than strive for perfection. This is for the simple reason that they have a captive audience, a constant influx of tourists who keep occupancy rates at a consistently high level. And prices are very high. Stay half an hour away from the city, and you will pay far less for a much larger room. So the hotels which really aim to please, despite their popularity, are the ones which get our highest praise.

- Murano glass chandeliers (hideous ones)
- Venetian marble floors (when coldly bare)
- Silk damask furnishing fabric (when overdone)
- 'Continental' breakfasts with inedible cardboard bread
- Hideous minibars
- Inadequate storage space
- Endless white-tiled bathrooms
- Too many bathrooms with shower only, no bathtub

READERS' REPORTS
To all the hundreds of readers who have written with comments on hotels, a sincere 'thank-you'. We attach great importance to your comments and absorb them into the text each year. Please keep writing: for further information see page 32.

CHECK THE PRICE FIRST
In this guide we have adopted the system of price bands, rather than giving actual prices as we did in previous editions. This is because prices were often subject to change after we went to press. The price bands refer to the approximate price of a standard double room (high season rates) with breakfast for two people. They are as follows:

under 100 Euros
100-150 Euros
150-220 Euros
220-280 Euros
280-350 Euros
over 350 Euros

To avoid unpleasant surprises, always check what is included in the price (for example, VAT and service, breakfast, afternoon tea) when making the booking.

HOW TO FIND AN ENTRY
In this guide, the entries are arranged in geographical groups. First, Venice is divided into its areas: San Marco, San Polo, Santa Croce, Castello, Dorsoduro, Cannaregio and the Lagoon Islands. Following this are entries from the area surrounding Venice, divided into Veneto, Lombardia, Friuli-Venezia Giulia and Trentino-Alto Adige.

Within each section the entries follow a set sequence:

Entries arranged alphabetically by city, town or nearest village. If several occur in or near one town, entries are arranged in alpha order by name of hotel.

To find a hotel in a particular area, use the maps following this introduction to locate the appropriate pages.

To locate a specific hotel, whose name you know, or a hotel in a place you know, use the indexes at the back, which list entries both by name and by nearest place name.

APARTMENTS IN VENICE

Venice is not only a hotel-city, but an apartment-city: many a Venetian makes his or her property earn its keep by dividing it into apartments. For the visitor, choosing an apartment rather than a hotel can be a happy and economical alternative: you'll feel (a little) like a local as you shop in the floating vegetable market near the Rialto Bridge.

For the widest choice, contact a rental agency such as **Venetian Apartments** (see below under Palazzetto San Lio); or try local resident Susan Schiavon, who runs **Apartments in Venice** (see below under Martinengo). She has 15 privately-owned apartments ranging from studios to three bedrooms and from £390 per week to £1,600 per week.

Below is small selection of some of our favourite apartments in the city and North-East Italy. They are available either through agencies or privately. Prices range very widely from around £400 a week to £2,000 a week for the flamboyant Venier apartment (see below).

In San Marco: **Palazzetto Pisani**, on the Grand Canal, has two apartments with maid and cook. Wonderful, faded grandeur. One room is large enough for 80 people. *Contessa Maria Pia Ferre (a Pisani descendant); tel/fax 041 5232550; e-mail info@palazzettopisani.com*

Palazzo del Giglio is a converted mansion with 19 smart flats. *Elena Fabiano; tel 041 2719111; e-mail hotelpalazzo@hotmail.com*

Martinengo is a charming book- and picture-filled apartment. The kitchen is delightfully homely and the principal bedroom (the apartment sleeps 5) is stylishly lined with old framed mirrors. *Susan Schiavon, Apartments in Venice; tel 0207 348 3800; website www.apartments-venice.com*

In Castello: the enigmatic, crumbly **Palazzetto San Lio** offers eight apartments with a genteel, slightly shabby feel – adding to the romance. *Venetian Apartments, 413 Parkway House, Sheen Lane, London SW14 8LS; tel 0208 878 1130; e-mail enquiries@venice-rentals.com*

Ca' Salvioni is a conversion of the *piano nobile* of a *palazzo*, with frescoes, Murano chandeliers, three large bedrooms and a splendid high-ceilinged salon, library, well-equipped kitchen and peaceful, shady garden. *Rosanna Giannotti; tel/fax 041 522 3046; e-mail casalvioni@tin.it*

In a tranquil backwater of **Dorsoduro**, **Palazzetto da Schio**, home of the da Schio family for 400 years, has three charming, comfortable apartments. *Contessa Anna da Schio; tel 041 5237937; e-mail avenezia@palazzettodaschio.it*

Out of Venice near Verona, **Foresteria Serègo Alighieri** has eight beautifully converted apartments in the former stables. *Conte Pieralvise Serègo Alighieri; tel 045 7703622; e-mail serego@seregoalighieri.it*

Venice and its lagoon

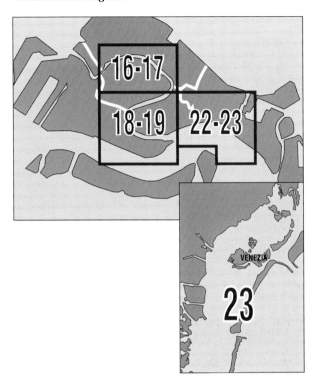

Lakes and mountains

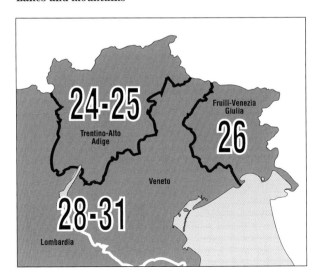

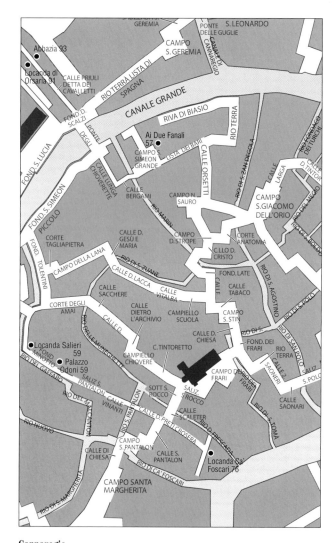

Cannaregio

Very much a residential area, full of charm and character, Cannaregio is bounded to the north by the Lagoon (Fondamente Nuove is the main starting point for vaporetti to the islands), and to the south by a long sweep of the Grand Canal. Most prized of the many lovely palazzi along here is the Ca' d'Oro, with its pink, sugar-spun Venetian Gothic façade. The bulk of tourists are drawn to Lista di Spagna and Strada Nova, two sections of the route from the station to the Rialto, leaving the rest of the district delightfully quiet at all times of the year. Don't miss the Ghetto, the world's oldest, nor the wonderfully over-the-top interior of Gesuiti, near Fondamene Nuove.

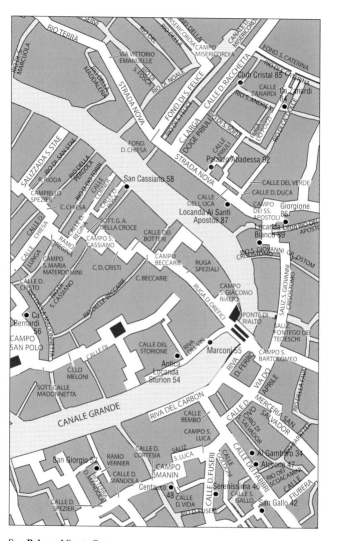

San Polo and Santa Croce

The sestiere of San Polo is lively and full of little shops, restaurants and bars, and of course, the colourful Rialto markets. Trading began here in the 11thC, and ever since, the erberia and pescheria markets have flourished. For just as long, the Rialto Bridge has attracted people; today it swarms with tourists, and the canal below is equally thick with river traffic. Built in 1588, it marks the centre of the city. Also in San Polo is the great Frari church, and Tintoretto's remarkable cycle of paintings in the Scuola di San Rocco. Santa Croce is mainly a humble area, with the vast car park, Piazzale Roma, as well as a stretch of palazzi along the Grand Canal, including one of our hotels.

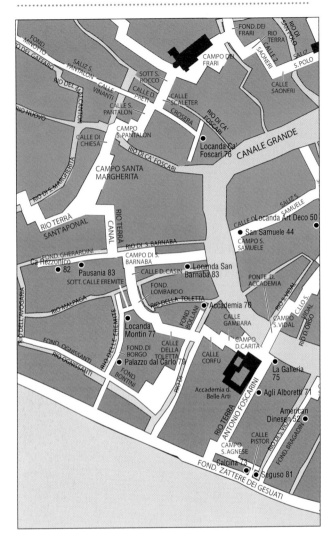

Dorsoduro

Only in 1854 was a second bridge constructed to cross the Grand Canal; in 1932 it was replaced with a temporary wooden structure, but, much loved, it has remained in place to this day as the Accademia Bridge which links the sestieri of San Marco and Dorsoduro. Bordered on one side by the Grand Canal, on the other by the wide Giudecca Canal, and criss-crossed by tributaries, Dorsoduro is tranquil and picturesque, yet close to the main sights. Its chief attractions are the Accademia Gallery and the Peggy Guggenheim Collection, as well as the churches of Santa Maria della Salute and Gesuati. Dig deeper and you will find the lovely and very old church of San Nicolò dei Mendicoli, the gondola boatyard, and charming little spaces such as Campiello Barbaro and Campo San

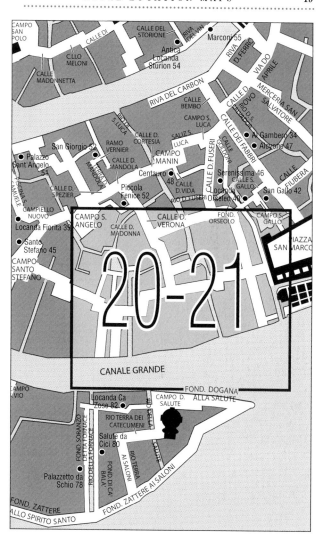

San Marco

Piazza San Marco is the heart of Venice, a fitting space from which to admire the great Basilica and Doge's Palace. Napoleon called it the 'most elegant drawing room in Europe' and on a balmy summer's night when the café orchestras are playing and the swirling daytime crowds have dwindled, his description is still apt. On one side of the Piazza is the Lagoon; on the other, narrow streets full of shops, both for tourists and locals, fan out over the network of canals. In this district you will also find the opera house, Teatro La Fenice – or what's left of it – the spacious Campo Santo Stefano and the charming Bovolo staircase, tucked away in a quiet corner. You will also find the greatest concentration of charming small hotels.

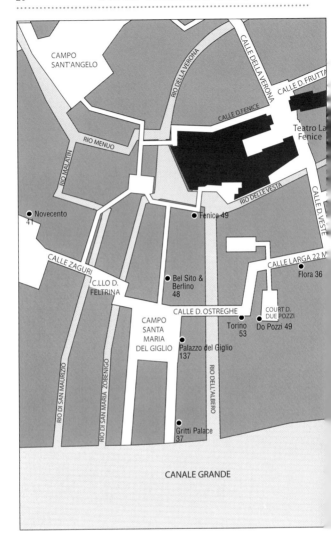

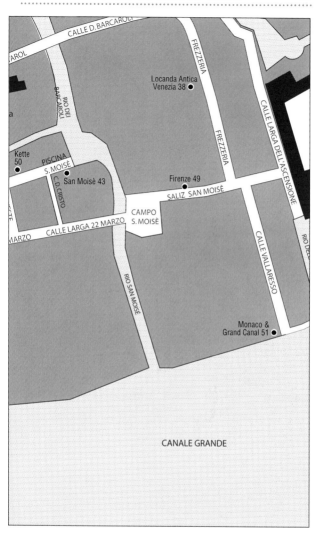

Castello
A marvellously varied district, Castello includes the mighty Riva degli Schiavoni, whose many hotels enjoy unrivalled views across the Lagoon to the island of San Giorgio Maggiore, with its landmark church of the same name by Palladio. Behind the waterfront lies a different Venice: quiet, dusty squares, pretty canals and lovely paintings – principally in San Giovanni in Bragora, Santa Maria Formosa, San Zaccaria, Scuola di San Giorgio degli Schiavoni, Fondazione Querini Stampalia and Santi Giovanni e Paolo. To the west is Arsenale, from where sprang the city's great maritime prowess.

Venetian Lagoon Islands
No visit to Venice is complete without a trip to at least some of the islands in the magical, mysterious Lagoon. Many centuries ago the people of the mainland were forced by invaders to seek refuge amongst the sandbanks; they built protective walls and thriving communities grew up, now long since disappeared. Murano has been a centre of glass-blowing since medieval times; San Michele is the cemetery island, and includes the tombs of famous artists and writers; Burano is packed with gaily painted houses; Torcello is the enigmatic cradle of the Venetian civilization, with only two beautiful churches to remind us of its days of supremacy; the Lido, developed in the 19th Century is both city suburb and seaside resort, and retains the faintly melancholy air of the once-fashionable. Its great hotels are filled with conventions, but A the smaller ones might make a good choice for families, who can combine playing on the beach with sightseeing in Venice.

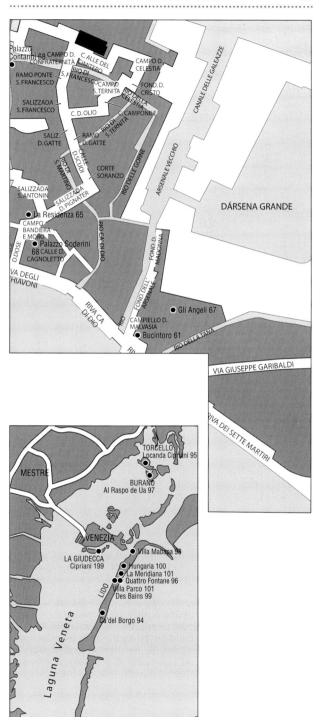

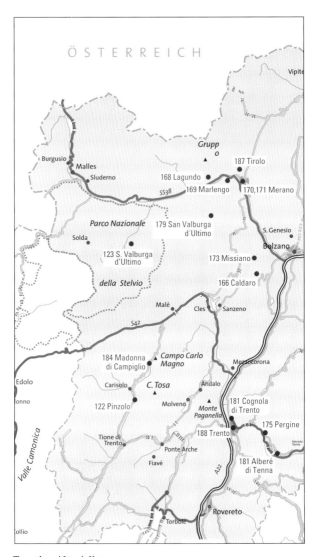

Trentino-Alto Adige

The province of Trentino-Alto Adige is a world away from Venice and its great plain. It feels like Austria, has a special autonomous statute and is largely German-speaking. Owners and staff of the Alpine hotels you will find in its mountains may not even speak Italian ... you are more likely to be greeted in German, and they may speak English. Place names are extremely confusing, as each town and village, mountain and valley has both an Italian and German name. We have given the Italian translation, occasionally referring to the German as well. Hotels are often Tyrolean chalets, with wooden furniture, ceramic stoves, tradi-

tional fabrics; the food too, is mainly Austrian: dumplings, goulash and sauerkraut feature on the simpler menus, while the more sophisticated hotels serve creative variations on the theme. The scenery amongst the Dolomites is breathtakingly beautiful, and there are plenty of activities to pursue both in winter and summer.

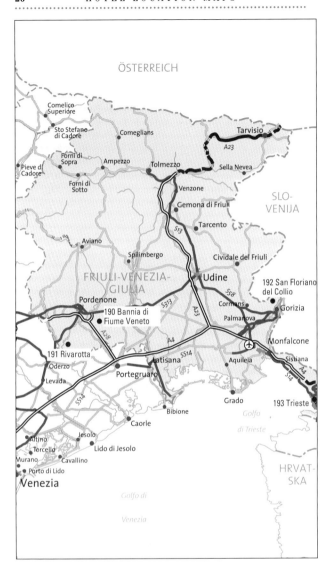

Friuli-Venezia Giulia

The province accounts for the eastern part of the Veneto plain as it curves towards the border with Slovenia. To the north and the border with Austria, it rises to the Carnic Alps with their Alpine meadows and pine forests. Some 20 years ago the area was devastated by an earthquake. Some of the most beautiful and verdant scenery in all Italy can be found in this corner of the country, and yet it is hardly visited, and hotels are thin on the ground There are some old fashioned hostelries in Tolmezzo and the beautifully situated spa town of Arta Terme. The main cities are Trieste, with its air of faded grandeur, and Udine, a busy industrial town with a lovely old piazza and cathedral. Our small selection of hotesl can be found mainly in the west of the province.

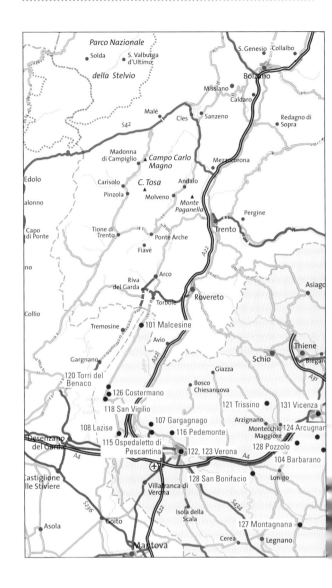

Veneto

The province of Veneto accounts for much of the great Veneto Plain, but to its north it thrusts through the mountains to reach the Austrian border. The bulk of our hotels are on the plain, in both countryside and in the plain's great cities, Vicenza, Padua and Treviso. If you want to stay within easy reach of Venice, there are plenty of choices. To the north of the province, where the foothills of the Dolomites begin to rise from the flat landscape, you will find some delightful places; the charming hilltop village of Asolo is particularly well served. To the west, there are choices in the vibrant and lovely city of Verona, in the fertile wine-country around it, and along the eastern shores of Lake Garda.

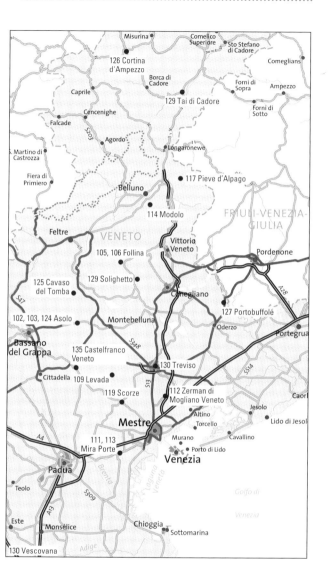

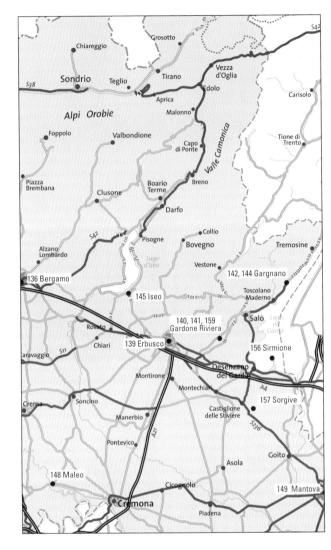

Lombardia

In this edition we have expanded the area covered to include the whole of Lombardia. One part of Lombardia where many of our featured hotels are is the area on the western shores of Lake Garda, the largest lake in Italy. It makes an ideal summertime playground, where you can windsurf, sail or cruise the lake by ferry. With a backdrop of snow-capped mountains, the shores are strung along with pretty villages, little harbours and waterfront promenades. To the south, the Sirmione Peninsula points into the lake, and the old town of Sirmione is the most picturesque of all.

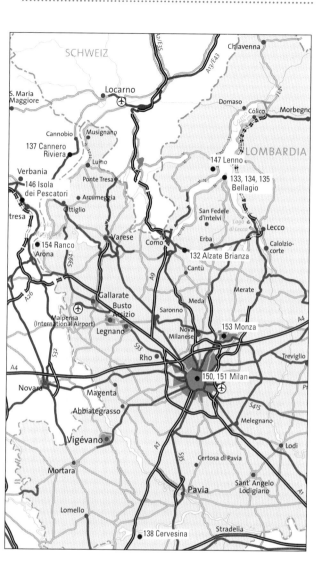

Reporting to the Guide

Please write and tell us about your experiences of small hotels, guest houses and inns, whether good or bad, whether listed in this edition or not. As well as hotels in Venice and Italy, we are interested in hotels in France, Spain, Austria, Germany, Switzerland and the U.S.A. We assume that reporters have no objections to our publishing their views unpaid.

Readers whose reports prove particularly helpful may be invited to join our Travellers' Panel. Members give us notice of their own travel plans; we suggest hotels that they might inspect, and help with the cost of accommodation.

The address to write to us is:

Editor, *Charming Small Hotel Guides*,
Duncan Petersen Publishing Limited,
31 Ceylon Road,
London W14 0PY.

Checklist
Please use a separate sheet of paper for each report; include your name, address and telephone number on each report.

Your reports will be received with particular pleasure if they are typed, and if they are organized under the following headings:

Name of establishment
Town or village it is in, or nearest
Full address, including postcode
Telephone number
Time and duration of visit
The building and setting
The public rooms
The bedrooms and bathrooms
Physical comfort (chairs, beds, heat, light, hot water)
Standards of maintenance and housekeeping
Atmosphere, welcome and service
Food
Value for money

We assume that in writing you have no objections to your views being published unpaid, either verbatim or in an edited version. Names of major outside contributors are acknowledged, at the editor's discretion, in the guide.

VENICE

SAN MARCO

AI DO MORI
~ TOWN GUESTHOUSE ~

TEL 041 5204817/5289293 **FAX** 041 5205328
E-MAIL reception@hotelaidomori.com **WEBSITE** www.hotelaidomori.com

WITH RECEPTION ON THE FIRST FLOOR and only a lantern discreetly displaying the name, the little Ai Do Mori is hard to spot. When you do arrive,
you are more than likely to find the vivacious owner divulging tips to her
guests: "Don't take a gondola on the Grand Canal. A *vaporetto* is much
cheaper. Take a gondola on the little canals and see a different Venice,
where everyday life carries on and tourists are far more sparse."

The modest, white-walled bedrooms are spacious and light. Nos 6 and 7
have rustic beams but by far the most endearing is the one Antonella
endearingly calls the "painters room". Up a steep staircase, tucked under
the eaves, it is small – just accommodating the double bed and a few carefully chosen pieces of furniture – but has a small suntrap of a roof terrace,
from where you can almost reach out and touch the figures on the Basilica
San Marco. With a table and chairs, it's just the place for a glass of *prosecco* in the sunshine.

In 2004, Antonella opened the Annex Bernardi just round the corner on
the edge of Piazza San Marco. The four rooms are clean and fresh, with
silk curtains at the windows and colours in pale gold and orange, plus the
advantage of modern bathrooms. A group could take all four rooms, with a
kitchenette at their disposal.

~

NEARBY Piazza San Marco, San Zulian.
LOCATION near junction with Calle Spadaria, just N of Piazzetta dei Leoni; vaporetto
San Marco
FOOD breakfast
PRICE €€
ROOMS 15; 14 double and twin, triple and family, 8 with bath, 2 with shower, 4
with washbasin; one single with washbasin; all rooms have phone, TV, air-
conditioning, hairdrier, safe
CREDIT CARDS MC, V **DISABLED** not suitable
PETS not accepted **CLOSED** 3 weeks Jan
PROPRIETOR Antonella Bernardi

VENICE

SAN MARCO

AL GAMBERO
~ TOWN GUESTHOUSE ~

Calle dei Fabbri, San Marco 4687, 30124 Venezia
TEL 041 5224384/5201420 **FAX** 041 5200431
E-MAIL hotelgambero@tin.it **WEBSITE** www.locandaalgambero.com

SANDRO ROSSI has gradually transformed his simple guesthouse, a one-time haven for students and backpackers, into a smart little hotel with pretty honey-coloured damask walls and striped curtains and small but comfortable bedrooms, all done up in the same Venetian vein with attractive repro furniture, tiled floors and marble bathrooms. All 27 rooms have now been renovated, and all have ensuite bathrooms and seasonal air-conditioning. Most of the bedrooms are off long corridors, up flights of marble stairs from the first-floor reception. There is no lift. Formerly classified as a one-star, the hotel now boasts three, but prices are still fairly modest for the San Marco location. Some rooms have attractive canal views; in high season rooms with views are the same price as those without views, though in low season they are more expensive.

From the little old-fashioned apricot and green breakfast room beyond the reception, Signor Rossi assures us that in summer you can hear the *gondolieri* serenades. The focal point of the room is a gleaming copper and brass *espresso* machine. On the ground floor, in bustling Calle dei Fabbri, the well known restaurant Le Bistrot de Venise serves 'antique' as well as traditional dishes. It's usefully open until 12.30 am and offers hotel guests a 10 per cent discount.

~

NEARBY Piazza San Marco, San Zulian.
LOCATION in shopping street just north of Piazza San Marco; vaporetto San Marco, Rialto or water taxi
FOOD breakfast
PRICE €€€
ROOMS 27 double and twin, all with bath or shower; all rooms have phone, TV, air-conditioning, minibar, hairdrier, safe
FACILITIES breakfast room
CREDIT CARDS MC, V **DISABLED** not suitable
PETS not accepted **CLOSED** never
PROPRIETOR Sandro Rossi

VENICE

FIRENZE

~ TOWN HOTEL ~

Salizzada San Moise, San Marco 1490, 30124 Venezia
TEL 041 5222858 **FAX** 041 5202668
EMAIL info@hotelfirenze.com **WEBSITE** www.hotelfirenze.com

WE CONTINUE to receive mixed reports of this central hotel, just moments from San Marco. Its distinguishing features are its rooftop terrace – reached from the top floor by an external staircase – where you can breakfast in summer whilst picking out the landmarks, and the three bedrooms with private terrace which cost no more than ones without. Situated in the main drag between San Marco and Santo Stefano, it's surrounded by designer shops and the wonderfully over-the-top façade of San Moisè.

The building itself is eye-catching, with a fine marble-and-iron art nouveau front; at the turn of the century it was an Austrian hat factory, as the splendid first floor windows announce. Inside, renovation has left the bedrooms uniform: unadorned Venetian marble floors (not cosy), peach-coloured walls, pale green headboards and matching cupboards, pretty Murano glass wall lights and white ruched net curtains. The first-floor breakfast room was designed to echo the famous café Florian in Piazza San Marco, with polished wood benches and tables lining the walls, but it doesn't quite come off and feels merely awkward. Choose the Firenze – managed with good humour by its owner, Signor Fabris – during the summer, when you can make use of the roof terrace.

~

NEARBY Piazza San Marco, Teatro La Fenice.
LOCATION 30 m from Piazza San Marco, alongside San Moise; vaporetto San Marco
FOOD breakfast
PRICE €€€€
ROOMS 25; 22 double, 3 single, all with bath; all rooms have phone, TV, air-conditioning, minibar, hairdrier, safe
FACILITIES breakfast room, rooftop terrace, lift
CREDIT CARDS AE, MC, V
DISABLED not suitable **PETS** accepted
CLOSED never
PROPRIETOR Paolo Fabris

VENICE

SAN MARCO

FLORA

~ TOWN HOTEL ~

Calle Larga XXII Marzo, 2283/a San Marco, 30124 Venezia
TEL 041 5205844 **FAX** 041 5228217
E-MAIL info@hotelflora.it **WEBSITE** www.hotelflora.it

SUCH IS THE POPULARITY of this small hotel, tucked away down a cul-de-sac close to San Marco, that to get a room here you have to book weeks, even months in advance. You only need to glimpse the garden to know why it is sought after. Creepers, fountains and flowering shrubs cascading from stone urns create an enchanting setting for breakfast, tea or an evening drink in summer.

The lobby is small and inviting, enhanced by the views of the garden through a glass arch; the atmosphere is one of friendly efficiency. There are some charming double bedrooms with painted carved antiques and other typically Venetian furnishings, but beware of other comparatively spartan rooms, some of which are barely big enough for one, let alone two. Coveted rooms include two on the ground floor facing the garden and the three spacious corner rooms, the topmost of which has a marvellous view of Santa Maria della Salute. The venerable Flora has been run by the charming Romanelli family, father, son and grandson, for over 40 years (young Gioele now runs his own place, the excellent Novecento; see p41). Plaudits continue to flow in to our office, though one mentions that the breakfast room felt crowded in the morning 'though the waiters were quick at juggling seating arrangements'.

~

NEARBY Piazza San Marco.
LOCATION 300 m from Piazza San Marco in cul-de-sac off Calle Larga XXII Marzo; vaporetto San Marco
FOOD breakfast
PRICE €€€€
ROOMS 44; 32 double and twin, 6 single, 6 family, all with bath or shower; all rooms have phone, TV, air conditioning, hairdrier, safe
FACILITIES reading room, breakfast room, bar, lift, garden
CREDIT CARDS AE, DC, MC, V **DISABLED** 2 rooms on ground floor
PETS accepted **CLOSED** never
PROPRIETORS Roger and Joel Romanelli

VENICE

SAN MARCO

GRITTI PALACE

~ TOWN HOTEL ~

Campo Santa Maria del Giglio, San Marco 2467, 30124 Venezia
TEL 041 794611 **FAX** 041 5200942 **E-MAIL** grittipalace@luxurycollection.com
WEBSITE www.luxurycollection.com/grittipalace

OF THE THREE GREAT HOTELS in Venice – the Danieli, the Cipriani and the Gritti – this is our favourite, and the one which most closely reflects the spirit of this incomparably beautiful city. In truth too large at nearly 100 bedrooms for our guide, it is nevertheless individual and intimate, and anyway no hotel guide to Venice would be complete without it.

All the bedrooms at this 15th century *palazzo* of Doge Andrea Gritti – which opened as a hotel in 1948 – are stunning, though it's not imposible to pickholes about lighting and so on considering the price. Of the eight exquisite Canal Views suites, our favourite is the Hemingway, in restful shades of pale green. Service is immaculate and the atmosphere patrician yet friendly. Under its new chef the beautifully sited restaurant is once more a destination for Venetian diners. The perks of being a guest here include access to museums and galleries outside the usual hours, free boat transfers to the Lido and a Pillow Menu featuring a choice of 12 types of pillow.

As Somerset Maugham pointed out, there are few greater pleasures than taking a drink on the terrace at sunset, the Salute opposite bathed in lovely colour. Before bed, he advises, glance at the portrait of old Andrea Gritti, who, after a tumultuous life, lived his last years here in peace.

~

NEARBY Teatro La Fenice; Piazza San Marco; Accademia.
LOCATION in *campo* on Grand Canal; vaporetto Santa Maria del Giglio or by water taxi
FOOD breakfast, lunch, dinner; room service
PRICE €€€€€€
ROOMS 93; 80 double and twin, 7 single, 6 suites, all with bath; all rooms have phone, TV, air-conditioning, minibar, hairdrier, safe
FACILITIES sitting room, dining room, bar, meeting room, lift, terrace
CREDIT CARDS AE, DC, MC, V
DISABLED no special facilities but access possible **PETS** accepted
CLOSED never **MANAGER** Marco Novella

VENICE

SAN MARCO

LOCANDA ANTICA VENEZIA

~ TOWN GUESTHOUSE ~

Frezzeria, San Marco 1672, 30124 Venezia
TEL 041 5208320 **FAX** 041 5230880
E-MAIL antica.venezia@libero.it **WEBSITE** www.hotelanticavenezia.com

A STONE'S THROW FROM PIAZZA SAN MARCO, we stumbled across this little-known, family-run *locanda* announced only by a buzzer and discreet brass plaque, and discovered some of the best-value rooms in Venice. The entrance is through a secluded brick-walled courtyard and up three flights of stone stairs. (Kind members of staff are on hand to help with your luggage.) At the top, you emerge into a long, thin reception area; don't be disappointed, there is more space and character in the bedrooms and public rooms one storey up.

The building is a 16th-century nobleman's house, with some of its original features still in evidence. In the cosy sitting area the supporting beams are exposed, and one of the three large, comfortable sofas nestles amongst them. This floor has been opened out to provide space for a small breakfast area as well, and a roof terrace beyond has a view of San Marco's massive brick Campanile and is the perfect place for drinks (served 24 hours).

The bedrooms are decorated in traditional Venetian fashion. A few are relentlessly blue, down to every item of painted, upholstered furniture. Our favourite is the spacious beamed top-floor 'suite'. The owners are very friendly and prices unbeatable for the location.

~

NEARBY Piazza San Marco; Bovolo staircase.
LOCATION just NE of the piazza, where Frezzeria makes a right-angle turn; vaporetto Vallaresso
FOOD breakfast
PRICE €€€
ROOMS 14 double and twin, triple, family, all with shower; all rooms have phone, TV, air conditioning, minibar, hairdrier, safe
FACILITIES sitting area, breakfast area, roof terrace
CREDIT CARDS AE, DC, MC, V **DISABLED** not suitable
PETS accepted **CLOSED** never
PROPRIETOR Daniele Saltorio

VENICE

SAN MARCO

LOCANDA FIORITA

~ TOWN GUESTHOUSE ~

Campiello Nuovo, Santo Stefano, San Marco 3457, 30124 Venezia
TEL 041 5234754 **FAX** 041 5228043
E-MAIL info@locandafiorita.com **WEBSITE** www.locandafiorita.com

IF YOU ARE LOOKING FOR ROCK-BOTTOM prices and a quiet yet central location, look no further than this bargain one star hotel, a red-painted villa tucked away in a quiet, little-visited square off Campo Santo Stefano. Rooms are small and functional, with modern white furniture which include desks, bedside tables, even beds. Our reporter found her bed surprisingly comfortable, but noted the skimpy towels and lack of shelves, though there was plenty of cupboard space in her room. 'With its beamed ceiling, mint-coloured walls and large windows it was a perfectly pleasant room in which to wake up,' she comments, 'especially when one reflects on what it cost'. No. 10 is the 'honeymoon room', with cupids painted on the wall and a tiny, rather public terrace. Breakfast is taken either at wooden tables set along the wall in the reception area, or, more comfortably, in your room. In summer, the terrace which runs along the front of the building is covered in a pergola of vines, and there are colourful flowers in window boxes.

A six-room annexe is located nearby, but it is not as pleasant (despite more facilities) and is more expensive than the main hotel.

~

NEARBY Piazza San Marco; Accademia gallery.
LOCATION a little square off Campo Santo Stefano/Calle dei Frati; vaporetto San Samuele
FOOD breakfast
PRICE €€
ROOMS 10; 8 double, 2 single, 9 with shower and WC, one without; all rooms have phone, fan, hairdrier, 5 have TV
FACILITIES reception/breakfast area, small terrace
CREDIT CARDS AE, DC, MC, V
DISABLED access difficult
PETS accepted
CLOSED never
PROPRIETOR Renato Colombera

VENICE

SAN MARCO

LOCANDA ORSEOLO
∼ TOWN HOTEL ∼

Corte Zorzi, San Marco 1083, 30124 Venezia
TEL 041 5204827 **FAX** 041 5235586
E-MAIL info@locandaorseolo.com **WEBSITE** www.locandaorseolo.com

W E'VE OFTEN HURRIED THROUGH little Campo San Gallo behind St Mark's Square, but never until recently pushed open the unsigned wrought iron gate that stands to one side. Do so, and you find yourself in a secret, silent mini-campo, complete with central well. Once there, you will have to look hard to locate the low-key front door of Locanda Orseolo. Step inside and you might be in a gorgeous compartment on the Orient Express, compact yet elegant, enveloping, richly coloured and furnished. But it's the gust of warmth from the young team at this equally young 15-room hotel that makes it really special. Led by Matteo (once a dentist but could be a film star) and Barbara, it includes their brothers, sisters and friends. In the morning, Matteo dons an apron and cooks pancakes and omelettes to order, Barbara serves and everyone chats. The comfortable bedrooms are gradually being transformed to echo the ground floor, complete with hand-painted murals and canopied beds. Secure one and you'll have a bargain.

The hotel, fashioned from a former private house and opened by Matteo (himself the son of a hotelier) and Barbara only in 2003, has become hugely popular with Americans. Reserved Brits and other northern Europeans may find the warmth of welcome almost too much, but they shouldn't – it's genuine.

∼

NEARBY Piazza San Marco; San Zulian.
LOCATION in tiny campo off Campo San Gallo, N of Piazza San Marco, E of Orseolo canal; vaporetto San Marco
FOOD breakfast
PRICE €€€€
ROOMS 15, all with bath or shower; all rooms have phone, TV, air-conditioning, minibar, hairdrier, safe
FACILITIES sitting room, breakfast room **CREDIT CARDS** AE, DC, MC, V
PETS accepted **DISABLED** access difficult **CLOSED** never
PROPRIETORS Peruch family

VENICE

SAN MARCO

NOVECENTO
~ TOWN HOTEL ~

Campo San Maurizio, San Marco 2683/84, 30124 Venezia
TEL 041 2413765 **FAX** 041 5212145
E-MAIL info@novecento.biz **WEBSITE** www.novecento.biz

OFF CAMPO SAN MAURIZIO, just around the corner from the Gritti Palace, the Novecento is a wonderful addition to the Venice hotel scene. It's attractive, enveloping, refreshingly different and run with touching commitment by young Gioele Romanelli, and his wife, Heiby. Gioele knows what he is doing: his father owns and runs the excellent Hotel Flora (p36).

It's a bit like walking into a Marrakech *riad*, with furniture, beds and fabrics imported from Morocco, Thailand and Pakistan, and a whiff of incense in the air. There are beamed ceilings, plaster walls, stained bottle glass windows, big cushions on the sitting room floor, amusing beds, superb bathrooms. Music plays in your room at the touch of a button. The old beamed Venetian house, just off the main route between San Marco and the Rialto, lends itself beautifully to its stylish makeover, which, the Romanellis tell us, is inspired by the great Fortuny, who was himself inspired by the Orient. With just nine bedrooms and a little courtyard garden, the atmosphere is cosy and intimate. Breakfast is a treat – wonderful cappuccino and pastries and other delicacies such as slices of feta surrounded by tiny strawberries.

~

NEARBY San Marco; Accademia gallery; Rialto.
LOCATION off Campo San Maurizio on Calle del Dose; vaporetto Santa Maria del Giglio
FOOD breakfast
PRICE ©©©-©©©©
ROOMS 9 double, 8 with bath, one with shower; all rooms have phone, TV, air conditioning,music, minibar, safe, hairdrier
FACILITIES honesty bar, sitting room, breakfast room, courtyard
CREDIT CARDS AE, DC, MC, V
DISABLED not suitable
PETS accepted
CLOSED never
PROPRIETORS Gioele and Heiby Romanelli

VENICE

SAN GALLO
~ TOWN HOTEL ~

Camp San Gallo, San Marco 1093a, 30124 Venezia
TEL 041 5227311/5289877 **FAX** 041 5225702
E-MAIL sangallo@hotelsangallo.it **WEBSITE** www.hotelsangallo.it

ALL YOU SEE FROM THE OUTSIDE is a rather dilapidated cinema, but don't be put off, the entrance to the San Gallo is up a flight of stone steps and through a heavy internal door. Buzz the buzzer and you will be admitted to a room that is a breath of fresh air with not a patch of silk damask in sight. This one large room fulfils the functions of reception, sitting and breakfast areas. Although the low ceiling bristles with unstained 14thC beams, it manages to be light and airy, and is freshly decorated in white with panels of mellow faux marble. Smart striped sofas and chairs cluster around wooden tables, and a little bar is tucked into one corner.

Franco Ferigo, the San Gallo's friendly owner, has lately upgraded and renovated the bedrooms, some of which are very small, though neat and spotlessly clean. They are done up simply, in pleasant if unremarkable Venetian style with traditional furnishings – velvet button bedheads, Murano chandeliers, busy patterned floor tiles. In lieu of a lift there are steep stairs to be negotiated. To compensate, however, there is a glorious roof terrace where in summer you can breakfast amidst the potted plants. And Piazza San Marco is just a few paces away.

~

NEARBY Piazza San Marco; San Zulian.
LOCATION N of Piazza San Marco, E of Orseolo canal; vaporetto San Marco
FOOD breakfast
PRICE €€€€
ROOMS 12; 8 double and twin, 2 with bath, 6 with shower; one single, 3 triple or family, all with shower; all rooms have phone, TV, air-conditioning, minibar/fridge, hairdrier
FACILITIES bar/breakfast room/sitting room, roof terrace
CREDIT CARDS MC, V
DISABLED not suitable
PETS accepted
CLOSED never
PROPRIETOR Franco Ferigo

VENICE

SAN MARCO

SAN MOISE

~ TOWN HOTEL ~

Piscina San Moise, San Marco 2058, 30124 Venezia
TEL 041 5203755 **FAX** 041 5210670
E-MAIL sanmoise@sanmoise.it **WEBSITE** www.sanmoise.it

THE INTERIOR IS VERY Venetian, and not to everyone's taste – more than a touch reminiscent of a high class brothel to us, with rather lurid colours on some of the walls and accompanying Murano glass chandeliers and wall lights that are appropriately garish examples of the genre. There are plenty of elegant touches, however, though the public rooms and landings are a bit of a hotch potch, there's grim modern lighting in the stairwell and some of the furniture is dark and uninteresting. Old magazines about cars and celebrities on every flat surface in the *salon* remind one of the dentist.

There are a handful of special rooms at the San Moisè – under the same ownership as the Marconi (see page 55) and the San Cassiano (see page 58) – which are well worth seeking out. One has splendid carved mahogany furnishings and steps up to a little bathroom. Two others have views straight down the Rio dei Barcaroli, a jolly and picturesque canal which is packed with gondolas and their camera-clicking cargo. Amongst the newly created suites, the best has a fireplace and terrace. The San Moisè is similar in many ways to its sister hotels which could be summed up as 'great potential but could do better'. Breakfast was poor on our last visit: knobbly scrambled egg and halved franfurters, plus all the usual cereals, juices and yoghurts. But the hotel's position, very central, yet tucked away at the end of a little street and on a canal, is enviable.

~

NEARBY Piazza San Marco, Teatro La Fenice.
LOCATION off Calle Larga XXII Marzo, 2 mins walk from Piazza San Marco
FOOD breakfast, lunch, dinner; room service during day
PRICE €€€€
ROOMS 16; 13 double, twin and triple, 4 with bath, 9 with shower; 3 single, all with shower; all rooms have phone, TV, air-conditioning, minibar, hairdrier, safe
FACILITIES breakfast room **CREDIT CARDS** AE, DC, MC, V
DISABLED not suitable **PETS** accepted **CLOSED** never
MANAGER Gianluca Serra

VENICE

SAN MARCO

SAN SAMUELE
~ TOWN GUESTHOUSE ~

Salizzada San Samuele, San Maro 3358, 30124 Venezia
TEL 041 5205165 FAX 041 5205165
E-MAIL info@albergosansamuele.it WEBSITE www.albergosansamuele.it

A BUDGET ESTABLISHMENT WITH YOUNG MANAGERS, a fresh lick of paint, 300-year old Venetian marble floors and a pleasant, airy feel to the bedrooms.

The *pensione* is installed on the upper floors of a pretty house in a wide street leading to the San Samuele *vaporetto* and *traghetto* landing stage. Ring the bell for admission, enter a pleasant little courtyard and start climbing the stairs, of which there are quite a few – this hotel is for the young and fit (and, with no air conditioning it can get pretty hot in summer time).

On our last visit, bedrooms were still looking pretty fresh, with a dash of colour in each, ordinary, mostly white furniture and chintzy, antique-style bedspreads on the skimpy-looking beds (a recent guest informs us that they are adequately comfortable). Bathrooms are modern, each enlivened by a jolly shower curtain. What gives these rooms the edge over others in the same price range, however, is the presence of not one but two large windows with views over the street (No. 10 is one of the best). The two rooms at the back make up in quiet what they lack in light. Breakfast, if you want it, is served in the rooms.

We have had good reader feedback about this modest, two-star establishment. Run by three friends, it's the sort of places that is much appreciated but hard to find: an affordable hotel that doesn't disappoint.

~

NEARBY Accademia gallery; Frari; Campo Santo Stefano.
LOCATION in quiet area of San Marco, between Campo Santo Stefano and Grand Canal; vaporetto San Samuele
FOOD breakfast
PRICE €€
ROOMS 10; 8 double, 2 single, 7 with shower; all rooms have phone
FACILITIES sitting room, breakfast room, bar
CREDIT CARDS not accepted DISABLED not suitable
PETS not accepted CLOSED never
PROPRIETORS San Samuele Association

VENICE

SAN MARCO

SANTO STEFANO

~ TOWN HOTEL ~

Campo Santo Stefano, San Marco 2957, 30124 Venezia
TEL 041 5200166 **FAX** 041 5224460 **E-MAIL** info@hotelsantostefanovenezia.com
WEBSITE www.hotelsantostefanovenezia.com

IF YOU FOLLOW THE POPULAR ROUTE from Piazza San Marco to the Accademia gallery you will walk across the Campo Santo Stefano, a lively square, popular as meeting place for locals, whose church has an alarmingly tilted campanile.

Close to all the activity stands the Santo Stefano, a well cared for little hotel housed in a distinctive 15th-century watchtower whose front rooms have views of the square (although these are prone to noise). Its owner, Roberto Quatrini, has made many improvements since he took over a few years ago, both to the bedrooms and to the small but elegant reception area and tiny breakfast room: contemporary furniture, prettily painted ceiling beams and pillars, and marble wall panels to match the floor. Bedrooms are now richly decorated, with patterned wallpaper and Venetian paintings, individually lit gilt mirrors and bedheads and Murano glass lamps. The refurbished bathrooms, with mosaic floors, all sport Jacuzzi water-massage and steam baths. Some rooms are very compact, but No. 11, with views across the campo, is particularly light and spacious. There is a tiny courtyard terrace at the back of the hotel as well as one in front, where you can sip a coffee and watch the world go by.

~

NEARBY Accademia gallery; Piazza San Marco.
LOCATION on large square about 500 m W of Piazza San Marco; vaporetto San Samuele
FOOD breakfast
PRICE €€€€
ROOMS 11; 6 double and twin, 2 single, 3 triple or quadruple, all with bath; all rooms have phone, TV, air-conditioning, minibar, hairdrier, safe
FACILITIES breakfast room, courtyard, lift, pavement terrace
CREDIT CARDS MC, V
DISABLED access difficult **PETS** accepted
CLOSED never
PROPRIETOR Roberto Quatrini

VENICE

SAN MARCO

SERENISSIMA

~ TOWN HOTEL ~

Calle Goldoni, San Marco 4486, 30124 Venezia
TEL 041 5200011 **FAX** 041 5223292
EMAIL info@hotelserenissima.it **WEBSITE** www.hotelserenissima.it

READERS' REPORTS CONFIRM that this is one of the most endearing and best-kept two-star hotels in town. Our inspector told us that she found it much more pleasant to stay here than in many a more expensive three-star, and given its very central location, she deemed it excellent value for money – a rare experience in Venice. Bedrooms are admittedly on the small side (a triple will give two people more room), but neat and pretty, with Venetian painted headboards, cupboards and bedside tables, and crisp bedlinen on the comfortable beds (though pillows are thin) and all with fast internet connection. The neat, tiled bathrooms have proper shower enclosures, not curtains. Try for a room with a view on to the sunny little square at the back, empty but for its central well and very peaceful. Both the charming first-floor breakfast room with its display of glass and the white-walled corridors are imaginatively hung with attractive and colourful modern paintings – these alone seem to lift the Serenissima from the rut. Breakfast is traditional Italian – Bel Paese and Fette Biscottate rusks and excellent hot chocolate as well as coffee. Downstairs in reception there is a little bar. A perfect example of the classic Italian *pensione*, the hotel has been looked after with great care by the same friendly family, Dal Borgo, since 1960.

~

NEARBY Piazza San Marco; Rialto; Bovolo staircase.
LOCATION between Piazza San Marco and Rialto, close to Calle dei Fabbri
FOOD breakfast
PRICE €€€
ROOMS 37; 29 double, twin and triple, 5 with bath, 24 with shower; 8 single, 2 with bath, 6 with shower; all rooms have phone, TV, air-conditioning, hairdrier
FACILITIES sitting area, breakfast room, bar
CREDIT CARDS AE, DC, MC, V
DISABLED not suitable **PETS** accepted
CLOSED after Carnival to mid-Mar
PROPRIETORS Dal Borgo family

VENICE

SAN MARCO

ALCYONE
TOWN HOTEL

Calle dei Fabbri, San Marco
4712, 30124 Venezia

TEL 041 5212508 **FAX** 041 5212942
E-MAIL info@hotelalcyone.com
WEBSITE www.hotelalcyone.com
FOOD breakfast
PRICE ⓔⓔⓔ
CLOSED never
PROPRIETORS Alessio Ricchi

B EFORE ITS RENOVATION a few years ago, this was an old-fashioned pensione called the Brooklyn. Though the current owners are proud of
their makeover, one suspects that the old hotel had more character
because the parts that have been left intact are charming. The pretty little breakfast room has waist-high painted panelling with gold velvet
above, dotted with ceramic plates; the stairwell is similar. The sugared
almond pink bedrooms are very small, done out in standard Venetian
style: purpose-made painted furniture, Murano glass wall lights, silk
damask bedcovers. We have had complaints of 'relaxed' service and stuffy
bedrooms in summer, though other remarks have been positive.

SAN MARCO

ANTICO PANADA
TOWN GUESTHOUSE

Calle Specchieri, San Marco 646,
30124 Venezia

TEL 041 5209088 **FAX** 041 5209619
E-MAIL info@hotelpanada.it
WEBSITE www.hotelpanada.com
FOOD breakfast
PRICE ⓔⓔⓔⓔ
CLOSED never
MANAGER Claudio Perelli

T HE REAL ATTRACTION OF THIS HOTEL is its bar. Cosy and wood-panelled,
with red velvet seats, it lives up to its name Ai Speci ('of mirrors' in
local dialect), as almost every inch of wall space is covered with antique
looking-glasses. Other pluses are a decent-sized and comfortable sitting
area, and freshly decorated bedrooms with attractive painted furniture.
Minuses are a staff who can at times muster only a cool welcome and an
easy win in any 'most hideous breakfast room' contest. While the 'superior'
rooms are decorated in Empire style, with Jacuzzis, there are also two
rooms in a small annexe, Cipro et Corfu, decorated in Biedermeier style,
with parquet floors. Further expansion is under way.

VENICE

SAN MARCO

BEL SITO & BERLINO
TOWN HOTEL

Campo Santa Maria del Giglio,
San Marco 2517, 30124 Venezia

TEL 041 5223365
FAX 041 5204083
E-MAIL info@hotelbelsito.info
WEBSITE www.hotelbelsito.info
FOOD breakfast
PRICE ⓔⓔⓔ **CLOSED** never
PROPRIETOR Luigi Gino Serafini

THE BEL SITO HAS its charms, including a flowery patio right on the *campo*, and given a sympathetic facelift one feels it could make a fine hotel. Too many of the rooms, however (they vary greatly), are small, skimpily furnished and worn at the edges, and the extensive reception room looks dowdy (although the long, mirrored breakfast room retains its old-fashioned dignity). There are two special rooms, worth a stay here if you can procure them: Nos 30 and 40, with wonderful close-up views of the exuberant baroque façade of Santa Maria Zobenigo, which you can almost reach out and touch. Also worthwhile are the rooms with views on to the canal; the others don't have a great deal to recommend them.

SAN MARCO

CENTAURO
TOWN HOTEL

Calle D Vida, Campo Manin,
30124 Venezia

TEL 041 5225832
FAX 041 5239151
E-MAIL info@hotelcentauro.com
WEB www.hotelcentauro.com
FOOD breakfast
PRICE ⓔⓔ
CLOSED never
PROPRIETOR Riccardo Tomasutti

A HOTEL THAT HAS BEEN in existence since the 17th century and in the Tomasutti family for much of the 20th and into the 21st. The current owner, Riccardo has transformed what was a fairly dingy two-star establishment into a smart three-star. Flock wallpaper has been jettisoned in favour of glossy paint effects; beams have been washed dark red with a yellow motif; the huge doors painted pale green. The cavernous breakfast room, freshly painted in yellow and white, still has its original parquet floor. Bedrooms, six with canal views, are generally airy, with Venetian marble floors and fabric-covered furniture. Many of them now sport a loud profusion of matching brocade stripes on both walls and bedcovers.

VENICE

SAN MARCO

DO POZZI
TOWN HOTEL

Calle Larga XXII Marzo 2373,
30124 Venezia

TEL 0473 222020 **FAX** 0473 447130
E-MAIL info@hoteldopozzi.it
WEBSITE www.hoteldopozzi.it
FOOD breakfast
PRICE €€€€
CLOSED never
PROPRIETOR Stefania Salmaso

IN A TINY, PALM-FRINGED COURTYARD, where café tables and chairs spill on to the pavement in summer, this hotel has the twin advantages of a quiet central location and its own restaurant, Da Raffaele, prettily set on a side canal. We are less inspired, however, by the hotel's dull interior: acres of silk damask cover the walls and furnishings are standard throughout. Our inspector regretted that there were no more original touches like the icons in the outer breakfast room. Bedrooms are serviceable and in generally good condition; some of the bathrooms are 'excruciatingly small'. A new annexe just round the corner, Favaro, has seven smart, well-equipped bedrooms which you may prefer.

SAN MARCO

FENICE
TOWN HOTEL

Campiello della Fenice, San
Marco 1936, 30124 Venezia

TEL 041 523 2333
FAX 041 5203721
E-MAIL fenice@fenicehotels.it
WEBSITE www.fenicehotels.com
FOOD breakfast
PRICE €€€€
CLOSED never
PROPRIETOR Michele Facchini

ONE OF THE BEST KNOWN small hotels in Venice, La Fenice et des Artistes, to give it its full name, has had a long and proud history of welcoming visiting artists to the adjacent Teatro Fenice opera house, which continues to this day, for the supporting cast at least. It's got plenty of old time character, at any rate in the series of dark, cosy and rather creaky sitting rooms, their walls plastered with paintings, signed photographs and ornate mirrors. The bedrooms, though, are less appealing, at least in our experience. On her last stay, our inspector reported that hers needed redecorating (though the bathrooms are in good condition), and had an uncomfortable bed. They do vary though: your comments appreciated.

VENICE

KETTE
TOWN HOTEL

Piscina San Moisè, San Marco 2053, 30124 Venezia

TEL 041 5207766
FAX 041 5228964
E-MAIL info@hotelkette.com
WEBSITE www.hotelkette.com
FOOD breakfast
PRICE €€€€
CLOSED never
PROPRIETOR Signor Baessato

RECENTLY REFURBISHED IN AN AMBITIOUSLY formal style of faux marble and much wood panelling, the Kette makes a smart and comfortable, if somewhat impersonal base. Displays of Murano glass and a few *objets d'art* add some character, as do the helpful, efficient staff.

The ground floor entrance (you can arrive by water taxi) is an arrestingly glossy sight, with a whirl of modern polychromatic marble floors in geometric patterns and large classical oil paintings on the walls. Bedrooms are traditional, with a masculine touch – dark wood furniture, carved headboards. A slick, comfortable base. The buffet breakfasts, in the original watergate hall, are well spoken of.

LOCANDA ART DECO
TOWN GUESTHOUSE

Calle delle Botteghe, San Marco 2966, 30124 Venezia

TEL 041 2770558
FAX 041 2702891
E-MAIL info@locandaartdeco.com
WEBSITE
www.locandaartdeco.com
FOOD breakfast **PRICE** €€€
CLOSED never
PROPRIETOR Judith Boulbain

A NEW KID ON THE SAN MARCO BLOCK, this miniature boutique hotel has been cleverly shoehorned into an old building, whose fine timbered ceilings bear witness to its age. No prizes for guessing its decorative theme: with a combination of carefully chosen antique and derivative furniture, the talented French owner has created a stylish art deco replica. A marble staircase with swirling wrought-iron banisters leads from the tiny reception, where you can relax on a leather club sofa, to the breakfast 'room' perched on a mezzanine above. Off landings lined with mirrors and framed posters from the '20s, the bedrooms have been tastefully decorated in white with wooden floors, pretty wardrobes and wrought-iron beds.

VENICE

SAN MARCO

MONACO ET GRAND CANAL
TOWN HOTEL

Calle Vallaresso, San Marco 1325, 30124 Venezia

TEL 041 5200211 **FAX** 041 5200501
E-MAIL mailbox@hotelmonaco.it
WEBSITE www.hotelmonaco.it
FOOD breakfast, lunch, dinner, room service **PRICE**
€€€€€€ **CLOSED** never
MANAGER Gabriele Machiorri

NOT MUCH ABOUT THIS TRADITIONAL grand hotel remains recognizable since its major makeover at the beginning of this decade, though the impeccably uniformed footmen and multilingual receptionists remain in place. Reception rooms and bedrooms are now slick, international-style spaces dressed in modern designer furniture and soothing tones of pale cream and beige. The location, of course, which is the hotel's chief attraction, hasn't changed either: right on the Grand Canal with magical views across to Salute and San Giorgio Maggiore, with masses of space to sit downstairs and enjoy them, including the sophisticated, intimate restaurant which, on last examination, served excellent food.

SAN MARCO

PALAZZO SANT'ANGELO
TOWN HOTEL

Ramo di Teatro, San Marco 3488, 30124 Venezia

TEL 041 2411452 **FAX** 041 2411557
E-MAIL
palazzosantangelo@sinahotels.it
WEBSITE
www.palazzosantangelo.com
FOOD breakfast
PRICE €€€€€€;
CLOSED never

WHAT'S SPECIAL ABOUT THIS glossy four-star hotel, part of the Italian Sina chain, is its front entrance right on the Grand Canal. With its own pier, you can approach by gondola or water taxi, on foot or by vaporetto (the Sant'Angelo stop is adjacent). Whichever way, it's a rare treat to enter a Grand Canal palazzo through it's original water entrance. Thereafter, it must be said that there is not much that's particularly characterful about the Sant'Angelo, a fairly new addition to the Venice hotel scene, and billed as one of its first 'boutique' hotels, but it is undoubtedly comfortable (as it should be for the price) with marble bathrooms and well furnished bedrooms. Breakfast, though, is only so-so.

VENICE

SAN MARCO

PICCOLA FENICE
TOWN SUITE HOTEL

Calle della Madonna, San Marco 3614, 30124 Venezia

TEL and **FAX** 041 5204909
E-MAIL
piccolafenice@fenicehotels.it
WEBSITE www.fenicehotels.com
FOOD breakfast **PRICE** €€€;
CLOSED Jan
PROPRIETOR Michele Facchini

T HIS SISTER HOTEL to the Fenice Hotel around the corner (see p49) consists of seven suites sleeping between two and six people, and may be an option for a stay in Venice of longer than a few nights (weekly rates are available). The topmost apartment, with little balcony overlooking the rooftops, would be perfect for a family. A recent inspector was not overly impressed with his first floor room, however: "It looked better in daylight than in the rather gloomy light cast by the greenish Murano chandelier. The furniture was minimal. Though there was a kitchenette, it was hard to imagine cooking a dish here that would gladden the heart".

SAN MARCO

SAN GIORGIO
TOWN HOTEL

Rio Terra della Mandola, San Marco 3781, 30124 Venezia

TEL 041 5235835
FAX 041 5228072
E-MAIL
info@sangiorgiovenice.com
WEBSITE
www.sangiorgiovenice.com
FOOD breakfast
PRICE €€€ **CLOSED** never
PROPRIETOR Valerio Bernardi

I F YOU WANT A QUIET LOCATION, yet close to the bustling main thoroughfare, consider the San Giorgio, tucked down a side street next to the Museo Fortuny. Bedrooms are small, neat, well cared for, with bathrooms of varying sizes, some with large shower cubicles. One room has an attractive carved wardrobe, others have pretty examples of Venetian painted furniture. Downstairs is a large, rather dark sitting/breakfast room. Valerio Bernardi is a splendid hands-on manager – and now owner – who dispenses better-than-average breakfasts and much advice and help to guests, including with bags (there's no lift). A simple hotel with excellent service.

VENICE

SAN MARCO

SAN ZULIAN
TOWN HOTEL

Piscina San Zulian, San Marco
535, 30124 Venezia

TEL 041 5225872
FAX 041 5232265
FOOD breakfast
E-MAIL desk@hotelsanzulian.com
WEBSITE www.hotelsanzulian.com
PRICE €€€€
CLOSED never
PROPRIETOR Mauro Girotto

A LITTLE HOTEL where public rooms and corridors are painted white, with colourful pictures and neat furniture and fittings. Bedrooms, though simple, are similarly fresh, well-equipped, with pretty furniture and white tiled bathrooms with properly enclosed showers. Rooms vary in size, so try for a larger one. One in particular breaks the mould, with a silk hanging above the bed and a charming ottoman at its foot, though there are attractive antiques elsewhere too. The 'honeymoon room' has a private terrace with views across the rooftops to the domes of San Marco (which helps to compensate for the minute bathroom). A free excursion to Murano is offered in the not inconsiderable price.

VENICE

ANTICA LOCANDA STURION
~ TOWN GUESTHOUSE ~

Calle del Storione, San Polo 679, 30125 Venezia
TEL 041 5236243 **FAX** 041 5228378
E-MAIL info@locandasturion.com **WEBSITE** www.locandasturion.com

FIRST YOU HAVE TO CONQUER THE STAIRS, a seemingly endless flight which rises like a ladder from the ground floor to the hotel on the third floor. The friendly receptionist must be used to her guests collapsing in front of her desk, for she refrained from smirking when this inspector presented herself gulping for air. There is no porter, but receptionists will help with the luggage.

Once you have recovered sufficiently to take in your surroundings, you will find them plush. Deep red silk fabric adorns the walls in several of the bedrooms (these are non-smoking), with pale silk damask in others. Furniture throughout is walnut and mahogany, with floors of Venetian marble or covered in deep red carpet. Two rooms look on to the Grand Canal. They are spacious for two people and can sleep two extra, one on a bed cleverly hidden during the day in a wooden box masquerading as a cupboard . We have, of late, received negative reports about the atmosphere and the stuffiness of the bedrooms. Some people find the place claustrophobic. A little library of guide books, mostly in English, adds a homely touch.

Locanda Sturion, found in a dark street by the Rialto hung with washing, has long been a hostelry. It stands on the site of a 13th-century house built for foreign merchants taking their wares to the market.

~

NEARBY Rialto; Rialto markets; Ca d'Oro.
LOCATION off Riva del Vin, close to Rialto bridge; vaporetto Rialto, San Silvestro
FOOD breakfast
PRICE €€€
ROOMS 11; 8 double, twin and triple, 3 family, 10 with bath, one with shower; all rooms have phone, TV, air-conditioning, minibar, hairdrier, safe
CREDIT CARDS AE, MC, V
DISABLED not suitable **PETS** accepted
CLOSED never
PROPRIETOR Signor Fragiacomo

VENICE

SAN POLO

MARCONI
~ TOWN HOTEL ~

Riva del Vin, San Polo 729, 30125 Venezia
TEL 041 5222068 **FAX** 041 5229700
E-MAIL info@hotelmarconi.it **WEBSITE** www.hotelmarconi.it

THE MARCONI IS A TYPICAL Venice hotel, encapsulating both what is right and what is wrong about many of them. As so often, the location is enviable (although since it is right by Rialto Bridge, overlooking a stretch of Grand Canal thick with gondolas and camera-clicking tourists, it appeals to those wanting action rather than peace and quiet). The building is a 16th-century *palazzo* with a 19th-century entrance hall which has a glass and wood frontage, marbled pillars, velvet hangings and a green and gold embossed ceiling. As for the bedrooms, best of all are the two rooms with balconies which overlook the Grand Canal, more expensive than the rest, but worth it. As for the others, they are fairly simple, though carved bedheads and damask curtains lend a grandiose, old fashioned air. There is double glazing throughout. And yet, although the hotel was renovated not so long ago, its dark wood fittings and rather dated fabrics give it a gloomy, rather musty air. And one senses that the staff are not as interested in their guests' well being as they might be. In other words a hotel that lacks a heart and coasts along rather than strives...or so we feel. Tell us if you disagree...reports please.

~

NEARBY Rialto Bridge; Rialto markets; Ca d'Oro.
LOCATION beside Rialto bridge, opposite the vaporetto landing stage; vaporetto Rialto
FOOD breakfast
PRICE €€€€
ROOMS 28; 23 double or triple, 3 single, 2 family, all with bath or shower; all rooms have phone, TV, air-conditioning, hairdrier, safe
FACILITIES breakfast room, terrace
CREDIT CARDS AE, DC, MC, V
DISABLED one room on ground floor
PETS accepted
CLOSED never
PROPRIETOR Franco Maschietto

VENICE

SAN POLO

CA'BERNARDI
TOWN BED AND BREAKFAST

Campiello Ca'Bernardi, San Polo
1321, 30125 Venezia

TEL 041 522 4923
FAX 041 099 7849
E-MAIL info@cabernardi.com
WEBSITE www.cabernardi.com
FOOD breakfast
PRICE €€
CLOSED never
PROPRIETORS Amelia Bonvini and
Deborah Veneziale

AMERICAN MOTHER AND DAUGHTER Deborah and Amelia have opened one of the most stylish B&Bs to have sprung up in Venice since the millennium. Close to San Silvestro vaporetto in a little *campiello* near the Rialto, it consists of four spacious bedrooms which sleep two, three or, in one case, four people, with desk and sitting area as well (and a brand new kitchen in the largest). With a warm palette and a slightly ethnic slant, the most has been made of each beamed and wood-floored room, named for their predominant colours such as 'Rose' and 'Yellow'. Best of all is the leafy courtyard, with attractive garden furniture, where breakfast is taken on sunny days (otherwise it is served in the room).

VENICE

SANTA CROCE

AI DUE FANALI

~ TOWN HOTEL ~

Campo San Simeon Grande, Santa Croce 946, 30135 Venezia
TEL 041 718490 **FAX** 041 718344
E-MAIL request@aiduefanali.com **WEBSITE** www.aiduefanali..com

A BAS RELIEF OF A SAINT inside the portico gives a clue to the hotel's origins as the Scuola of the Church of San Simeon Grande next door, in an elongated *campo* which is off the tourist track and soothingly crowd-free. By Venetian standards, this ancient building is quite unexceptional from the outside, but within, you will find a glossy little hotel, stylishly furnished by its talented owner, Marina Ferron, who also owns the San Simeon Apartments. The polished marble and stone floor of the ground-floor reception/sitting room is strewn with Persian rugs and dotted with fine antiques. The walls are hung with oil paintings and gilt-framed mirrors. Nick-nacks on the marble fireplace and fresh flowers create a homely feel.

There are great views from both the smart third-floor breakfast room (all green marble and wood) and the small roof terrace, perched on stilts on top of the building like a jetty out-of-water. Bedrooms are on the small side, but simply and tastefully decorated, with painted bedheads and modish stone-tiled bathrooms. All in all, a handy yet off-the-beaten-track address that provides Venetian sophistication without San Marco prices.

~

NEARBY station; Scalzi; San Giacomo dell'Oro.
LOCATION across the Grand Canal from the station.
FOOD breakfast
PRICE €€€
ROOMS 17; 10 double, twin and triple, 7 with bath, 3 with shower; 7 single, 2 with bath, 5 with shower; all rooms have phone, TV, air-conditioning, minibar, hairdrier, safe
FACILITIES breakfast room, sitting area, lift, roof terrace
CREDIT CARDS AE, DC, MC, V
DISABLED possible, but no special facilities
PETS not accepted
CLOSED never
PROPRIETOR Marina Ferron

VENICE

SANTA CROCE

SAN CASSIANO
~ TOWN HOTEL ~

Calle della Rosa, Santa Croce 2232, 30135
TEL 041 5241768 **FAX** 041 721033
E-MAIL info@sancassiano.it **WEBSITE** www.sancassiano.it

ARRIVING BY BOAT at San Cassiano's private jetty on the Grand Canal is considerably easier than finding your way by foot through a maze of tortuous, narrow alleyways from the nearest *vaporetto* or *traghetto* point (ask for a brochure to be sent so that you can follow its map). It also means that you can appreciate the 14th-century *palazzo*'s best feature: its deep red Gothic façade which faces the Grand Canal's greatest glory, the Ca' d'Oro. As befits such a building, the San Cassiano Ca' Favretto (to give the hotel its full name) has some grandiose rooms inside, and the six bedrooms facing the canal are splendid – indeed you should be tempted to look elsewhere if you can't secure one. The light, elegant breakfast room with huge windows and waterfront views is also a delight.

It could be perfect. Our latest inspector succinctly describes why it isn't. 'One or two deft touches would make this old building very smart indeed. The snug bar could be made wonderful but probably won't be. The place needs tightening up a little. Our first-floor room overlooking the Ca' d'Oro had fashionable dark red polished plaster walls and no pictures, which was as it ought to be. Real gilt on the bed-head. Good reproduction furniture. Bath rather short, but attractive, new and well-kept bathroom. The plants in the window boxes were dead, symptomatic of the slightly slack management. Wonderful barley-sugar turned wooden handrail on the steep staircase (no lift). Breakfast pretty ordinary.'

~

NEARBY Ca' d'Oro; Rialto Bridge; Rialto markets.
LOCATION on Grand Canal, opposite Ca' d'Oro; vaporetto San Stae or water taxi
FOOD breakfast
PRICE €€€€€
ROOMS 36; 20 double and twin, 12 triple and family, 4 single all with bath or shower; all rooms have phone, TV, air-conditioning, minibar, hairdrier, safe
FACILITIES sitting room, breakfast room, bar **CREDIT CARDS** AE, MC, V
DISABLED 2 rooms specially adapted **PETS** accepted **CLOSED** never
PROPRIETOR Franco Maschietto

VENICE

SANTA CROCE

LOCANDA SALIERI
TOWN HOTEL

*Fondamenta Minotto, Santa
Croce 160, 30135 Venezia*

TEL 041 5212508 **FAX** 041 5212942
E-MAIL info@locandasalieri.com
WEBSITE www.locandasalieri.com
FOOD breakfast
PRICE € **CLOSED** never
PROPRIETOR Judith Boulbain

IN A VERY QUIET CANALSIDE CORNER OF THE Santa Croce district, well placed for the station and Piazzale Roma, and just moments from the Grand Canal, this sister hotel to Locanda Art Deco (see page 50) makes a very acceptable one-star budget establishment, having been renovated in 2004. The ten bedrooms are plain, as you might imagine, but fresh, with clean white walls, smart bedspreads, floaty curtains and even little tables and chairs. Each one has an ensuite gaily tiled bathroom (with good showers and hairdrier). Some rooms have views on to the Gaffaro Canal, some on to Tolentino church, others over rooftops. Through the hotel you can book boat tours, concerts, restaurants, even a relaxing massage.

SANTA CROCE

PALAZZO ODONI
TOWN HOTEL

*Fondamenta Minotto, Santa
Croce 151, 30135 Venezia*

TEL 041 2759454 **FAX** 041 2759454
E-MAIL info@palazzoodoni.com
WEBSITE www.palazzoodoni.com
FOOD breakfast
PRICE €€€
CLOSED never
PROPRIETOR Alessandro Fabris

THE OWNERS OF PALAZZO ODONI have been in situ for five generations, but it was one of the first inhabitants for whom the house is named: Andrea Odoni, celebrated 16th-century art and antiques collector. Just a few doors along from the Locanda Salieri (see above) it has been converted into a modest hotel with more than a little character, thanks to its familial touch. Bedrooms (with minibars) are decorated in a rather *ad hoc* fashion, with original pieces of furniture mixed with new, and well appointed bathrooms. As so often with Venetian *palazzos*, the inconsequential exterior belies the (faded) grandeur of the public rooms. (A brass plaque and a buzzer are the only signs that this is no longer a private house.) Breakfast is an adequate self-service affair.

VENICE

CASTELLO

BISANZIO
~ TOWN HOTEL ~

Calle de la Pietà, Castello 3651, 30122 Venezia
TEL 041 5203100 **FAX** 041 5204114
EMAIL email@hotelbisanzio.com **WEBSITE** www.hotelbisanzio.com

T HE BIG PLUS POINT of this straightforward tourist hotel – which you may choose if comfort and modern amenities rather than character is your prime objective – is the bedrooms, at least the good ones, which cost very little more than the not-so-good ones. The latter are mainly dull boxes, while the former are light and airy bargains. Best are the eight rooms with private terraces and rooftop views. No. 34, for example, has a space-enhancing lobby leading to a bathroom tiled in pale green *corto Veneziano* tiles on one side, and on the other a large terrace with views of St Mark's *campanile*. No. 82 has a smaller terrace, but the room is large and light with a capacious bath and attractive marble basin (as are all the basins in this hotel). The rooms with double bed and bunk beds make an excellent choice for a family. Furnishings are mostly of the modern painted wood variety and floors and doors are insulated, cutting down outside noise to a minimum.

As for the public spaces, the lobby is both functional and stylish, with white walls, beamed ceilings, twinkly halogen lights, marble floors, several separate sitting areas and a cosy bar – and bland, uniform furniture. There is a large breakfast room where a generous buffet is served.

~

NEARBY Riva degli Schiavoni, Piazza San Marco.
LOCATION just off Riva degli Schiavoni, behind La Pietà; vaporetto San Zaccaria or water taxi
FOOD breakfast
PRICE €€€€€
ROOMS 43; 35 double, twin and triple, 2 suites, 2 single, 4 family, 20 with bath, 23 with shower; all rooms have phone, TV, air-conditioning, minibar, safe, hairdrier
FACILITIES sitting room, bar, breakfast room, courtyard, lift
CREDIT CARDS AE, DC, MC, V
DISABLED no special facilities
PETS accepted **CLOSED** never
PROPRIETORS Busetti family

VENICE

CASTELLO

BUCINTORO
~ TOWN HOTEL ~

Riva San Biagio, Castello 2135, 30122 Venezia
TEL 041 5223240 **FAX** 041 5235224
E-MAIL info@hotelbucintoro.com **WEBSITE** www.hotelbucintoro.com

WE KNOW A COUPLE who splashed out on the Londra Palace (which they liked very much) for the first few days of their stay in Venice and then sharply downgraded to the Bucintoro – which they almost preferred. Apart from the wonderful views across St Mark's Basin, which the two hotels share, the contrast could not be greater. Rooms at this basic *pensione*, little changed since the Bianchi family bought it more than 30 years ago, are as plain as a pikestaff; breakfast is frugal (the coffee is good); and the sitting room, despite its newly upholstered armchairs, remains unappealing.

The secret of its success is its position: every clean and simple room has a lagoon view and is flooded with Venetian light. Corner rooms, beloved by artists (Whistler, Dufy and Marquet are past guests) are the best, with windows on to both the lagoon and San Marco (try for Nos 1, 7, 9, 11). Room No. 4 is one of the pleasantest, with large bed, pretty bedspread, airy curtains and the waters of the lagoon gently lapping below. No. 26 can fit up to four people and has a fair-sized bathroom. The modest cement-rendered building with tables outside in summer is conveniently close to the Arsenale vaporetto stop. The great cruise ships that now ply the lagoon are an unwanted addition to the scene.

~

NEARBY Arsenale; Naval Museum; Piazza San Marco.
LOCATION on the waterfront, at the far end of Riva degli Schiavoni; vaporetto Arsenale or water taxi
FOOD breakfast
PRICE €€€
ROOMS 28; 22 double, twin and triple, 17 with bath, 5 with shower, 6 single, 5 with shower, 1 with basin; all rooms have phone, fan on request, hairdrier
FACILITIES breakfast room, sitting room, terrace
CREDIT CARDS MC, V **DISABLED** not suitable
PETS not accepted **CLOSED** Dec, Jan
PROPRIETORS Bianchi family

VENICE

CASTELLO

CASA VERADO

～ TOWN HOTEL ～

Campo SS. Filippo e Giacomo, Castello 4765, 30122 Venezia
TEL 041 5286138 **FAX** 041 5232765
EMAIL info@casaverardo.it **WEBSITE** www.casaverardo.it

THIS IS A PLACE WITH A PAST: built in the 16th century as a nobleman's *palazzo,* it became a Jewish school during World War I, and then in 1930 was converted into a one-star hotel. The Mestre family bought it in 1999, totally revamped it, and opened it as a polished three star. The remarkable thing is that, throughout its various incarnations, so few of its splendid features were interfered with. You can still see the original well in the courtyard garden and, inside, gorgeous inlaid mosaic floors and heavy wooden doors. With its perfect proportions, moulded ceiling and light streaming in from windows at either end, the *piano nobile* is an inspired choice for the breakfast room. Less inspired are the reproduction chairs that furnish it, at odds with the well-chosen Fortuny lamps and Austrian mirror.

We've grown accustomed to being disappointed by Venetian bedrooms, but that's not the case here. The best are the corner rooms, wonderfully light and overlooking the canal on two sides. Many have antiques, Florentine or Liberty beds, parquet floors, old frescoes, mouldings and painted ceilings. No. 305 has a private terrace. A comfortable, safe choice, but it just misses that personal, home-from-home feel.

～

NEARBY Piazza San Marco; Santa Maria Formosa.
LOCATION follow Calle drio la Chiesa NE of Campo SS. Filippo e Giacomo just across Ponte Storto; vaporetto San Zaccaria
FOOD breakfast, lunch, dinner; room service
PRICE €€€€
ROOMS 22 double and twin, triple, family, all with bath or shower; all rooms have phone, TV, air conditioning, minibar, hairdrier, safe
FACILITIES sitting room, bar, breakfast room, lift, 2 roof terraces, courtyard
CREDIT CARDS AE, DC, MC, V
DISABLED one specially adapted room **PETS** accepted
CLOSED never
PROPRIETOR Mestre family

VENICE

CASTELLO

LONDRA PALACE
~ TOWN HOTEL ~

Riva degli Schiavoni, Castello, 30122 Venezia
TEL 041 5200533 **FAX** 041 5225032
EMAIL info@hotelondra.it **WEBSITE** www.hotelondra.it

THE POSITION MIDWAY ALONG THE RIVA is, of course, magnificent, with no fewer than 100 of the hotel's bedroom windows affording matchless views across the lagoon to the island of San Giorgio Maggiore. No wonder Tchaikovsky found it a congenial place in which to write his Fourth Symphony in 1877. Then there were two adjacent hotels, both opened in 1860; they merged in 1900, and today, after a costly refit in the 1990s, the Londra Palace is undoubtedly one of the premier hotels in the city. Of course, it's too large for our guide, strictly speaking, but we include it (along with the Gritti Palace) because we think it stands out clearly from Venice's other large, luxury hotels. One of its best features is that every room has been given the same lavish attention. The standard is high, and the quality of the Biedermeier furniture and the original paintings used throughout is exceptional. Rooms with a view are more expensive – secure one if you can. In the morning, heavy shutters keep them deliciously dark and quiet; open them and you lie in bed listening to the peaceful slap of waves on the quay. Service is smooth and the twinkly concierge endears himself to everyone. The food in the restaurant, Do Leoni, was, on our last visit, excellent.

~

NEARBY Piazza San Marco; San Giorgio in Bragora, San Zaccaria.
LOCATION midway along the waterfront, 2 mins walk from San Marco; vaporetto San Zaccaria, San Marco or water taxi
FOOD breakfast, lunch dinner; room service
PRICE €€€€€€
ROOMS 53; 33 double and twin, 20 junior suites, all with bath; all rooms have phone, TV, air-conditioning, minibar, safe, hairdrier
FACILITIES sitting room, dining room, bar, terrace, sundeck, lift
CREDIT CARDS AE, DC, MC, V
DISABLED no special facilities **PETS** accepted
CLOSED never
PROPRIETOR Ugo Samueli

VENICE

CASTELLO

METROPOLE

~ TOWN HOTEL ~

Riva degli Schiavoni, Castello 4149, 30122 Venezia
TEL 041 5205044 **FAX** 041 5223679
E-MAIL venice@hotelmetropole.com **WEBSITE** www.hotelmetropole.com

OF THE HALF DOZEN OR MORE HOTELS along the Riva degli Schiavoni, with its matchless views of the lagoon, this is our favourite. Still in private hands, it has endearing touches (the owner, Signor Beggiato, is a collector: everywhere you look are carved angels, lecterns, church pews, corkscrews, crucifixes, calling card cases, fans) and a core of twinkle-eyed staff who have been there forever. It's a canny choice in winter, when the velvet-hung *salone*, its table heaped with cakes at tea-time, the intimate bar and the small wood-panelled and muralled restaurant (a former chapel where Vivaldi taught singing to orphan girls), are most inviting; the latter makes a cosy and comfortable place in which to lunch or dine. But it's a good hotel for summertime too: the large, quiet garden at the back, filled with flowers, makes the perfect place for a drink or a stroll.

In the morning, the generous buffet breakfast is served in a pretty room, a vision in candy pink and white, decorated with antique fans. Bedrooms vary from traditional (such as cosy no. 350 with private *altana*) to wildly kitsch (complete with flying cherubs in no. 251). It's a busy tourist hotel in a bustling location, but it has character, atmosphere, and a genuinely warm heart.

~

NEARBY Piazza San Marco, San Zaccaria.
LOCATION midway along the Riva, next to the church of La Pietà; vaporetto San Zaccaria, Arsenale or water taxi
FOOD breakfast, lunch, dinner; room service
PRICE €€€€€
ROOMS 72; 56 double and twin, 3 single, 10 junior suites, 3 family; all rooms have phone, TV, air conditioning, minibar, safe, hairdrier
FACILITIES breakfast room, sitting room, dining room, lift, garden
CREDIT CARDS AE, DC, MC, V
DISABLED access possible
PETS accepted
CLOSED never
PROPRIETORS Beggiato family

VENICE

LA RESIDENZA

~ TOWN HOTEL ~

Campo Bandiera e Moro, Castello 3608, 30122 Venezia
TEL 041 5285315 **FAX** 041 5238859
E-MAI info@venicelaresidenza.com **WEBSITE** www.venicelaresidenza.com

L A RESIDENZA APPEALS to true lovers of Venice who appreciate the chance
to stay in the grand Gothic *palazzo* which dominates this dusty and
enigmatic square, whose little church, San Giovanni in Bragora is one of
the city's most appealing.

Just to enter is an experience: huge doors swing open to reveal an
ancient covered courtyard and stone steps leading up to a vast baroque
hall with beautifully coloured, lavishly carved plaster walls. Taking breakfast here in the early morning light is a rare treat, though the hushed
atmosphere can be a little oppressive.

This, however, is not a grand hotel, but a modest two-star in immodest
surroundings. Those devotees – and these were many – who appreciated
the combination of grotty, kitsch and antique in the bedrooms under the
hotel's former ownership mourn the fact that they have all now been renovated (calm and pretty, but standard); other, more recent guests, appreciate the modernizations and feel that as long as the central hall remains
unchanged, La Residenza retains it special appeal.

By the way, the famous smell – of cats? or is it boiled cabbage? – seems
to have retreated to the hallway; some say it's gone altogether.

~

NEARBY San Giorgio degli Schiavoni; Arsenale.
LOCATION on small square 100 m behind Riva degli Schiavoni; vaporetto Arsenale,
San Zaccaria
FOOD breakfast
PRICE €€€
ROOMS 14; 12 double and twin, 2 single, all with bath or shower; all rooms have
phone, TV, air conditioning, minibar, safe, hairdrier
FACILITIES sitting room, breakfast area
CREDIT CARDS MC, V
DISABLED not suitable **PETS** accepted
CLOSED never
PROPRIETOR Giovanni Ballestra

VENICE

B&B SAN MARCO
TOWN BED-AND-BREAKFAST

Fondamenta San Giorgio degli Schiavoni, Castello 3385, 30122 Venezia

TEL 041 5227589
E-MAIL info@realvenice.it
WEBSITE www.realvenice.it
FOOD breakfast **PRICE** €
CLOSED never
PROPRIETOR Marco Scurati

FROM THE ROOMS on the third floor of this delightful private house, there are fine views over the rooftops as well as of San Giorgio degli Schiavoni and its adjacent canal and little bridge – typically Venetian. The three bedrooms are neat and pretty, decorated with a sure touch and a domestic hand. The brass or mahogany beds are piled with cushions, there are pictures on the walls and pretty bedside tables with ornaments and bedside lamps. The rooms are large enough for a third bed. There is also a two bedroom apartment with its own kitchen. For the rest, breakfast is taken in Marco's own large kitchen any time until 11am. Everyone lends a hand – the antithesis of staying in a hotel and a very welcome change.

CANADA
TOWN HOTEL

Campo San Lio, Castello 5659, 30122 Venezia

TEL 041 5229912
FAX 041 5235852
E-MAIL booking@canadavenice.com
WEBSITE www.canadavenice.com
FOOD breakfast
PRICE € € € **CLOSED** never
PROPRIETOR Signor Brusaferro

TWO ROOMS ONLY are worth having here: the ones at the very top, each with its own wooden-railed terrace looking out across tiled roofs and church façades to the campanile of St Mark's. Though simple and straightforward, their carved mahogany and studded velvet bedheads add a touch of pomp, and the bathrooms are clean and neat. They cost no more than any other room, but the bonus of the terrace makes them distinctly good value. You will have to climb endless stairs to reach reception, and yet more to get to the bedrooms, so only the fit need apply. A simple hotel with some character. We found the staff friendly.

VENICE

CASTELLO

GLI ANGELI
TOWN BED-AND-BREAKFAST

Campo de la Tana 2161, 30122 Venezia

TEL 041 5230802
FAX 041 2415350
E-MAIL theangels@email.it
WEBSITE www.gliangeli.net
FOOD breakfast
PRICE €
CLOSED never
PROPRIETOR Sonia Pisciutta

THIS LITTLE FAMILY-RUN B&B (the owners live upstairs) is found in one of the most genuine corners of Venice, moments from the imposing entrance to the Arsenale dockyards and close to the local shopping street Via Garibaldi, where the washing hangs in colourful rows across the wide street, and there are ice cream parlours and *pizzerie* as well as a market. It's a bit on the twee side, to be honest, but run with charm and commitment by Sonia Pisciutta. It consists of three bedrooms furnished in Venetian style, with fabric draped as coronets above the beds and some ornate pieces of furniture dotted about. The largest, Camera Oro, has a kitchen and sleeps up to four people. The others are for two people.

CASTELLO

PAGANELLI
TOWN HOTEL

Riva degli Schiavoni, Castello 4182, 30122 Venezia

TEL 041 5224324
FAX 041 5239267
E-MAIL hotelpag@tin.it
WEB www.hotelpaganelli.com
FOOD breakfast
PRICE €€€
CLOSED never
PROPRIETORS Paganelli family

THIS MODEST, FRIENDLY PLACE gives itself no airs at all – in fact the wood-veneer-clad entrance, filled with leather chairs, looks remarkably unprepossessing – but it shares the same lagoon views as much more august and expensive hotels on the Riva. And the simple, pleasant bedrooms far exceed the public rooms. They are furnished with pretty, delicate painted pieces, and gauze curtains flutter at the shuttered windows. Largest and smartest rooms face the waterfront: No. 6 is our favourite. Breakfast is served in an annexe in an adjoining side street, where a number of bedrooms are also located. It's a simple affair – as you would guess – but the coffee is good.

VENICE

CASTELLO

PALAZZO CONTARINI
TOWN HOTEL

*Salizzada San Guistina, Castello
2926, 30122 Venezia*

TEL 041 2770991
FAX 041 2777021
E-MAIL info@palazzocontarini.com
WEBSITE www.palazzocontarini.com
FOOD breakfast
PRICE ⓔⓔⓔⓔ   CLOSED never
MANAGER Christina Abele

IN A CHARMING AND UNTOURISTY AREA of Castello, this splendid, historic *palazzo* has recently been converted by a hotel chain, Tivigest, into a small hotel. It's a particularly good bet for small groups of friends looking for full or partial self-catering, especially if you choose one of the more expensive apartments, which are grand and richly furnished. The non-self catering bedrooms and the communal rooms, however, are less carefully furnished, and breakfast, in a cramped room off the splendid *salone,* is of the cardboard bread and packet butter variety. It's the sort of place where one wishes that a private owner was behind it – nearly there but not quite. It has a lovely courtyard.

CASTELLO

PALAZZO SODERINI
TOWN BED-AND-BREAKFAST

*Campo Bandiera e Moro, Castello
3611, 30122 Venezia*

TEL 041 2960823
FAX 041 2417989
E-MAIL info@palazzosoderini.it
WEBSITE www.palazzosoderini.it
FOOD breakfast
PRICE ⓔⓔ   CLOSED never
PROPRIETOR Manuel Orio

IF MODERN MINIMALISM is your thing, and you like to be surrounded by it wherever you go (or if you just want to avoid clichéd 'Venetian style' decoration at all costs) then head for this cutting edge b&b in the lovely Campo Bandieri e Moro, where you will also find the Hotel Residenza (see page 67). The three bedrooms are seriously pared-down, with white-covered king size beds, white walls, white furniture – you get the picture. There are marble bathrooms with showers, plus (of course) WiFi internet connection for computers, satellite TVs, safes and minibars. Best is the lovely garden – not white at all but green and very pretty.

VENICE

CASTELLO

WILDNER
TOWN HOTEL

Riva degli Schiavoni, Castello
4161, 30122 Venezia

TEL 041 5227463
FAX 041 5265615
E-MAIL
wildner@veneziahotels.com
WEBSITE www.veneziahotels.com
FOOD breakfast
PRICE €€€
CLOSED never
PROPRIETOR Nicola Fullin

T WO LONG-STANDING BUDGET options tucked between the four-star palaces along the Riva degli Schiavoni are the Paganelli (see page 69) and the Pensione Wildner. The same family has run the Wildner for nearly 40 years, maintaining an air of solid respectability amid the hubbub of the waterfront. All the bedrooms are similar in their old-fashioned simplicity, but the ones to try for are those with a view across the lagoon which are no more expensive than the rest. Some can sleep four, which makes a useful option for families or friends on a budget. The stream of tourists along the Riva by day (empty at night), and the cruise ships that now ply the lagoon, are an increasing drawback to staying in this location, however.

VENICE

DORSODURO

ACCADEMIA
~ TOWN HOTEL ~

Fondamenta Bollani, Dorsoduro 1058, 30123 Venezia
TEL 041 5210188 **FAX** 041 5239152
E-MAIL info@pensioneaccademia.it **WEBSITE** www.pensioneaccademia.it

STILL ONE OF THE BEST LOVED hotels in Venice, the Accademia continues to exert its considerable charm on a stream of contented guests. Despite modernizations such as sliding front doors and air conditioning, both the hotel and its staff have the knack of making guests feel like travellers from another, more genteel, age rather than modern-day tourists.

The Accademia's privileged canalside location is both convenient and calm, but what really distinguishes the *pensione* is its gardens – the large canal-side patio, where tables are scattered among plants in classical urns, and the grassy rear garden where roses and fruit trees flourish. Built in the 17th century as a private mansion, Villa Maravege retains touches of grandeur, and most of the furnishings are classically Venetian (the Murano chandeliers for once tasteful and harmonious). Perfect for sitting and relaxing is the finely furnished first floor landing, while the bedrooms have inlaid wooden floors and antiqued mirrors. The airy breakfast room has crisp white tablecloths and a beamed ceiling; but, weather permitting, guests will inevitably opt to start their day in the garden. The price of a room here feels good value for money these days compared to similar hotels.

~

NEARBY Accademia gallery; Scuola Grande dei Carmini.
LOCATION where the Toletta and Trovaso canals meet the Grand Canal; vaporetto Accademia or water taxi
FOOD breakfast
PRICE €€€
ROOMS 29; 22 double and twin, 9 with bath, 13 with shower, 7 single, 6 with shower; all rooms have phone, TV; most have air conditioning, hairdrier, safe
FACILITIES breakfast room, bar, sitting room, garden
CREDIT CARDS AE, DC, MC, V
DISABLED no special facilities **PETS** accepted
CLOSED never
PROPRIETOR Giovanna Salmaso

VENICE

DORSODURO

AGLI ALBORETTI
~ TOWN HOTEL ~

Rio Terrà Foscarini, Dorsoduro 884, 30123 Venezia
TEL 041 5230058 **FAX** 041 5210158
E-MAIL alborett@gpnet.it **WEBSITE** www.aglialboretti.com

THE ALBORETTI IS DISTINGUISHED by its warm welcome, and genuine family atmosphere. Reception is a cosy wood-panelled room with paintings of Venice on the walls and a model of a 17th-century galleon in its window; the ground floor sitting room is small, but a second sitting room on the first floor makes a comfortable retreat (the TV is rarely used); the terrace behind the hotel, entirely covered by a pergola and set simply with tables and chairs, is a delight, especially for a leisurely breakfast in summer. The building's fourth floor is now part of the hotel, and includes another terrace for guests.

The style of the bedrooms is predominantly simple, some with a nautical theme, and most with an antique or two. Like the rest of the hotel, they are well cared for and spotlessly clean, but the bathrooms, though totally renovated, are tiny, as are some of the rooms. None are large, but three are recommended for their garden views, and one also has a balcony on which you can breakfast.

Signora Linguerri runs a sophisticated restaurant next door, a favourite with Venetians, where you can eat in the pretty dining room or outside under the pergola; she is an expert on wine and her list offers an interesting selection.

~

NEARBY Accademia gallery; Zattere; Gesuati.
LOCATION alongside the Accademia gallery; vaporetto Accademia
FOOD breakfast, lunch, dinner
PRICE €€€
ROOMS 23; 13 double and twin, 5 single, 5 family rooms, all with bath or shower; all rooms have phone, modem point, TV, air conditioning, minibar, hairdrier
FACILITIES sitting rooms, dining room, bar, lift, terrace
CREDIT CARDS AE, MC, V
DISABLED no special facilities **PETS** accepted
CLOSED Jan occasionally; restaurant Wed, Thur lunch
PROPRIETOR Anna Linguerri

VENICE

DORSODURO

AMERICAN-DINESEN

~ TOWN HOTEL ~

Rio di San Vio, Dorsoduro 628, 30123 Venezia
TEL 041 5204733 **FAX** 041 5204048
E-MAIL reception@hotelamerican.com **WEBSITE** www.hotelamerican.com

Its owners want to change the hotel's name – The American – back to the original: Dinesen. At present it is officially called both. Set in a peaceful backwater of Dorsoduro, yet conveniently close to the Accademia and the Grand Canal, it's a quiet, dignified hotel with murmuring guests in spacious reception rooms and a tiny terrace where you can take breakfast under a pergola in summer. The public areas have a sombre Edwardian air, with wood panelling and silk damask on the walls, tapestry or velvet upholstered chairs, oriental rugs on Venetian mosaic floors, frilly white curtains and potted plants. Corridors are also panelled in wood, with little tables and chairs placed here and there. Bedrooms vary in size, as do the bathrooms, and though unexceptional they have pretty Venetian painted furniture (with minibars mercifully disguised as free-standing cupboards), ornate gilt mirrors and attractive Paisley-print bedspreads.

If you choose the American, you should do what you can to secure one of the nine bedrooms that overlook the canal. Nos 101 and 102 are particularly recommended, with three canal-facing French windows on two sides, and narrow balconies from where you can watch the water traffic drift by.

~

NEARBY Accademia gallery; Zattere; Santa Maria della Salute.
LOCATION midway along canal, which runs between Grand Canal and Giudecca Canal; vaporetto Accademia or water taxi
FOOD breakfast
PRICE €€€€
ROOMS 28; double and twin and single, all with bath or shower; all rooms have phone, TV, air conditioning, minibar, hairdrier, safe
FACILITIES sitting area, breakfast room, terrace
CREDIT CARDS AE, MC, V
DISABLED no special facilities
CLOSED never
PROPRIETOR Salvatore Sutera Sardo

VENICE

DORSODURO

LA CALCINA
~ TOWN HOTEL ~

Fondamenta Zattere ai Gesuati, Dorsoduro 780, 30123 Venezia
TEL 041 5206466 **FAX** 041 5227045
E-MAIL info@lacalcina.com **WEBSITE** www.lacalcina.com

THE HOUSE WHERE RUSKIN LIVED is hard to resist, both for its historical connection and for its location facing the sunny straits of the Giudecca
canal. The simple *pensione*, inherited by a go-ahead young couple, is
nowadays a stylish small hotel whose calm, uncluttered rooms provide a
welcome antidote to an excess of Venetian rococo. The pretty ground floor
reception rooms include a cosy, informal bar/restaurant/café, La Piscina,
just the place for a light meal and a glass or two of wine.

Unlike many hotels in the city there is a marked difference in price
between the rooms at the front, with views across the glittering water, and
the darkish back rooms, which have no view, but are equally comfortable.
Most expensive are the corner rooms, where the sun streams in from two
directions. None of the rooms is large, but all compensate with cool cream
walls, warm parquet floors, furniture from the original pensione and
gleaming bathrooms with heated towel rails. Meals are served in summer
on the terrace in front of the hotel, or on the lovely, sunny floating deck on
the Giudecca (or you can book the romantic rooftop altana for two), and
in winter in the marble-floored restaurant/bar with a picture window, so
that even if you opt for a bedroom at the back you can still enjoy the vista.
Several comfortable apartments in a nearby house are also available.

~

NEARBY Gesuati church; Accademia gallery.
LOCATION on W side of San Vio canal; vaporetto Zattere or water taxi
FOOD breakfast, light snacks, lunch, dinner
PRICE €€
ROOMS 29; 3 suites; 19 double and twin, 2 with bath, 20 with shower, 7 single, 1
with bath, 3 with shower, 3 with washbasin; all rooms have phone, air
conditioning, hairdrier, safe; apartments also available with space for 2
FACILITIES breakfast room/bar, sitting area, terrace, roof terrace
CREDIT CARDS AE, DC, MC, V
DISABLED not suitable **PETS** not accepted **CLOSED** never
PROPRIETORS Alessandro and Debora Szemere

VENICE

DORSODURO

CA'PISANI
~ TOWN HOTEL ~

Dorsoduro 979/a, 30123 Venezia
TEL 041 2401411 **FAX** 041 2771061
E-MAIL info@capisanihotel.it **WEBSITE** www.capisanihotel.it

BLATANTLY FLYING IN THE FACE of Venetian hotel tradition, the Ca' Pisani, built in the shell of a deep-pink 16th-century *palazzo*, is cool, hip and undeniably chic.

Inside, the overall style is designer minimalist, but the odd original feature (brick arches, roof beams, painted coffered ceilings, marble floors), and the collection of fine '30s and '40s beds, mirrors and wardrobes softens this to a certain extent. Decorative themes are consistent throughout both public areas and bedrooms. Silver (above the reception area, in bedroom furniture, in mirror frames, on light fittings, in steel chair frames) is a staple and lightens dark ebony, pale acid-green and pale violet paintwork, and black and orange leather chairs. Warm, hardwood floors and wood doors are all given a contemporary twist. Bathrooms, in either deep mauve or palest grey marble specked with silver, are straight from the pages of a design magazine. The bedrooms have Bang&Olufsen phones and TVs and electrically-operated window blinds. Biscuit-coloured bedcovers and cushions look smart against crisp white linen sheets. Breakfast is served in the basement restaurant where you can also enjoy a light meal. Reports would be welcome: we have heard one or two grumbles.

~

NEARBY Accademia gallery; Guggenheim museum.
LOCATION between the Accademia and Zattere; vaporetto Accademia, Zattere
FOOD breakfast, lunch, dinner
PRICE €€€€€
ROOMS 29; 23 double and twin, 4 junior suites, 2 studios, all with bath; all rooms have phone, TV, air conditioning, minibar, hairdrier
FACILITIES sitting room, restaurant, bar, Turkish bath, terrace
CREDIT CARDS AE, DC, MC, V
DISABLED 2 specially adapted rooms
PETS accepted
CLOSED never
PROPRIETORS Serandrei family

VENICE

DORSODURO

LA GALLERIA

~ TOWN HOTEL ~

Accademia, Dorsoduro 878/a, 30123 Venezia
TEL 041 5232489 **FAX** 041 5204172
E-MAIL galleria@tin.it **WEBSITE** www.hotelgalleria.it

ANYONE WHO CRAVES A WINDOW on the Grand Canal, yet is on a shoestring, should head for La Galleria. Its position, right by the Accademia bridge and gallery, and next to the vaporetto stop (where all the boats plying the Grand Canal call, unlike many of the stops along the way) is superb, unless, that is, you don't like the idea of the throng that mills around outside the gallery during the day.

Access is through an improbable entrance next to a craft gallery, whereafter you climb a flight of steepish steps and travel back some 90 years, for this quaint little ten-room hotel in a very old and creaky building appears frozen in the Edwardian era. Dark red flock paper covers the walls; floors are mostly plain wooden boards; the furniture is traditional Venetian – silk and gilt bedheads, large old-fashioned wardrobes, beds and chandeliers; and there are few amenities. Stick to the larger rooms on the Grand Canal – others are simply too small. Best is No. 10 which can sleep four and has a glorious painted ceiling, and only costs 35 euros more than a standard double room with bathroom. Breakfast is served in your room and the staff are charming.

~

NEARBY Accademia gallery; Grand Canal.
LOCATION at NE corner of Campo della Carità, next to the Accademia bridge; vaporetto Accademia or water taxi
FOOD breakfast
PRICE €€
ROOMS 10; 8 double and twin, 2 with bath; one single; one family with bath; all rooms have phone
FACILITIES sitting area
CREDIT CARDS not accepted
DISABLED not suitable
PETS accepted
CLOSED 2 to 3 weeks in winter
PROPRIETOR Luciano Benedetti

VENICE

DORSODURO

LOCANDA CA' FOSCARI

~ TOWN HOTEL ~

Calle della Frescada, Dorsoduro 3888-3887/b, 30123 Venezia
TEL 041 710401/710817 **FAX** 041 710817
E-MAIL info@locandacafoscari.com **WEBSITE** www.locandacafoscari.com

YOU WILL NEED HELP FINDING Calle Frescada, a little lane tucked almost out of sight and unmarked on most maps: take Calle Larga Foscari towards the Frari, and at the junction with Crosera, turn right. Calle Frescada runs across the end, and the hotel faces down Crosera. Happily our inspector's maddening search for this little one-star hotel was worth the effort – Ca' Foscari is a cut above. Somehow its charming, modest exterior – smart front door and bell pull, little lantern displaying its name – tells the story, and the interior does not disappoint, nor the welcome from Valter and Giuliana Scarpa and their daughter Sara.

On the ground floor is a little breakfast room. A couple of flights of stairs, and you are in a fresh, white corridor with white-painted doors leading to the bedrooms. These are modest, as you would expect, but pristine, with lacy curtains, pretty bedspreads and white-tiled minute bathrooms, or, in rooms without bathrooms, decent basins. Note that the communal bathroom only has a shower, not a bath. The metal-framed beds are much more comfortable than they look. An excellent budget hotel in a bustling residential neighbourhood. A group of 22 to 28 can take the whole place, dinner (cooked by Signor Scarpa) and breakfast included, for £34 a night each.

~

NEARBY Scuola Grande di San Rocco; Frari; Accademia gallery.
LOCATION between Campo San Tomà and Palazzi Foscari; vaporetto San Tomà
FOOD breakfast
PRICE €€
ROOMS 11; 6 double and twin, 3 with shower, 3 with basin only; one single with shower, 2 triples without shower, 2 family rooms without shower; communal bathroom with shower
FACILITIES breakfast room
CREDIT CARDS MC, V
DISABLED not suitable **PETS** not accepted
CLOSED mid-Nov to mid-Jan, late Jul
PROPRIETOR Valter Scarpa

VENICE

DORSODURO

LOCANDA MONTIN
~ COUNTRY HOTEL ~

Fondamenta di Borgo, Dorsoduro 1147, 30123 Venezia
TEL 041 5227151 **FAX** 041 5200255
E-MAIL reserve@locandamontin.com **WEBSITE** www.locandamontin.com

WE'VE FEATURED THIS FRIENDLY *antica locanda* in our Venice guide since the first edition, but always as a short entry. Now, with the rising cost of the city's conventional hotels, its 12 modest rooms seem to us to offer an attractive, reasonably priced alternative, and we've decided to upgrade it to a long. In the same family for generations (and now run by the younger members), it used to attract a devoted following among the glitterati from Ezra Pound to Jimmy Carter. Fame was assured when in 1970 the pergola-shaded garden became the setting for a scene in a film featuring Tony Musante and Florinda Bolkan, *Anonimo Veneziano*. Although it still has charisma, with paintings jostling for space on the walls, the restaurant is rather living off its reputation, serving ordinary food – the speciality is fish – at highish prices.

Leading off a magnificent beamed landing, furnished with ornate pieces, bedrooms are large and slightly tatty with few frills but plenty of character. Some have their original stone floors; others have new wooden ones. Typically walls are pale and covered in paintings and prints, and the furniture is a ragbag of modern wood and handsome wrought-iron beds. Six rooms overlook the canal, and six the garden: No. 11 (on the canal side) is particularly popular.

~

NEARBY Carmini; San Trovaso; Accademia gallery; Zattere. .
LOCATION on quiet Eremite canal between the Grand Canal and Zattere and between the Accademia and Frari
FOOD breakfast
PRICE €€
ROOMS 12 single, double and twin, triple, family, 7 with bath or shower, 5 with basin; all rooms have phone, air conditioning
FACILITIES sitting area, restaurant, garden **CREDIT CARDS** AE, DC, MC, V
DISABLED not suitable **PETS** accepted
CLOSED 10 days Aug, 2-3 weeks Jan
PROPRIETORS Carrettin family

VENICE

DORSODURO

PALAZZETTO DA SCHIO

APARTMENTS IN PRIVATE HOUSE

Fondamenta Soranzo, Dorsoduro 316/b, 30123 Venezia
TEL and **FAX** 041 5237937
E-MAIL avenezia@tin.it **WEBSITE** www.palazzettodaschio.it

FONDAMENTA SORANZO IS A TRANQUIL backwater lined with attractive houses, including this red-painted palazzetto, home of the da Schio family for the past 300 years. The present incumbent, Contessa da Schio, lives on the ground floor and *piano nobile* while other parts of the house have been converted into four charming and comfortable apartments, available from any period of time from two days to three months. Note, though, that the apartments are considerably less expensive when taken per week or per month, rather than per night. They are largely furnished with family antiques, including pictures and mirrors, with modern bits and pieces to fill the gaps. The topmost apartment (not for those who don't like stairs) has wide views and large sitting rooms, while the apartments on the mezzzanine floor have views of the canal and the garden and cosy, antique-filled living rooms.

The entrance hall of the palazzetto, lit by precious Venetian torch lamps and opening on to the garden, is splendid. This, and the fine three-bedroom piano nobile apartment, can be hired for parties at any time of the year and is available to stay in for one month in the summer.

NEARBY Santa Maria della Salute; Accademia; Zattere.
LOCATION on canal between Grand and Guidecca Canals; vaporetto Salute or water taxi
FOOD none
PRICE €€
ROOMS 4 apartments, 2 with one bedroom, 2 with 2 bedrooms; all with phone, kitchen and bathroom; phone; maid service
CREDIT CARDS not accepted
DISABLED not suitable
PETS not accepted
CLOSED never
PROPRIETOR Contessa Anna da Schio

VENICE

DORSODURO

PALAZZO DAL CARLO
TOWN BED-AND-BREAKFAST

Fondamenta di Borgo, Dorsoduro 1163, 30123 Venezia
TEL 041 5226863 **FAX** 041 5226863
E-MAIL info@palazzodalcarlo.com **WEBSITE** www.palazzodalcarlo.com

YOU'D NEVER GUESS what lay behind this front door as you hurried past, perhaps on your way to eat at the venerable Montin almost next door (see page 77). Unless, that is, you are lucky enough to be a guest of its owner, Roberta dal Carlo.

After a career in the business of building and restoration, Roberta – charming, elegant and infectiously warm – returned to her family palazzo, redecorating and restoring it herself to its present state of perfection. Delicate 18th century stucco ceilings and a superb Venetian marble terrazzo floor are the decorative highlights, with the prettiest of pale green for the walls and comfortable sofas in which to sink. The combination of sophistication and homeliness, along with Roberta's warmth, quickly puts guests at ease and often as not, ready to chat. There are three attractive bedrooms, each very different and each with a compact but ultra-stylish bathroom. The bedroom at the top – which sleeps three if needed – opens on to a fabulous terrace. Sit and gaze at the view across to Giudecca (until, that is, it is suddenly blocked by the bizarre sight of a horizontal skyscraper – or cruise ship – gliding past). Breakfast, taken communally, is a treat, with the best and freshest ingredients.

NEARBY Carmini; San Trovaso; Accademia gallery; Zattere.
LOCATION on quiet Eremite canal between the Grand Canal and Zattere and between the Accademia and Frari; vaporetto Ca'Rezzonico/Accademia.
FOOD breakfast
PRICE ©©
ROOMS 2 double or twin, one double or triple, all with bath
FACILITIES sitting room with TV, breakfast room
CREDIT CARDS MC, V
DISABLED not suitable
PETS accepted
CLOSED Jan
PROPRIETOR Roberta dal Carlo

VENICE

DORSODURO

SALUTE DA CICI
~ TOWN HOTEL ~

Fondamenta di Ca' Balà, Dorsoduro 222, 30123 Venezia
TEL 041 5325404 **FAX** 041 5222271
E-MAIL info@hotelsalute.com **WEBSITE** www.hotelsalute.com

A LONG-TIME FAVOURITE OF OURS, this calm, civilized hotel occupies a palazzo on a small canal in an interesting area between the Accademia and
Salute. If you've had your fill of Baroque churches, it's also perfectly
placed for a visit to the Guggenheim Collection and a blast of abstract
expressionism.

The façade is charming and typically Venetian: peeling stucco and rose-
coloured brick, Gothic windows and stone balconies decked with flowers.
And the interior doesn't disappoint. It has a classically elegant lobby of
columns and marble floors beneath exposed rafters. A little bar is
reserved for guests and a tiny sheltered garden offers a few sunny tables
for a drink. Interconnecting basement rooms, dating from the time when
this was a pensione, provide breakfast areas. Corridors lead off a beautifully furnished first-floor landing to simple white-painted bedrooms with
high ceilings, Venetian marble floors and furniture that ranges from
antique to utility. There's only a small difference in price, so request a
room on the canal or, if you're willing to sacrifice character for comfort, go
for one of the nine modern rooms in the annexe.

NEARBY Gugggenheim Collection; Santa Maria della Salute.
LOCATION just S of Rio Calle Terra Nuovo, 5 minutes walk E of Salute; vaporetto
Salute or water taxi
FOOD breakfast
PRICE €€
ROOMS 50 double and twin, single, triple and family, all with bath or shower; all
rooms have phones
FACILITIES bar, sitting area, breakfast room, garden
CREDIT CARDS not accepted
DISABLED not suitable
PETS not accepted
CLOSED mid-Nov to Christmas, Jan to Mar (or Carnival if earlier)
PROPRIETOR Sebastiano Cagnin

VENICE

DORSODURO

SEGUSO
~ TOWN HOTEL ~

Zattere ai Gesuati, Dorsoduro 779, 30123 Venezia
TEL 041 5286858 **FAX** 041 5222340
E-MAIL pensioneseguso@tiscali.it **WEBSITE** www.pensioneseguso.com

SITTING ON THE SUNNY PROMENADE of the Zattere, lapped by the choppy waters of the wide Giudecca canal, gives you the distinct feeling of being by the seaside. This open setting, with a grand panorama across the lagoon, is just one of the charms of the Seguso (which is right beside the Calcina, page 73). A *pensione* in the old tradition, it is family-run, friendly and solidly old-fashioned – some people love it, others don't, depending on their taste (we do). And (unlike most hotels in Venice) prices are modest; the Seguso is not noted for its food, but half board here costs no more than bed-and-breakfast alone in hotels of similar comfort closer to San Marco.

The best bedrooms are the large ones at the front of the house, over-looking the canal – though for the privilege of the views and space you may have to forfeit the luxury of a private bathroom (only half the rooms have their own facilities). The main public rooms are the dining room, prettily furnished in traditional style, and the modest sitting room where you can sink into large leather chairs and peruse ancient editions of travel writing and guidebooks. Breakfast is taken on the front terrace – delightful. Fellow guests are often friendly, interesting and great Venice enthusiasts. Group bookings (maximum 30 people) are accepted, though not in September and May. A survivor from another age.

NEARBY Accademia gallery; Gesuati church.
LOCATION 5 mins' walk S of Accademia, overlooking Giudecca canal; vaporetto Zattere or water taxi
FOOD breakfast, lunch, dinner
PRICE ©©©
ROOMS 36; 31 double and twin, 5 single, 9 with bath, 9 with shower; all rooms have phone
FACILITIES dining room, sitting room, lift, terrace
CREDIT CARDS AE, MC, V
DISABLED access possible **PETS** accepted
CLOSED mid-Dec to mid-Feb
PROPRIETORS Seguso family

VENICE

DORSODURO

CASA REZZONICO
TOWN BED-AND-BREAKFAST

Fondamenta Gheradini,
Dorsoduro 2813, 30123 Venezia

TEL 041 2770653 **FAX** 041 2775435
E-MAIL info@casarezzonico.it
WEBSITE www.casarezzonico.it
FOOD breakfast
PRICE €€ **CLOSED** never
PROPRIETOR Matteo Veronese

A PRETTY TWO-STOREY BUILDING with awnings fluttering in the breeze from the upper windows, Casa Rezzonico stands right on charming Rio di San Barnaba, lined by working boats moored alongside.Its seven bedrooms, while fairly simple, are a cut above, with decent reproduction antique furniture (and some antiques too): carved bedheads, matching bedside tables and big roomy wardrobes. Floating white curtains hang from wooden rails and the beds are dressed in pretty floral bedspreads. As so often in Venice, the terrazzo or parquet floors, while genuine and in keeping, make for a rather uncosy air. Some rooms overlook the canal, others the hotel's best feature: its grassy garden.

DORSODURO

LOCANDA CA' ZOSE
TOWN HOTEL

Calle del Bastion 193/b,
Dorsoduro, 30123 Venezia

TEL 041 5226635 **FAX** 041 5226624
E-MAIL info@hotelcazose.com
WEBSITE www.hotelcazose.com
FOOD breakfast
PRICE €€€ **CLOSED** never
PROPRIETORS Graziella and Velentina Campanati

O NE OF A CROP OF NEW locandas that have sprung up throughout Venice, this is the latest project of a pair of charming sisters and, in our opinion, their formula – despite being a formula – is a winning one. Split between two 17th-century buildings, the 12 bedrooms are all decorated in similar fashion, with painted, gilt-edged furniture and traditional-style fabrics. The exposed rafters remain the only clue to the buildings' age. Everything is fresh and bright: from the newly sponge-painted walls to the immaculate well-lit bathrooms. The comfortable rooms have power showers, minibars, satellite TVs and orthopaedic-sprung beds. The main breakfast room (there's another in the annexe) is painted white with dainty upholstered chairs. Excellent value in low season.

VENICE

DORSODURO

LOCANDA SAN BARNABA
TOWN HOTEL

Calle del Traghetto, Dorsoduro 2486, 30123 Venezia

TEL 041 2411233 **FAX** 041 241 3812
E-MAIL info@locanda-sanbarnaba.com
WEBSITE www.locanda-sanbarnaba.com **FOOD** breakfast
PRICE €€€ **CLOSED** never
PROPRIETOR Silvia Okolicsanyi

IN THE PAST, WHEN WE HAVE POPPED our heads into this small hotel, one of the first of the new breed of locandas to emerge in the 1990s, we have never particularly warmed to it, feeling it a little sterile. But readers' letters have convinced us otherwise, and they speak of a warm welcome, reasonable prices and simple bedrooms (13 of them in all) which are simply but individually and thoughtfully decorated with a mix of antiques and textiles. One has an original fresco on the ceiling. There's a small courtyard and roof terrace, and no bridge to cross to the nearest vaporetto stop.

DORSODURO

PAUSANIA
TOWN HOTEL

Fondamenta Gherardini, Dorsoduro 2824, 30123 Venezia

TEL 041 5222083
FAX 041 5222989
E-MAIL info@hotelpausania.it
WEBSITE www.hotelpausania.it
FOOD breakfast
PRICE €€€€
CLOSED never
PROPRIETOR Guido Gatto

SEVERAL CRITICAL LETTERS FROM READERS have prompted us to reduce our entry on this hotel, just along from Casa Rezzonico, to a short one. It lies close to the last surviving floating vegetable shop in Venice – a colourful barge on the San Barnaba canal. The building is a weathered Gothic palazzo with distinctive ogee windows. Inside, timbered ceilings, Corinthian columns, an ancient well-head and a battered but beautiful stone staircase are features of the original building. Bedrooms are all decorated in the same tastefully restrained style, though one of our correspondents felt that they needed attention, and another complained of being given a room that was unacceptably "small and dank".

VENICE

CANNAREGIO

CA' ZANARDI

~ *TOWN BED-AND-BREAKFAST* ~

Calle Zanardi, Cannaregio 4132, 30131 Venezia
TEL 041 2410220 FAX 041 5237716
E-MAIL ecgroup@tin.it *WEBSITE* www.best-of-italy.com/zanardi

IT'S A REAL VENETIAN EXPERIENCE finding your way on foot to 16th-century palazzo Ca'Zanardi, lost in a jumble of streets, bridges, alleys and canals in a very real part of Cannaregio (yet, really, only five minutes from Ca' d'Oro and moments from Fondamente Nuove). Once you get there, seeing Venice minus the tourists on the way, you will find a palazzo largely unchanged and still redolent of the city's golden age. As well as letting the six bedrooms on a bed-and-breakfast basis when they are available, the palazzo's French owner hires the whole place (ballroom, music rooom, dining room, executive office, terrace) for private parties and Carnival events – including masked balls – and a perfect and very genuine venue it makes: lavish and decadent yet lived-in and mellow with age; in short, affordable glory of another age.

You enter through a little courtyard into the *androne* – the vast hall where the gondolas were kept (and one is still parked) – then climb the staircase to the *piano nobile*. Here is the vast ballroom, with its impressive ceiling and marble terrazzo floor, and the more intimate music room, dripping in gold and crystal. The simply equipped bedrooms are in keeping, with splendid Venetian beds and plenty of gilt, mirrors and brocade. Breakfast on the terrace is a treat.

~

NEARBY Ca' d'Oro; Fondamenta Nuove.
LOCATION between Grand Canal and Fondamenta Nuove, E of Rio di Gesuiti
FOOD breakfast
PRICE €€
ROOMS 6 double and twin, all with bath or shower; all rooms have hairdrier
FACILITIES ballroom, dining room, music room, terrace
CREDIT CARDS MC, V
DISABLED not suitable
PETS not accepted
CLOSED never
PROPRIETOR Nicolas Arnita

VENICE

CANNAREGIO

CLUB CRISTAL
~ TOWN HOTEL ~

For further information all nationalities should contact: Liz Heavenstone, 188 Regent's Park Road, London NW1 8XP **TEL** (0044)207 722 5060 **FAX** (0044) 207 586 3004 **E-MAIL** info@sancassiano.it **WEBSITE** www.sancassiano.it

THE SETTING COULD HARDLY BE MORE IDEAL, at least for those seeking a peaceful backwater: an airy, palatial town house overlooking a tree-lined courtyard and a little canal in a quiet residential corner of Cannaregio, yet only five minutes' walk from the Ca' d'Oro. It is the family home of Susan Schiavon, an Englishwoman ("not pure English; lots of other nationalities come into it besides") who has lived in Venice many years and lets five of its bedrooms to discerning visitors for whom she is a fund of knowledge about the city.

An elegant white marble staircase leads to the *piano nobile* and a high-ceilinged sitting room filled with books and squashy sofas and armchairs – this is, as we said, very much a private house with normal clutter about the place; don't expect apple-pie order. A perfect breakfast is served on the plant-filled terrace beyond. The bedrooms, entered through original doors painted with birds and flowers, vary in size, some large; all are full of character, with family furniture, comfortable beds, and crisp linen. Susan serves dinner by arrangement, and you should take advantage of her accomplished home cooking at least once. Emphatically a home, not a hotel. Couples often return, and lone women feel particularly at ease.

~

NEARBY Ca' d'Oro; Gesuiti; Rialto.
LOCATION on a small canal between Ca' d'Oro and Gesuiti; vaporetto Ca' d'Oro
FOOD breakfast; dinner by arrangement
PRICE €–€€
ROOMS 4 double, one single, all with bath or shower; all rooms have hairdrier
FACILITIES sitting room, dining room, terrace
CREDIT CARDS AE, DC
DISABLED not suitable
PETS not accepted
CLOSED never
PROPRIETOR Susan Schiavon

VENICE

GIORGIONE
~ TOWN HOTEL ~

SS. Santi Apostoli, Cannaregio 4587, 30131 Venezia
TEL 041 5225810 **FAX** 041 5239092
E-MAIL info@hotelgiorgione.com **WEBSITE** www.hotelgiorgione.com

I F YOU'RE COMING TO VENICE with teenage children, this comfortable four -
star hotel could be a wise choice. When sightseeing begins to pall, they
can retreat to the pool table or the well-equipped games room. Unlike
many Venetian hotels, there is plenty of sitting space downstairs, a cosy
bar and large secluded garden with a pond and no shortage of tables and
chairs. The occasional column, arch and exposed beam are reminders that
this is a 15th-century palazzo, although bland decoration doesn't always
make the best of these features. Silk damask swagged curtains and upholstered sofas and chairs furnish the public rooms; while many of the bedrooms look twee and dated.

Some of the standard double rooms are on the small side, so for a few
extra euros, opt for a superior room or, better still, for a bit more, one of
the 'loft suites', tucked into the eaves with its own terrace, where you can
eat a lazy breakfast or sip a prosecco at sunset, the rooftops of the city
spread out before you. Breakfast downstairs is a generous buffet of fruit,
cereal, rolls, salami and eggs, served in a large white room decorated with
bad frescoes.

~

NEARBY Ca' d'Oro; Santi Apostoli; Miracoli.
LOCATION just off Campo Santi Apostoli to the north; vaporetto Ca' d'Oro
FOOD breakfast
PRICE €€€€€
ROOMS 76; 66 double, twin and single, 10 suites, all with bath; all rooms have
phone, TV, air-conditioning, minibar, safe, hairdrier
FACILITIES sitting areas, breakfast room, games room, bar, lift, garden
CREDIT CARDS AE, DC, MC, V
DISABLED access possible
PETS not accepted
CLOSED never
PROPRIETOR Signor Zanolin

VENICE

CANNAREGIO

LOCANDA AI SANTI APOSTOLI
~ TOWN HOTEL ~

Strada Nova, Cannaregio 4391, 30131 Venezia
TEL 041 5212612 **FAX** 041 5212611
E-MAIL aisantia@tin.it **WEBSITE** www.locandasantiapostoli.com

BE ON THE LOOKOUT FOR A PAIR of handsome dark green doors which herald the discreet entrance of this converted *palazzo*. Beyond is a scruffy courtyard and a quirky lift that takes you up to the third floor. What lies in store for you here is totally unexpected: a lovely apartment that has been transformed by the Bianchi Michiel family into an elegant, if pricey, B&B, one of the first, and still one of the best *locandas* to open in recent years in the city. The sitting room is the epitome of style: oil paintings hang on glossy apricot walls; heavy lamps rest on antique tables; sofas and chairs are covered in quiet chintz or swathed in calico. At the far end, a triptych of wood-framed windows overlooks the Grand Canal. Ornaments and books left casually around make it feel more like a home than a hotel.

Large and individually decorated, the bedrooms have been done out in glazed chintzes and stunning strong colours. Like the sitting room, they are dotted with antiques and pretty china knick-knacks. The two on the Grand Canal are considerably dearer than the rest. Stefano also owns a one-bedroom apartment on the second floor, with a vibrant green colour scheme, no view of the canal, but a sunny roof terrace.

~

NEARBY Ca' d'Oro; Santi Apostoli; Miracoli.
LOCATION just E of Campo Santi Apostoli; vaporetto Ca' d'Oro
FOOD breakfast
PRICE €€€€; apartment prices on request
ROOMS 11 double and twin, 6 with bath, 4 with shower; all rooms have phone, TV, air conditioning, minibar, hairdrier
FACILITIES breakfast room, sitting room, lift
CREDIT CARDS AE, DC, MC, V
DISABLED not suitable
PETS accepted
CLOSED Jan to mid-Feb, 2-3 weeks in Aug, sometimes 2 weeks in Dec
PROPRIETOR Stefano Bianchi Michiel

VENICE

CANNAREGIO

LOCANDA ANTICO DOGE
~ TOWN HOTEL ~

Campo SS Apostoli, Cannaregio 5043, 30131 Venezia
TEL 041 2411570 **FAX** 041 2443660
E-MAIL info@anticodoge.com **WEBSITE**: www.anticodoge.com

DON'T BE PUT OFF BY FIRST IMPRESSIONS at the Antico Doge. Its entrance may not be to your taste, but the long, wide peach-coloured hallway, decorated with glitzy white Murano glass lights and garish paintings of Venice, gives little hint of the charm and splendour that lies one floor up. Keep going, pausing at the small reception desk (where you will find a friendly and professional welcome) and, mounting the stairs, you will soon arrive on the *piano nobile* of this privately owned palazzo with a long history. The central *salone*, which doubles as a breakfast room and bar, is resplendent in gold, with vases of fresh flowers. Bedrooms drip with silk, brocade and damask on walls, windows and beds. Huge chandeliers, gilt mirrors, antique furniture and fine rugs on parquet floors complete the picture. In one suite hangs a picture of a startled looking Doge Marin Falier, whose mansion this once was.

Close to the Rialto, in a delightfully domestic and watery area of Cannaregio, just round the corner from both the Locanda Ai Santi Apostoli (previous page) and the Locanda Leon Bianco (next page), the Antico Doge is, like them, a cut above many similar bed and breakfast establishments.

~

NEARBY Santi Apostoli; Miracoli; Rialto.
LOCATION across little bridge on W side of Campo Santi Apostoli; vaporetto
Ca'd'Oro
FOOD breakfast
PRICE €€€€
ROOMS 15, all double or twin; 7 with shower, 8 with bath; all rooms have phone,
TV, air conditioning, minibar, safe, hairdrier
FACILITIES bar, breakfast room
CREDIT CARDS AE, MC, V
DISABLED access possible; stairlift **PETS** not accepted
CLOSED never
PROPRIETOR Mariella Bazzetta

VENICE

LOCANDA LEON BIANCO
∽ TOWN HOTEL ∽

Corte Leon Bianco, Cannaregio 5629, 30131 Venezia
TEL 041 5233572 **FAX** 041 2416392
E-MAIL info@leonbianco.it **WEBSITE** www.leonbianco.it

IF WINDOWS ON TO THE GRAND CANAL are your heart's desire, but you are on a budget, then here, along with La Galleria (see page 75) is the answer. The Leon Bianco is hidden away in an enclosed courtyard, behind a sturdy door in the wall, and approached by stone steps rising up a cavernous brick-walled stairwell. The spacious, simple rooms have carved mahogany beds, big old cupboards, undulating floors and immense tilted wooden doors. Three look over the Grand Canal, with wonderful views of the Rialto market and the traghetto that plies back and forth across the canal, while a fourth, though it lacks a view, is equally romantic, with a dramatic fresco of Moors and camels taken from a painting by Veronese emblazoned across one wall. The locanda, only a few years old, but old-fashioned in feel, occupies one floor of an old *palazzo* and has a reception area and seven large, attractive bedrooms with small, modern bathrooms. Although it doesn't offer the services or address of the ritzy San Marco hotels, the modest prices are irresistible by comparison. A word of warning, however: a reader wrote to us to complain that her booking was cancelled in a preremptory fashion, with little help given to finding alternative accommodation. More reports, please.

∽

NEARBY Santi Apostoli; Miracoli; Rialto.
LOCATION in courtyard between Santi Apostoli and Santa Giovanni Crisostomo canals; vaporetto Ca' d'Oro, Rialto
FOOD breakfast
PRICE €€€
ROOMS 7; 6 double and twin with shower, one family with bath; all rooms have phone
FACILITIES none
CREDIT CARDS AE, DC, MC, V
DISABLED not suitable
PETS not accepted
CLOSED never
PROPRIETORS Spellanzon family

VENICE

LOCANDA DEL GHETTO
~ TOWN HOTEL ~

Campo del Ghetto Nuovo, Cannaregio 2892, 30131 Venezia
TEL 041 2759292 **FAX** 041 2757987
E-MAIL ghetto@veneziahotels.com **WEBSITE**: www.veneziahotels.com

SURROUNDED ON ALL SIDES BY WATER, the Campo del Ghetto Nuovo is the evocative, rather melancholy heart of what was the world's first Jewish ghetto. Quiet and contemplative, it lies only five minutes walk from heaving Lista di Spagna yet within easy reach of the peaceful Cannaregio backwaters. This stylish, nine-room locanda opened in early 2002, in a building which dates from the 15th century. Several of the rooms have original decorated wooden ceilings.

Seen from the Campo, the reception area glows invitingly from behind big windows under a little portico. On the ground floor is a small breakfast room overlooking the canal while upstairs, the light and airy bedrooms, though varying in shape and size, are all done out in the same elegant, understated style; pale cream walls, honey-coloured parquet floors, pale gold bedcovers and curtains, smart reproduction furniture, brass fittings and soft lighting. Two have small terraces on the Campo while another, (the smallest), has two original Gothic windows and an ancient fireplace serving as a bed head. Bathrooms are super-smart and even equipped with phones.

~

NEARBY Train station; Madonna del Orto; Jewish museum.
LOCATION in Campo del Ghetto Nuovo, ten minutes walk from the train station. vaporetto Ponte Guglie, San Marcuola
FOOD breakfast
PRICE €€€€
ROOMS 9 double and twin, all with bath; all rooms have phone, TV, air-conditioning, minibar, safe
FACILITIES breakfast room, sitting area
CREDIT CARDS AE, MC, V
DISABLED one ground floor room **PETS** not accepted
CLOSED never
PROPRIETOR Alessandra Mascharo

VENICE

CANNAREGIO

LOCANDA DI ORSARIA
~ TOWN HOTEL ~

Calle Priuli, Cannaregio 103, 30121 Venezia
TEL 041 715524 **FAX** 041 715433
E-MAIL info@locandaorsaria.com **WEBSITE** www.locandaorsaria.com

IN A STREET WITH ITS FAIR SHARE OF HOTELS, Locanda di Osaria is by far the smallest and by far the most charming. The front door, flanked by bay trees, leads straight into a pretty breakfast-cum-reception room which, though the size of a shoe-box, seats 12 for a slap-up buffet breakfast each morning. Wooden furniture, fresh flowers and a tapestry hung on a wall lend a country air, echoed upstairs in the simply, yet tastefully furnished bedrooms. We were amazed and pleased by their size in comparison with the ground floor. The windows are big too, and – of great significance in summer – this is the only hotel in Venice, the owner claims, where all the rooms have mosquito screens. Terracotta floors and white-painted walls, both upstairs and down, loose-weave chintz bedspreads, and attractive plain wood furniture (we loved the 'dressing chests') mark the style as more Tuscan than Venetian.

Since the retirement of the ebullient Renato Polesel, a larger-than-life character who presided over this diminutive gem for a number of years, Pietro, his equally friendly and helpful son, has been running the hotel.

~

NEARBY station; Scalzi; Palazzo Labia; San Geremia.
LOCATION next to the station; vaporetto Ferrovia
FOOD breakfast
PRICE €€€
ROOMS 8; 5 double and twin, 3 triple, all with shower; all rooms have phone, TV, air-conditioning, minibar, safe, hairdrier
FACILITIES breakfast room
CREDIT CARDS AE, DC, MC, V
DISABLED one room on ground floor
PETS accepted
CLOSED 3 weeks early Dec
PROPRIETORS Pietro Polesel

VENICE

CANNAREGIO

PALAZZO ABADESSA
~ TOWN HOTEL ~

Calle Priuli, Cannaregio 4011, 30131 Venezia
TEL 041 2413784 **FAX** 041 5212236
E-MAIL info@abadessa.com **WEBSITE**: www.abadessa.com

THE ABADESSA WILL NOT CHARM EVERYONE, but those it does will adore it. The narrow passageway opposite the Ca' d'Oro, past the offices of the local Communist party, though peaceful and safe, might deter women on their own. So take a water taxi – or better still, a gondola – to the Abadessa's private watergate on the workaday Rio Santa Sofia. Your arrival will be greeted with recorded 18th-century music and great enthusiasm from the ebullient Signora Maria-Luisa Rossi whose home this is (bought some 20 years ago). If it is early evening you will be invited to join the other guests for a glass or two of Prosecco on the house. Guests really do seem to make friends here. There are 12 rooms, one or two of which, hung with dark silk damask and cavernous, are a bit gloomy, but they all have centuries-old painted beams, frescoed ceilings and *trompe l'oeil* walls, furnished with appropriate antiques, with much gilt, silk and velvet about the place. There is no restaurant, but the breakfast is outstandingly good. A great advantage is the large and pretty garden, laid to lawn, which gives a very welcome sense of space and peace. The point of the Abadessa, a *residenza d'epoca* (protected historic building) is to make you feel that you are staying in a private palace and the public rooms are genuinely palatial. And there is Signora Rossi.

~

NEARBY Ca' d'Oro; Strada Nova.
LOCATION just off Strada Nova, opposite the Ca' d'Oro vaporetto stop
FOOD breakfast
PRICE ©©©©©
ROOMS 12 double and twin, 4 with bath, 8 with shower; all rooms have phone, TV, air-conditioning, minibar, hairdrier
FACILITIES breakfast room
CREDIT CARDS AE, DC, MC, V
DISABLED not suitable **PETS** accepted
CLOSED never
PROPRIETORS Signor and Signora Rossi

VENICE

ABBAZIA
TOWN HOTEL

Calle Priuli dei Cavaletti,
Cannaregio 68, 30121 Venezia

TEL 041 717333
FAX 041 717949
E-MAIL info@abbaziahotel.com
WEBSITE www.abbaziahotel.com
FOOD breakfast
PRICE €€€€
CLOSED never
MANAGER Franco de Rossi

IF YOU HAVEN'T GUESSED ITS origins from the name, then the interior is sure to provide a clue. High-ceilinged corridors are peppered with doors to almost monastic bedrooms. The former abbey's refectory has been converted to a sitting room of vast proportions, with wood-panelling, a stunning stone floor and perfectly preserved pulpit jutting out from one wall. Even the welcoming staff don't quite succeed in overcoming the feeling of austerity (it was home to the Barefoot Carmelite Friars of Venice). We recommend bedrooms 302 and 303, both spacious with huge windows and walk-in cupboards. Best of all is the delightful mature garden.

VENICE

LAGOON ISLANDS

CA' DEL BORGO
~ VILLAGE HOTEL, LIDO ~

Piazza delle Erbe, Malamocco, Lido, 30126 Venezia
TEL 041 770749 **FAX** 041 770799
E-MAIL info@cadelborgo.com **WEBSITE** www.cadelborgo.com

IF YOU ARE LOOKING FOR SOMEWHERE calm and refined in which to install a group of friends, Ca' del Borgo could be an answer; as well as operating as an ordinary hotel, it is particularly well suited to private parties.

Ca' del Borgo stands in a wide, quiet street in Malamocco. A handsome town house, it was renovated a few years ago for private use, then sold to the owners of Villa Mabapa (see page 98), who have now relinquished it to Signor Decol. It retains the air of a gracious and civilized home, with eight spacious, comfortable and smartly decorated bedrooms with a large terrace and a little garden with a stone well. A grandiose entrance hall with a beamed ceiling and oriental rugs sets the tone. Bedrooms have parquet floors, oriental rugs, excellent beds, perhaps deep red silk damask on the walls, perhaps a colour scheme of yellow and blue. Bathrooms are marble, with efficient showers. Service is discreet.

A car would be useful. The hotel is out of the way, and will transfer guests to the Ca' del Moro sports and health club, which they are entitled to use; they also have use of the Hotel Excelsior's beach. Free bikes are provided.

~

NEARBY Venice; Lagoon Islands.
LOCATION in Malamocco village, 6 km SW of Santa Maria Elisabetta; parking; vaporetto Santa Maria Elisabetta, then taxi or hotel minibus, or by hotel water taxi
FOOD breakfast
PRICE €€€
ROOMS 8 double and twin, 3 with bath (two with Jacuzzi), 5 with shower; all rooms have phone, TV, air-conditioning, minibar, hairdrier, safe
FACILITIES breakfast room, sitting room, terrace; catering facilities available
CREDIT CARDS AE, DC, MC, V
DISABLED one specially adapted room on ground floor
PETS accepted
CLOSED Dec, Jan
PROPRIETOR Fabrizio Decol

VENICE

LAGOON ISLANDS

LOCANDA CIPRIANI
~ RESTAURANT-WITH-ROOMS, TORCELLO ~

Torcello, 30012 Burano, Venezia
TEL 041 730150 **FAX** 041 735433
E-MAIL info@locandacipriani.com **WEBSITE** www.locandacipriani.com

THE TINY LAGOON ISLAND OF TORCELLO is the cradle of the Venetian civilization, yet all that remains are two serenely beautiful religious buildings, the church of Santa Fosca, and the Byzantine cathedral. The latter has a haunting mosaic of the Madonna, and from its campanile, there is a wonderful view of the lagoon. When the tourists drift home at the end of the day, Torcello's magic takes hold, and only the half dozen or so residents, and the handful of guests at the Locanda Cipriani are there to share the privilege. In the past, these have included Hemingway, Chaplin and Paul Newman; and the entire British royal family have lunched here. The inn, opened in 1934 by Giuseppe Cipriani and still in the family, has six bedrooms: simple and homely yet sophisticated, with polished wood floors, attractive pictures on white walls, writing desks, *objets d'art*, comfortable sofas and armchairs. Air conditioning has been installed, but mercifully not televisions, and bathrooms are up to date.

The Locanda's *raison d'être* has always been its restaurant. Though it is a memorable experience to eat here, either in the rustic dining room or on the lovely terrace overlooking the cathedral, prices are steep, reflecting not so much the quality of the food, but its long-standing fame. Romance, however, is guaranteed. In fact, we can think of nowhere more romantic to stay in all of northern Italy.

~

NEARBY Venice (40 mins); lagoon islands.
LOCATION in centre of island, overlooking the cathedral; vaporetto Torcello (line LN from Fondamente Nuove)
FOOD breakfast, lunch, dinner
PRICE €€€€
ROOMS 6; 3 double with sitting rooms, 3 single, all with bath; all rooms have phone, air conditioning
FACILITIES sitting room, dining room, bar, terrace, garden **CREDIT CARDS** AE, MC, V
DISABLED not suitable **PETS** accepted **CLOSED** Jan to mid-Feb
PROPRIETOR Bonifacio Brass

VENICE

QUATTRO FONTANE
~ SEASIDE HOTEL ~

Via Quattro Fontane 16, 30126 Lido, Venezia
TEL 041 5260227 **FAX** 041 5260726
E-MAIL info@quattrofontane.com **WEBSITE** www.quattrofontane.com

THE LONGER WE LINGERED at the Quattro Fontane, the more it grew on us, until it became one of our very favourite Venetian hotels. At first the 150-year-old mock Tyrolean building struck us as rather gloomy and suburban, but we soon warmed to the charmingly decorated reception rooms, particularly the *salone* and the little writing room. Beautiful and unusual mementos of the owners' travels are dotted around the hotel on walls and shelves – carved wooden figures, painted shells, model ships, puppets, porcelain, stamps, a collection of rare Sicilian paintings on glass. In the baronial dining room, with its cavernous hearth and bold red chairs, service is directed with courtesy by the now elderly long-serving head waiter: the two sisters who own the hotel (their former family home) and live on the premises, have retained their dedicated senior staff for many years.

The bedrooms in the main building have plenty of character and are individually decorated with great taste, full of interesting things. Those in the 1960s annexe are more streamlined, but here too each is different, attractive and cosy, with gaily tiled bathrooms. In warm weather you can eat on the wide tree-filled terrace that encircles the hotel. Long may the wonderful Quattro Fontane continue to beguile us.

~

NEARBY Venice; Lagoon Islands.
LOCATION set back from seafront on S side of Lido, near Casino; vaporetto Santa Maria Elisabetta
FOOD breakfast, lunch, dinner
PRICE €€€€
ROOMS 58; 54 double, 4 single, 35 with bath, 23 with shower; all rooms have phone, TV, air conditioning, hairdrier, minibar, safe
FACILITIES sitting room, writing room, dining room, bar; tennis court and beach cabins available **CREDIT CARDS** AE, DC, MC, V
DISABLED access difficult **PETS** accepted
CLOSED Nov to April
PROPRIETORS Bente and Pia Bevilacqua

VENICE

LAGOON ISLANDS

AL RASPO DE UA

~ RESTAURANT-WITH-ROOMS, BURANO ~

Via Galuppi 560, 30012 Burano, Venezia
TEL 041 730095 **FAX** 041 730397

IF YOU WANT AN INTERESTING EXPERIENCE, local colour and indeed charm at probably the lowest price in the Venetian Lagoon, then this could be it. And Venice is only a 40-minute vaporetto ride away. (The photograph shows Burano's waterfront.)

Al Raspo da Ua is a restaurant at the heart of the meltingly pretty island of Burano, with its brightly daubed little houses, on a pedestrian thoroughfare, close to a canal. To be truthful, it is flanked by lace and souvenir shops, and picture postcard stands, but the restaurant itself is bustling and well turned out, clearly the most popular on the island, packed at lunchtime in season. The back room, hung with fishing nets, has its share of characters, and the staff, when we visited, seemed to be good types.

When evening comes, and the day trippers depart to the city, the charming location should start to work its spell. This is no more, or less, than a simple restaurant with rooms to let above (the only facility for lodgers, apart from the bedrooms, is a side entrance for their use) but the rooms are cheerful enough, clean and fairly recently equipped, with just one communal bathroom. This place is a well-kept secret: make sure you book ahead.

~

NEARBY Venice; Lagoon Islands.
LOCATION at centre of island, on pedestrian thoroughfare, 5 mins walk from landing stage; vaporetto Burano
FOOD breakfast, lunch, dinner
PRICE €
ROOMS 5 double; one communal bathroom with shower only, plus one further WC
FACILITIES restaurant, sitting area
CREDIT CARDS AE, DC, MC, V
DISABLED not suitable
PETS accepted
CLOSED Jan; restaurant closed Wed
PROPRIETORS Mario Bruzzese and Giuliano Padouan

VENICE

LAGOON ISLANDS

VILLA MABAPA
SEAFRONT HOTEL, LIDO

Riviera San Nicolò 16, Lido, 30126 Venezia
TEL 041 5260590 **FAX** 041 5269441
E-MAIL info@villamabapa.it **WEBSITE** www.villamabapa.it

SET PEACEFULLY IN A GARDEN OVERLOOKING THE LAGOON, Villa Mabapa is one of the Lido's most popular hotels, although in the past our readers have been less than enthusiastic, criticising the cool, dismissive attitude of the reception staff, the dowdy decoration and the banal food. The hotel is now part of the Best Western chain, whose standards are generally high, and so we expect there have been improvements: reports please.

Villa Mabapa consists of three buildings. The villa itself, built as a family home in the 1930s, contains the high-ceilinged public rooms and some traditional-style bedrooms. The best are on the first floor. Our inspector reports that hers, although a lovely room with a huge sweep of windows overlooking the lagoon, was haphazardly furnished and rather bare. The bedrooms in the annexe, although recently redecorated, are rather dull, and all the same. The hotel acquired the villa next door a few years ago, and here there are nine further rooms. At the rear of the main hotel is a garden which is overlooked by the dining room, but the best place to eat is on the terrace, with wonderful sunset views.

And the name? It contains the first syllables of the words *mamma, bambino* and *papà*. These days, it is the *bambino* who is in charge.

NEARBY Venice; Lagoon Islands.
LOCATION on Lagoon side of the Lido; 15 mins walk from Santa Maria Elisabetta landing stage; in gardens; parking; vaporetto San Nicolò (infrequent stop),Santa Maria Elisabetta or by water taxi
FOOD breakfast, lunch, dinner
PRICE €€€€
ROOMS 69; 53 double and twin, 15 single, one suite, all with bath or shower; all rooms have phone, TV, air-conditioning, hairdrier,safe
FACILITIES sitting room, breakfast room, dining room, bar, lift, terrace, garden
CREDIT CARDS AE, DC, MC, V
DISABLED some rooms on ground floor **PETS** accepted
CLOSED never
PROPRIETOR Signor Vianello

VENICE

LAGOON ISLANDS

CIPRIANI
RESORT HOTEL, GIUDECCA

Giudecca 10, 30133 Venezia

TEL 041 5207744
FAX 041 5207745
E-MAIL info@hotelcipriani..com
WEBSITE www.hotelcipriani.com
FOOD breakfast, lunch, dinner;
room service
PRICE €€€€€€
CLOSED never
MANAGER Natale Rusconi

WE HAVE HEARD differing opinions about the world-famous Cipriani and its two suite annexes with butler service, Palazzo Vendramin and the newer Palazzetto. Our own view is that it is astonishingly overpriced, but if you are happy to accept that, then you can relax and enjoy its principal assets: the peaceful location and the fabulous pool. On the subject of which, one past visitor told us: 'On a hot day we went for lunch, for which we were content to pay a great deal, then asked if our young daughter could swim in the deserted pool. We were told she could not – house rules. We returned gratefully to the Gritti.'

LAGOON ISLANDS

DES BAINS
SEAFRONT HOTEL, LIDO

*Lungomare Marconi 17, Lido,
30126 Venezia*

TEL 041 5265921 **FAX** 041 5260113
E-MAIL desbains@sheraton.com
WEBSITE
www.sheraton.com/desbains
FOOD breakfast, lunch, dinner;
room service **PRICE**
€€€€€ **CLOSED** never
MANAGER Giulio Polegato

THOUGH STRICTLY TOO LARGE TO QUALIFY for this guide, the grand turn-of-the-century Des Bains is the best hotel on the Lido. With its flower-filled garden, swimming pool, dining terrace and private beach lined with bamboo huts, its facilities are unrivalled. Rooms are expensive but special offers can cut their costs by more than a third. Painted cream inside and out, its elegant, chandeliered, parquet-floored salons evoke memories for most visitors of the setting for Visconti's film version of *Death in Venice*, the novel Thomas Mann wrote here. Its refined Edwardian atmosphere has survived a takeover by the Sheraton chain.

VENICE

LAGOON ISLANDS

HUNGARIA
TOWN HOTEL, LIDO

*Gran Viale, Santa Maria
Elisabetta 28, 30126 Venezia*

TEL 041 2420060 **FAX** 041 5264111
E-MAIL
villaparco@hotelsvenice.com
WEBSITE www.hotelvillaparco.com
FOOD breakfast
PRICE ⓔⓔⓔⓔⓔ
CLOSED never
MANAGER Signor Bonetto

IF YOU LOVE ART DECO, THEN YOU SHOULDN'T MISS the extraordinary Hungaria, in the principal street of the Lido's hub, Santa Maria Elisabetta. Built in 1905, this Renaissance-style extravaganza has a façade covered in poly-chromatic majolica tiles and – amazingly – its original furniture in all the bedrooms, made by a famous Italian ebonist, Eugenio Quarti. But don't get too excited: despite all this, despite sensitive modernization to include air-conditioning, TV, phone, minibars, modern bathrooms and so on, the place has a slightly bland feel to it, and on our last visit it wasn't terribly lively. However, with the excellent Signor Bonetto, lately of the Hotel Metropole, in charge, things will only improve.

LAGOON ISLANDS

LA MERIDIANA
TOWN HOTEL

*Via Lepanto 45, Lido, 30126
Venezia*

TEL 041 5260343
FAX 041 5269240
E-MAIL info@lameridiana.com
WEBSITE www.lameridiana.com
FOOD breakfast
PRICE ⓔⓔⓔ
CLOSED early Nov to Carnival
PROPRIETOR Gianluca Regazzo

ALTHOUGH NOT RIGHT ON THE BEACH, La Meridiana has the sedate and quite agreeably old-fashioned air of a seaside hotel, which was purpose-built in the 1930s in rustic style, and where little seems to have changed since. Venetian marble floors and dark three-quarters panelled walls keep the ground floor refreshingly cool in summer. In winter, it has a more noticeably antiquated feel. In the main building, bedrooms are large and fairly recently decorated. Numerous casement windows make them light and airy, and some have French doors on to a terrace. There are also nine rooms in a connecting annexe.

VENICE

LAGOON ISLANDS

VILLA PARCO
TOWN HOTEL, LIDO

Via Rodi 1, Lido, 30126 Venezia

TEL 041 5260015
FAX 041 5267620
E-MAIL
villaparco@hotelsvenice.com
WEBSITE www.hotelvillaparco.com
FOOD breakfast
PRICE €€€
CLOSED never
MANAGER Lea Zollino

SET BACK FROM THE ROAD, through wrought-iron gates, in a romantic, if overgrown garden full of poplars, oleanders and statuary, this 19th-century villa still looks impressive despite its now peeling paint. The area is a quiet residential one, a few minutes' walk from the waterfront. The villa itself is in the art nouveau style, though furnishings are mainly modern. Airy bedrooms are 'clean and comfortable', according to a recent report which also commends the 'helpful staff'. Breakfast is served in a small room in the basement or, from May to September, under a canopy in the pretty garden.

VENETO

ASOLO

AL SOLE

～ TOWN HOTEL ～

Via Collegio 33, 31011 Asolo, Treviso
TEL 0423 951332 **FAX** 0423 951007
E-MAIL info@albergoalsole.com **WEBSITE** www.albergoalsole.com

FROM A GLORIOUS POSITION, perched above the Piazza Maggiore on the steep hill up to the massive fortress, the Rocca, this 16th-century villa has a splendid view of the medieval town with its higgledy-piggledy streets. Its deep pink and cream façade is original and appealing, while the trendy, hi-tech interior – hallmark of the dynamic young owner Silvia de Checchi – makes a dramatic contrast.

Almost every room has white rough-cast walls and mellow wood floors, enlivened by daring colour combinations for fabrics and furniture. Although the look is mainly cool and modern, a few antiques and the occasional bowl and pitcher hark back to the past. Recalling former stars in Asolo's firmament, such as 'Eleanor Duse' and 'Gabriele d'Annunzio', the bedrooms are all different; the former has light painted furniture, the latter, ornate church-style pieces. Some rooms have huge claw-foot baths; some have massage showers, just one of the many four-star comforts. Perhaps the ultimate of these are the state-of-the-art loos for the ground floor, which electronically flush, lift and then replace the seat, complete with hygenic paper cover, at the appropriate times. A panoramic restaurant, La Terrazza, has now been opened, and the hotel also has a small fitness centre .

～

NEARBY Palladian villas; Possagno (10 km).
LOCATION at the top of Piazza Maggiore; private car park
FOOD breakfast, dinner
PRICE €€€
ROOMS 23; 14 double and twin, 2 with bath, 12 with shower, 8 single, 2 with bath, 6 with shower, one suite with bath; all rooms have phone, TV, air conditioning, minibar, hairdrier, safe
FACILITIES breakfast room, sitting room, dining room, bar, fitness centre, lift, terrace **CREDIT CARDS** AE, MC, V
DISABLED 2 specially adapted rooms **PETS** accepted
CLOSED never
PROPRIETOR Silvia de Checchi

VENETO

ASOLO

VILLA CIPRIANI
~ COUNTRY VILLA ~

Via Canova 298, 31011 Asolo, Treviso
TEL 0423 523411 **FAX** 0423 952095
E-MAIL villacipriani@sheraton.com **WEBSITE** www.sheraton.com/villacipriani

ASOLO IS A BEAUTIFUL MEDIEVAL hilltop village commanding panoramic views, a jewel of the Veneto. The Villa Cipriani, a jewel of the Sheraton Group, now part of the huge Starwood Group, is a mellow ochre-washed house on the fringes of the village, its deceptively plain entrance leading into a warm reception area which immediately imparts the feeling of a hotel with a heart (and a house with a past: it was once the home of Robert Browning). Today it is graced by the prettiest of flower-filled gardens, and meals are served on the terrace or in the restaurant overhanging the valley. As for the gracious and comfortable bedrooms, make sure you ask for one with a view, and try for an 'exclusive' rather than a 'superior' double. The latter are not particularly spacious, while the former include a sitting area; two rooms have terraces.

Villa Cipriani is a relaxing country hotel, whose views, comfort, peaceful garden and good food make it particularly alluring. However, some reports complain of prices that were hard to justify, also mentioning intrusive wedding parties and brash clientele. Others have been full of praise.

~

NEARBY Palladian villas; Possagno (10 km).
LOCATION on NW side of village; with garage parking
FOOD breakfast, lunch, dinner; room service
PRICE ©©©©©©
ROOMS 31; 29 double and twin, 2 single, all with bath; all rooms have phone, TV, air conditioning, minibar, hairdrier
FACILITIES sitting room, dining rooms, bar, meeting room, lift, terrace, garden
CREDIT CARDS AE, DC, MC, V
DISABLED access difficult
PETS accepted
CLOSED never
MANAGER Hermann Gatti

VENETO

BARBARANO

IL CASTELLO
~ AGRITURISMO ~

Via Castello 6, 36021 Barbarano, Vicenza
TEL 0444 886055 **FAX** 0444 777140
E-MAIL castellomarinoni@tin.it **WEBSITE** www.castellomarinoni.it

IL CASTELLO REFERS TO THE handsome Villa Godi-Marinoni, built in the 17th century on the ruins of an ancient castle which looks down over the medieval village of Barbarano. Occupied for the last century by the Marinoni family, it retains the original perimeter walls of the castle and its cellars. There is a Renaissance garden and a citrus garden, the lemon trees standing in rows of terracotta pots. To the south stretches the family's vineyard; *grappa*, olive oil and honey are also produced.

As you enter Il Castello through stone gates and a cobbled, covered way, the family villa is on the right, and the guest house ahead, overlooking a large walled courtyard. Adjacent is a converted barn, used for concerts, exhibitions and wedding parties; guests can meet and chat here if they like.

There are four separate apartments, for which reservations must be made on a weekly basis (unless made 10 days before arrival), each sleeping up to five people (the minimum is two), and all with fully equipped kitchens and bathrooms. Rooms, white-painted and airy, with Venetian marble floors, are somewhat spartan in feel, despite the use of old family furniture throughout. English is spoken.

~

NEARBY Vicenza (22 km); Padua (32 km); Verona (34 km).
LOCATION on S side of Barbarano; follow signs to Il Castello in village; in own grounds with parking
FOOD none
PRICE €
ROOMS 4 apartments with kitchen and bathroom each sleeping up to 5 people
FACILITIES garden, produce shop
CREDIT CARDS not accepted
DISABLED access possible
PETS not accepted
CLOSED never
PROPRIETORS Lorenzo Marinoni and family

VENETO

FOLLINA

VILLA ABBAZIA
~ TOWN HOTEL ~

Via Martiri della Libertà, 31051 Follina, Treviso
TEL 0438 971277 **FAX** 0438 970001
E-MAIL info@hotelabbazia.it **WEBSITE** www.hotelabbazia.it

THE HOTEL CONSISTS of two buildings: a 17th-century palazzo and, adjacent, an enchanting little art nouveau villa. Standards of decoration and comfort in both are exceptionally high – rarely have we met hoteliers (brother and sisters) more keen to please their guests – and the Abbazia is now a Relais et Châteaux hotel. If you find the lobby and balconied breakfast area a bit much – a sugary pink confection of candy-striped walls strewn with roses, draped tables and floral china – you will not be disappointed by the bedrooms. Each one is individually decorated, and all are delightful: sophisticated and very feminine in English style, full of thoughtful touches. Three rooms have private balconies, at no extra cost. Best of all is the villa with its pillared portico, carved flourishes on its four façades and sweeping staircase. Its rooms have lovely parquet floors and antique furniture. The Abbazia's restaurant, La Corte, is beautifully decorated with stone walls and pillars and an enchanting mural depicting the highlights of the region as seen from a balcony. If you want to eat out, try Da Gigetto in Miane (where you should be sure to visit the wine cellars).

The Zanons have prepared a helpful list of local information, including bicycle routes. They also run a gift shop, La Volta, next door, and have now opened a second hotel across the street, dei Chiostri (see next page).

~

NEARBY 11th-century abbey; Palladian villas; Asolo (20 km).
LOCATION in town centre, facing the abbey; car parking
FOOD breakfast, lunch, dinner; room service
PRICE €€€
ROOMS 18; 11 double and twin, 7 suites, all with shower, bath or Jacuzzi; all rooms have phone, TV, safe, hairdrier; 12 have air conditioning
FACILITIES breakfast room, sitting room, dining room, tea room, terrace, garden; garage, bicycles **CREDIT CARDS** AE, DC, MC, V
DISABLED not suitable **PETS** accepted
CLOSED Jan
PROPRIETORS Zanon family

VENETO

FOLLINA

HOTEL DEI CHIOSTRI
~ TOWN HOTEL ~

Piazza del Municipio 20, 31051 Follina, Treviso
TEL 0438 971805 **FAX** 0438 974217
E-MAIL info@hoteldeichiostri.com **WEBSITE** www.hoteldeichiostri.com

NOT CONTENT WITH CREATING from scratch their lovely hotel, Villa Abbazia (see previous page) Giovanni Zanon and his sisters have now opened a second hotel right across the street in this quiet hill town in prosecco wine country. It's a strange place to find two luxury hotels and visitors to the area are now thoroughly spoilt for choice. Both are stylish and run with friendly professionalism, but while the Abbazia is full of feminine frills, the Hotel dei Chiostri, built on the ruins of an old monastery, and right beside the cloister of the 11th-century abbey, is much more slick and masculine, designed to attract businessmen as well as tourists.

Whether the style is your cup of tea or not, it's superb value for money. The 15 bedrooms have been beautifully decorated and kitted out by Ivana, who has a talented eye for colour and detail. Though the rooms are all different, they share bold colour schemes, spacious desks, large comfortable beds, lovely bathrooms and up-to-date gadgetry. Only breakfast is served in the Chiostri, in a pretty yellow ground-floor room; for lunch and dinner, the hotel shares the Abbazia's attractive restaurant, Il Corte. Beneath the hotel is secure garage parking for guests' cars.

~

NEARBY 11th-century abbey; Palladian villas; Asolo (20 km).
LOCATION in town centre, next to the abbey; car parking
FOOD breakfast; room service
PRICE €€€
ROOMS 15; 8 double with bath, 7 junior suites with Jacuzzi; all rooms have phone, TV, air-conditioning, minibar, hairdrier, safe
FACILITIES breakfast room, lift; garage
CREDIT CARDS AE, DC, MC, V
DISABLED access possible
PETS not accepted
CLOSED never
PROPRIETORS Zanon family

VENETO

GARGAGNAGO

FORESTERIA SEREGO ALIGHIERI
~ COUNTRY VILLA APARTMENTS ~

37020 Gargagnago di Valpolicella, Verona
TEL 045 7703622 **FAX** 045 7703523
E-MAIL serego@seregoalighieri.it **WEBSITE** www.seregoalighieri.it

IN 1353, THE SON OF DANTE, who had been exiled in Verona, bought Casal dei Ronchi, and there his direct descendants have lived ever since. Today, overseen by Count Pieralvise Serego Alighieri, the estate is a prosperous producer of Valpolicella wines (much improved in recent years and shaking off their 'cheap and nasty' reputation) as well as olive oil, balsamic vinegar, honey, jams and rice. The family home is a lovely yellow ochre building fronted by formal gardens which overlook the vineyards. Beyond are the former stables, now beautifully converted to make eight apartments, simple yet sophisticated, sleeping two to four people. In each one you find a gleaming chrome kitchen, country furniture, soothing green cotton fabrics, white walls and marble bathrooms. No. 8 spirals up a slim tower: minute sitting room, stairs to a minute kitchen, more stairs to the bedroom. Open a door in the bedhead and there's a tiny window behind. No. 1 is the most spacious, with dining table and elegant chairs. Breakfast is served in a room decorated with old family photographs on the ground floor. Wine tasting can be arranged for eight people or more. There are some good restaurants nearby.

~

NEARBY Verona (18 km); Lake Garda (14 km).
LOCATION signposted off the road from Pedemonte to San Ambrogio, 18 km NE of Verona; in own extensive grounds with ample car parking
FOOD breakfast
PRICE apartment sleeping 2-4 people €€€ per night; weekly rates available
ROOMS 8 apartments for 2, 3 or 4 people, each with kitchen, bathroom with shower, phone, TV, air conditioning
FACILITIES reception, breakfast room, terrace meeting room, estate produce shop
CREDIT CARDS AE, DC, MC, V
DISABLED not suitable
PETS accepted
CLOSED Jan
PROPRIETOR Conte Pieralvise Serego Alighieri

VENETO

LAZISE

ALLA GROTTA
~ TOWN GUESTHOUSE ~

Via Fontana 8, 37017 Lazise, Verona
TEL and **FAX** 045 7580035

THE PRETTY AND COLOURFUL little fishing port of Lazise (with a busy Tuesday market) is an ideal base for exploring Lake Garda and Verona, which is close by. Less popular than Sirmione, it is noted for the quality of its fish restaurants, one of which is Alla Grotta, an ochre red building in a delightful location overlooking the little harbour, always full of congenial activity and from which you can take trips on the lake.

In the smart, spacious dining room, with rustic stone walls and a *forno al legno* in the centre for grilling fresh fish, we enjoyed a delicious lunch of grilled sardines and sea bass, served with excellent mixed salads. The restaurant is the *raison d'être* of family-owned and run Alla Grotta, but upstairs there are also 14 neat, well-turned-out bedrooms, which are in heavy demand during high season (book well in advance). With the exception of the two suites, which are furnished in more dramatic style (one has a distinctly Japanese look with a large bamboo screen separating sleeping and sitting areas), they could not be described as characterful, and don't pretend to be anything other than standard hotel bedrooms. However they are of a fair size and decorated with a bit of colour and imagination, and the odd piece of country furniture. The suites have lake views. There is no sitting room for residents. Readers' reports welcome.

~

NEARBY Sirmione (11 km); Peschiera (8 km); Verona (22 km).
LOCATION in the town centre, overlooking the harbour; car parking nearby
FOOD breakfast, lunch, dinner
PRICE €
ROOMS 14; 12 double, 2 suites, all with bath or shower; all rooms have phone, TV
FACILITIES dining room, bar, terrace
CREDIT CARDS MC, V
DISABLED access difficult
PETS not accepted
CLOSED mid-Dec to mid-Feb; restaurant Tue
PROPRIETORS Barato family

VENETO

LEVADA

GARGAN

~ COUNTRY GUESTHOUSE ~

Via Marco Polo 2, Levada di Piombino Dese, Padova
TEL 049 9350308 **FAX** 049 9350016
E-MAIL gargan@gargan.it **WEBSITE** www.gargan.it

THE SETTING IS RURAL, on a working farm, and the farmhouse is typical –
attractive enough, but not especially prepossessing. A donkey brays in
the garden. We walked in quite unprepared for the level of sophistication
of this *agriturismo;* it's in a league of its own. The ground floor comprises
a hallway with cool white walls and beams painted pale green, plus five
interconnecting dining rooms. Furnished only with antiques, these rooms
have delicate lace curtains, timbered ceilings, and an array of pictures on
their white walls. Our visit coincided with Sunday lunch, and every table
was immaculately laid with a white cloth, fine china and gleaming silver;
an open fire crackled in the hearth.

The ingredients used in the delicious dinners are mainly produced on
the farm. Signora Calzavara is in charge of the cooking and provides a full
American breakfast and other meals when required.

The six bedrooms are enchanting. Floors are strewn with rugs; most
have wrought-iron bedheads and fine walnut furniture. It's best to book by
e-mail or fax unless you speak Italian.

~

NEARBY Palladian villas; Venice (20 km); Padua (26 km).
LOCATION 20 km N of Venice, in Levada take Via G. Carducci opposite the church
and turn left into Via Marco Polo; in own garden with car parking
FOOD breakfast, lunch, dinner
PRICE €
ROOMS 6; 4 double and twin, 2 family rooms, all with shower; all rooms have TV
FACILITIES dining rooms, sitting area, garden
CREDIT CARDS not accepted
DISABLED access difficult
PETS not accepted
CLOSED Jan, Aug
PROPRIETORS Calzavara family

VENETO

MALCESINE

BELLEVUE SAN LORENZO
~ LAKESIDE HOTEL ~

Loc. Dosde Feri, 37018 Malcesine, Lago di Garda, Brescia
TEL 0457 401598 **FAX** 0457 401055
E-MAIL info@bellevue-sanlorenzo.it **WEBSITE** www.bellevue-sanlorenzo.it

AN ENTHUSIASTIC REGULAR guest of the Bellevue San Lorenzo alerted us to this hotel on the shores of Lake Garda, entreating us to overlook its large number of rooms and its use by (upmarket) tour groups and focus instead on its qualities.

With its own steps down to the Lungolago, the hotel is situated on the main road outside Malcasine (a bit hairy for walkers, as there is no pavement) and consists of the main villa, a fine old house, with public rooms, and attached, the newer restaurant with rooms above. Other bedrooms (less desirable) are in villas in the grounds of mature gardens filled with olive, cypress and magnolia trees and scattered with contemporary sculpture. Bedrooms are comfortable, if unremarkable. A collection of contemporary art decorates the walls in both the older and the newer buildings.

What stood out for our readers, and subsequently our inspector, was the friendliness of the staff, particularly the hard-working receptionists who both speak several languages and for whom nothing is too much trouble. The grounds are very attractive, and the sun terrace by the pool makes a pleasant place to while away the hours. Food is somewhat variable, but can often be excellent. Most of all, given the standards and facilities, the bill at the Bellevue represents real value for money.

~

NEARBY Ferry services to villages and towns around Lake Garda.
LOCATION on hill overlooking Lake Garda, 1 km outside Malcesine
FOOD breakfast, lunch, dinner
PRICE €€
ROOMS 50; 46 double and twin, one suite, 3 junior suites, all with bath; all rooms have phone,TV, air conditioning, minibar, safe, hairdrier
FACILITIES sitting room, dining room, bar, lift, terrace, garden, swimming pool, wellness centre, wine room **CREDIT CARDS** AE, DC, MC, V
DISABLED no special facilities **PETS** not accepted
CLOSED Nov to Apr
PROPRIETOR Ruggiero Togni

VENETO

Mira Porte

VILLA FRANCESCHI

~ VILLA HOTEL ~

Via Don Minzoni 28, 30034 Mira Porte, Venezia
TEL 041 4266531 **FAX** 041 5608996
E-MAIL info@dalcorsohotellerie.com **WEBSITE** www.dalcorsohotellerie.com

VILLA FRANCESCHI IS THE latest venture of the hands-on Dal Corso family whose other Mira Porte hotel, Villa Margherita (see page 113), is a stalwart of this guide. More luxurious and more romantic than its older sister, the hotel is split between two 16th-century buildings, set in attractively landscaped gardens and painstakingly restored over several years by the family. The main part, the 'Barchessa', contains reception, breakfast and meeting rooms, plus 16 bedrooms, and across the 'Campiello', a paved terrace designed to be a lively summer gathering place, the 'Padronale' is a gorgeous small-scale Palladian villa with nine bedrooms. Double doors, several metres high, open into its impressively proportioned hall, and the high-ceilinged rooms leading off it are equally grand, classically furnished with fabrics the colour of jewels and Murano chandeliers.

Although it has less panache, the main building is exceedingly comfortable. Inviting armchairs and sofas fill the large reception/sitting room, where the day's newspapers in various languages hang on rods, brasserie-style. Bedrooms are less opulent but cosier than those in the Padronale. There is also a gazebo-style breakfast room and a meeting room for up to 100 people (seminars are held here quite regularly, so phone first if you want to avoid them). The family restaurant is nearby.

~

NEARBY Venice (10 km); Padua (20 km).
LOCATION on banks of Brenta at Mira Porte at the E end of Mira, in own grounds with ample parking
FOOD breakfast; lunch and dinner at Ristorante Margherita
PRICE ©©
ROOMS 25; 19 double and twin, 6 suites, 22 with bath, 3 with shower; all rooms have phone, TV, air conditioning, minibar, hairdrier, safe
FACILITIES sitting room, bar, breakfast room, restaurant (1 km away), lift, terrace, garden **CREDIT CARDS** AE, DC, MC, V
DISABLED two specially adapted rooms **PETS** accepted **CLOSED** never
PROPRIETORS Dal Corso family

VENETO

MOGLIANO VENETO

VILLA CONDULMER
~ COUNTRY VILLA ~

Via Preganziol 1, 31020 Mogliano Veneto, Treviso
TEL 041 5972700 **FAX** 041 5972777
E-MAIL info@hotelvillacondulmer.com **WEBSITE** www.hotelvillacondulmer.com

F OR THE PRICE OF A VENICE three-star hotel you can stay in this impressive 18th-century villa 20 minutes away. One very satisfied couple wrote to say that they will do just that whenever they visit the city again.

Flanked by annexes, Villa Condulmer stands four-square in a miniature park designed by Sebatoni. From the moment you walk in you will, like our correspondents, be struck by the sheer scale, not only of the rooms but of the furnishings. The vast central hall is decorated with baroque stucco in subtle colours, inset with murals. Two extravagantly large Murano chandeliers hang from the high ceiling, but comfortable armchairs make it a room to relax in, not just admire. A pair of grand pianos bear witness to Verdi's visits here. The more dilapidated is his; the other, a copy. The dining room ('delicious food') is in restful pale green and white, and there is an intimate stuccoed bar. The most exotic, and expensive, bedrooms are the upstairs suites The double rooms in the main villa are decorated in bright silk damasks, but we prefer the more restrained annexe rooms, where the peace and quiet, the comfortable beds and the heavy linen sheets should guarantee a good night's sleep.

~

NEARBY Palladian villas; Venice (18 km).
LOCATION 12 km S of Treviso, N of road to Mogliano Veneto; in own grounds with ample parking.
FOOD breakfast, dinner
PRICE €€€€
ROOMS 43 double, twin, single, junior suites, 8 apartments, all with bath or shower; all rooms have phone, TV, air conditioning, minibar, hairdrier
FACILITIES breakfast room, bar, sitting rooms, meeting room, TV room, dining rooms, garden, swimming pool, tennis courts, 9- and 18-hole golf
CREDIT CARDS AE, DC, MC, V
DISABLED access difficult **PETS** accepted
CLOSED never
PROPRIETOR Davide Zuin

VENETO

MIRA PORTE

VILLA MARGHERITA

~ VILLA HOTEL ~

Via Nazionale 416, 30034 Mira Porte, Venezia
TEL 041 4265800 **FAX** 041 4265838
E-MAIL info@dalcorsohotellerie.com **WEBSITE** www.dalcorsohotellerie.com

THIS COUNTRY VILLA IN THE VENETIAN HINTERLAND stands on the Brenta
Riviera overlooking a flat, industrial landscape but offering peace,
seclusion and acres of real estate for your money, while being well placed
for excursions into Venice, which is just ten kilometres away.

Villa Margherita was built in in the 17th century as a nobleman's country retreat and has been a hotel since 1987, now part of the Romantik
group. Readers are impressed with the standard of furnishings and service; 'not cheap but worth it', comments one. The yellow and blue breakfast room is gloriously light, with French windows on to the garden, while
the sitting room has murals (the principal one portrays a bevy of naked
nymphs cavorting on the banks of the Brenta), an open fireplace and
some beautiful lamps, vases and clocks. You will find fresh fruit and flowers in the thoroughly comfortable bedrooms, the best of which lead to the
breakfast terrace.

The Dal Corso family is the driving force behind the hotel and its highly
regarded restaurant, 200 metres away across a terrifying road. A lively
place, it specializes in mouthwatering seafood dishes. The family have
opened a new, deluxe hotel, Villa Francheschi (see page 111), nearby.

~

NEARBY Venice (10 km); Padua (20 km).
LOCATION on banks of Brenta at Mira Porte at the E end of Mira, in own grounds
with ample parking
FOOD breakfast; lunch and dinner at Ristorante Margherita
PRICE €€€
ROOMS 19; 18 double and twin, 3 with bath, 15 with shower; one single with
shower; all rooms have phone, TV, air conditioning, minibar, hairdrier
FACILITIES breakfast room, sitting room, bar, restaurant (200 m away), terrace,
garden, jogging track **CREDIT CARDS** AE, DC, MC, V
DISABLED several rooms on ground floor **PETS** accepted
CLOSED never
PROPRIETORS Dal Corso family

VENETO

MODOLO

FULICIO MIARI FULCIS

~ AGRITURISMO ~

Località Modolo, 32124 Castion, Belluno
TEL and **FAX** 0437 927198
E-MAIL agriturismofmf@libero.it **WEBSITE** www.dolomiti.com/miari

THE *RAISON D'ETRE* OF THE little hamlet of Modolo is the beautiful 16th-century Villa Miari, quite a surprising find in this rural backwater. Nearby is the home of Fulcio Miari Fulcis, nephew of the present owner of Villa Miari, his charming Milanese wife and their children. And this is very much a home; in winter wood is piled up outside, in summer brightly coloured bedclothes hang out of the window to air; children and family pets potter about. There is a pinball machine and a barbecue area. Fulcio is a ski instructor at nearby Nevegàl and also keeps horses, organizing riding expeditions for his guests.

The handsome, green-shuttered farmhouse is typical of the area with the main two-storey building abutting a broad three-storey tower: this wing is reserved for guests. Bedrooms are homely and charming, with a profusion of armchairs and ottomans and an assortment of gaily patterned fabrics. You have a one-in-six chance of occupying a huge hand-carved four-poster from Thailand. Large wood-framed windows give views of the rising hills, and there are rustic beamed ceilings, wooden floors and old doors.

~

NEARBY Belluno (7 km); Nevegàl ski area (10 km).
LOCATION from Belluno, follow signs for Nevegàl; after Castion, turn left signposted Modolo; the house is on the right; car parking
FOOD breakfast
PRICE €
ROOMS 6; 4 double and twin, 2 family; 3 communal bathrooms
FACILITIES sitting room, breakfast room, sauna, barbecue, garden, horse-riding
CREDIT CARDS not accepted
DISABLED not suitable
PETS accepted
CLOSED never
PROPRIETOR Fulcio Miari Fulcis

VENETO

OSPEDALETTO DI PESCANTINA

VILLA QUARANTA

~ COUNTRY VILLA ~

Via Brennero, 37026 Ospedaletto di Pescantina, Verona
TEL 045 6767300 **FAX** 045 6767301
E-MAIL info@villaquaranta.com **WEBSITE** www.villaquaranta.com

OSPEDALETTO EARNED ITS NAME as a stopping-off point on the way to and from the Brenner pass; the 13th-century Chapel of Santa Maria di Mezza Campagna, with its Ligozzi frescoes, was where travellers put up. This now forms one side of the Villa Quaranta's pretty inner courtyard: the remainder of the buildings are 17th-century. Yet though the hotel's setting, in lovely grounds, is impressive, and its main building imposing, the atmosphere is one of quiet informality. In the restaurant, for example, you are confronted by a vast stone staircase, awe-inspiring frescoed walls, stone-arched doors and tiled floors; yet the ambience is relaxed and the food good value.

The hotel is now a Best Western, and other considerable changes have taken place recently. Bedrooms proliferated a few years ago; new ones are spacious, if uniform, with luxury bathrooms, tasteful reproduction furniture, brass fittings, deep-pile carpets. There's a piano bar, pool, terrace bar ... and across the park a luxurious beauty and fitness centre ... and a disco. This last caused a blot on our otherwise happy stay as the roar of revellers' engines continued into the small hours.

~

NEARBY Verona (9 km; minibus to opera); Lake Garda (12 km).
LOCATION on SS12, 15 km NW of Verona; in own park with ample parking
FOOD breakfast, lunch, dinner
PRICE ⑤⑥⑥
ROOMS 70; 59 single, double and twin, 11 suites, all with bath; all rooms have phone, TV, air-conditioning, minibar, hairdrier
FACILITIES sitting room, dining rooms, bar, TV room, swimming pool, 2 tennis courts (one indoor), fitness/beauty centre, meeting centre, park with lake
CREDIT CARDS AE, DC, MC, V
DISABLED access possible
PETS not accepted
CLOSED hotel never; restaurant Mon
MANAGER Michaela Tommasi

VENETO

PEDEMONTE

VILLA DEL QUAR

~ COUNTRY VILLA ~

Via Quar 12, 37020 Pedemonte, Verona
TEL 045 6800681 **FAX** 045 6800604
E-MAIL info@villadelquar **WEBSITE** www.villadelquar.it

SITUATED IN THE FERTILE VALPOLICELLA valley, this 'typical patrician dwelling' is nowadays a luxury hotel, a member of Relais et Châteaux. The ebullient owner and her family live in the fine main villa, while her hotel occupies the east wing. Public rooms in particular make a great impression. The galleried sitting room, an enclosed arcade with beamed roof, is delightfully light, airy and sophisticated. The Michelin-starred restaurant, Arquade, which consists of two dining rooms – resplendent with mirrors, Venetian torches and a vast Murano glass chandelier – is also extremely attractive and makes a delightful place in which to eat. The reception room, doubling as a library and tea room, overlooks the swimming pool. Bedrooms are restrained, masculine, many with lovely old cupboard doors. Bathrooms feel luxurious, swathed in prettily coloured marble. If you take a suite, ask for the one with a terrace, which is no more expensive.

In summer, a white awning covers the terrace and the immaculate pool sparkles invitingly. The villa's setting, though quiet, is in uneventful countryside not quite in keeping with its interior, though it is surrounded by a sea of vines.

~

NEARBY Verona (11 km); Lake Garda (20 km).
LOCATION in Pedemonte follow signs for Verona and hotel at traffic lights; after about 1,500 m turn right for hotel; in own grounds with ample car parking
FOOD breakfast, lunch, dinner; room service
PRICE €€€€€
ROOMS 27; 18 double and twin, 9 suites, all with bath; all rooms have phone, TV, air conditioning, minibar, hairdrier, safe
FACILITIES sitting room, restaurant, breakfast room, bar, terrace, swimming pool, small gym
CREDIT CARDS AE, DC, MC, V
DISABLED rooms on ground floor **PETS** accepted
CLOSED mid-Jan to mid-Mar
PROPRIETORS Evelina Acampora and Leopoldo Montresor

VENETO

PIEVE D'ALPAGO

DOLADA

RESTAURANT-WITH-ROOMS

Via Dolada 21, Plois, 32010 Pieve d'Alpago, Belluno
TEL 0437 479141 **FAX** 0437 478068
E-MAIL dolada@tin.it **WEBSITE** www.dolada.it

A TWISTING ROAD LEADS FROM the Alpago valley to Pieve, and then corkscrews on up to the little hamlet of Plois. Albergo Dolada turns out to be a handsome building with faded apricot walls and green-shuttered windows with a little garden which looks out over snow-capped mountains and the Santa Croce lake and valley far below (there are wonderful walks from the door).

Built in 1923, Dolada has been owned and run as an inn by four generations of the De Prà family. The much vaunted kitchen (one Michelin star, with another in the offing) is overseen by Enzo De Prà, aided by his son Riccardo, while his wife Rossana, a professional *sommelier*, and daughter Benedetta (whose husband is head barman at the Cipriani in Venice) are a cheeful and friendly presence front of house. 'The food' our reporter comments, 'was divine, and the welcome could not have been more friendly. I would recommend the white bedroom, for its spaciousness, if you can get it, but don't worry if not.' The modern bedrooms are named for their colour schemes; the pink one can come as a bit of a shock the morning after an evening of serious over-indulgence in the elegant restaurant, but a long walk in the hills, with wonderful views all around, should sort things out.

NEARBY Belluno (20 km); Nevegàl ski area (18 km).
LOCATION in the hamlet of Plois, signposted from Pieve d'Alpago; ample parking
FOOD breakfast, lunch, dinner
PRICE €€
ROOMS 7 double and twin, all with shower; all rooms have phone, TV,
FACILITIES restaurant, terrace, garden
CREDIT CARDS AE, DC, MC, V
DISABLED no special facilities
PETS accepted
CLOSED restaurant closed Mon and Tues lunch
PROPRIETORS De Prà family

VENETO

SAN VIGILIO

SAN VIGILIO

~ LAKESIDE HOTEL ~

San Vigilio, 37016 Garda, Verona
TEL 045 7256688 **FAX** 045 7256551
E-MAIL info@punta-sanvigilio.it **WEBSITE** www.punta-sanvigilio.it

IN GENERAL THE EAST SIDE OF LAKE GARDA is less upmarket than the west but this hotel's idyllic setting, on a lush peninsula, Punta San Vigilio, dotted with olive trees and cypresses, is a conspicuous exception. The property is owned by Conte Agostino Guarienti, who lives in the 16th-century villa that dominates the headland. An air of discreet exclusivity pervades the hotel (royalty are among regular guests) yet the atmosphere is far from stuffy. It is sophisticated, yet with the intimacy of a well-worn country house. Of the public rooms, our favourite is the elegant dining room, right on the lake, with a comfortingly creaky wooden floor. A ceramic stove occupies one corner and sideboards display plates and bottles. You can eat in here, on a little arched veranda or under huge white umbrellas on the terrace where terracotta pots overflow with flowers. Next door is a cosy sitting room.

The seven bedrooms in the main house are all different, though they have beautiful antiques and fabrics in common. Only one has no view. Other bedrooms, or rather suites, are in separate buildings and more rustic in style. In the evening the place comes into its own: with the day trippers gone, guests can wander the peninsula or sit with a drink at one of the Taverna's vine-shaded tables. Whether you arrive by car through an avenue of cypress trees, or, even more magically, by boat, you will find this a gem of a hotel.

~

NEARBY Garda (2 km); Verona (45 km); ferry services (4 km).
LOCATION 2 km W of Garda, on promontory; parking available 150 m away
FOOD breakfast, lunch, dinner
PRICE ⓔⓔⓔⓔⓔ
ROOMS 14; 11 double and twin, 3 suites, all with bath or shower; all rooms have phone, TV, air conditioning, minibar, hairdrier; most rooms have safe
FACILITIES sitting room, dining room, bar, terrace, walled garden
CREDIT CARDS AE, DC, MC, V **DISABLED** not suitable **PETS** accepted
CLOSED Nov to just before Easter
PROPRIETOR Conte Agostino Guarienti

VENETO

SCORZE

VILLA SORANZO CONESTABILE

~ TOWN VILLA ~

Via Roma 1, 30037 Scorzè, Venezia
TEL 041 445027 **FAX** 041 5840088
E-MAIL info@villasoranzo.it **WEBISTE** www.villasoranzo.it

STANDING AT THE CENTRE of the hard-working town of Scorzè, this aristo-cratic villa dates back to the 16th century, but was remodelled in the 18th century in elegant neoclassical style. Visible from its earliest period (especially if you take room No. 1) are fragments of gorgeous School of Veronese frescoes. There are also fine ceilings and floors, an impressive double staircase and a park modelled in the early 19th century in Romantic English style. The spacious first floor rooms are somewhat staid but full of character, recalling the last century when they were the bed-rooms of the noble Conestabile family, retaining their lofty proportions, and, in some cases, original *faux* marble walls. Rooms on the second floor, formerly the household quarters, are plainer but spacious and furnished in different styles.

On a spring visit our inspector reports that she ate alone in the dining room, but was comforted by the familial ambience, with copper pans hang-ing from the ceiling and old dressers laden with wine bottles, and by a simple but well-prepared set menu. She also notes that her visit was marred by one of the coolest welcomes in reception that she can remem-ber, and detected little in the way of a thaw on her return recently. However, other satisfied guests have encountered much friendlier staff; more reports please.

NEARBY Riviera del Brenta; Venice (24 km); Padua (30 km).
LOCATION in Scorzè, 24 km NW of Venice; in own grounds with ample car parking
FOOD breakfast, dinner
PRICE ⓔⓔ
ROOMS 20; 14 double and twin, 3 single, all with bath or shower, 3 suites; all rooms have phone, TV
FACILITIES sitting room, dining room, bar, breakfast room, terrace, garden
CREDIT CARDS AE, DC, MC, V **DISABLED** not suitable **PETS** accepted
CLOSED restaurant only, Sat, Sun
PROPRIETORS Martinelli family

VENETO

TORRI DEL BENACO

GARDESANA

~ LAKESIDE HOTEL ~

Piazza Calderini 20, 37010 Torri del Benaco, Verona
TEL 045 7225411 **FAX** 045 7225771
E-MAIL info@hotel-gardesana.com **WEBSITE** www.hotel-gardesana.com

TORRI DEL BENACO IS ONE of the showpiece fishing villages which are dotted along the shore of Lake Garda, and Gardesana, the former harbourmaster's office, is in a plum position. It is a real treat to tuck into the chef's speciality fish soup on the delightful first-floor dining terrace which overlooks the central *piazza*, 14th-century castle and bustling port. The wrought-iron balustrade is decked with cascading geraniums, the tables are elegant, the waiters smartly uniformed, and the food, particularly the fish, fresh and delicious. It makes a perfect vantage point for watching the boats come and go, and the changing colours of the lake. Drinks can also be taken on the ground-floor terrace, which extends out on to the *piazza*.

The building has a long history, as its exterior would suggest, with its stone arches and mellow stucco walls; but the entire interior has been smartly modernized in recent years to produce an essentially modern and very comfortable, if simple, hotel. The green and white bedrooms are almost all identical: wooden floors, wooden furnishings, soft fabrics, plenty of little extras. If you can, try to book one of the corner rooms; these have the advantage of facing both the lake and the *piazza*; otherwise choose a third floor room, overlooking the lake with balcony.

~

NEARBY Bardolino (11 km); Malcesine (21 km); Gardaland.
LOCATION in town centre, on waterfront, in pedestrian zone; unload at hotel, private parking 150 m away
FOOD breakfast, dinner
PRICE €
ROOMS 34; 31 double, 3 single, all with shower; all rooms have phone, TV, air conditioning (Jul and Aug)
FACILITIES dining room, bar, lift, terrace
CREDIT CARDS AE, DC, MC, V
DISABLED no special facilities **PETS** not accepted
CLOSED Nov and Dec
PROPRIETOR Giuseppe Lorenzini

VENETO

TRISSINO

RELAIS CA'MASIERI
~ COUNTRY RESTAURANT-WITH-ROOMS ~

Località Masieri, Via Masieri, 36070 Trissino, Vicenza
TEL 0445 490122 **FAX** 0445 490455
E-MAIL info@camasieri.com **WEBSITE** www.camasieri.com

THE COUNTRYSIDE AROUND industrial Arzignano is uninspiring, but things improve as you wind your way to Masieri through willow-fringed meadows. Through wrought-iron gates and at the end of a long drive, the sight of Ca' Masieri itself, a fine old shuttered mansion with swimming pool and shady terrace further lifts the spirits. In our case, they were immediately cast down, because we were late and the chef had just gone home: we had been dreaming of the much-vaunted food all morning. The sight of the charming little restaurant, its walls decorated with delicate 18th-century frescoes, only made our disappointment worse. Had we been in time, we might have had the salad of crayfish tails followed by risotto with herbs, and then the casserole of pigeon.

The bedrooms are in an adjacent building which retains its old wooden beamed ceilings, but is otherwise furnished in contemporary style. Two rooms have spiral metal staircases from a sitting area up to the mezzanine beds. No. 201 is huge, with a terrace overlooking the hills and Trissino. There are pretty bedspreads in William Morris leaf-print, curvy modern tables, and stylish bathrooms with walls painted the colour of aluminium.

NEARBY Vicenza (21 km); Verona (49 km).
LOCATION from Trissino, follow signs to Masieri, and in Via Masieri to Ca' Masieri up a private drive; ample car parking
FOOD breakfast, lunch, dinner
PRICE €€
ROOMS 12; 5 double, 2 single, 5 apartments, all with shower; all rooms have phone, TV, air conditioning, minibar
FACILITIES sitting room, bar, breakfast room, dining room, terrace, swimming pool
CREDIT CARDS AE, MC, V
DISABLED not suitable
PETS accepted
CLOSED never; restaurant closed Sun, Mon lunch
PROPRIETOR Angelo Vassena

VENETO

VERONA

GABBIA D'ORO
~ TOWN HOTEL ~

Corso Portoni Borsari 4a, 37121 Verona
TEL 045 8003060 **FAX** 045 590293
E-MAIL gabbiadoro@easyasp.it **WEBSITE** www.hotelgabbiadoro.it

THIS STYLISH HOTEL in a 17th-century palazzo, luxurious but never ostenta-
tious, boasts an attention to detail rarely encountered nowadays. A
small, beautifully wrapped gift awaits your arrival, and the staff are as
charming and polished as the hotel itself. The public rooms, entered
through massive wood doors with gilt decoration, are comfortable as well
as elegant: there are plenty of places in which to sit and relax, and sofas
are large and deep. Wooden floors, beams and brickwork are much in evidence; the sitting room shares one wall with the Gardello Tower.
Furnishings, chandeliers, silver-framed photographs, ornaments and
antiques are always in keeping. Little lamps lend a glow to the panelled
bar, and the new orangery is restful, with its green-and-white colour
scheme and view to the terrace.

Frescoes, restored or reproduced from the originals, recur as friezes
both downstairs and in the bedrooms. Suites outnumber doubles. In
almost all, beds are shrouded in a canopy of antique lace. No. 404, dark
red with sloping walls, rafters, and nooks and crannies, is so romantic
that it's normally chosen for honeymooners. Prices are high, but we felt
justifiably so.

~

NEARBY Piazza delle Erbe; Loggia del Consiglio; Arena.
LOCATION in medieval centre of the city, S of Porta Borsari; garage parking available
FOOD breakfast
PRICE €€€€€€
ROOMS 27; 8 double and twin, 19 suites, all with bath or shower; all rooms have
phone, TV, air conditioning, minibar, hairdrier, safe
FACILITIES breakfast room, sitting room, orangery, bar, meeting room, lift, terrace
CREDIT CARDS AE, DC, MC, V
DISABLED access difficult
PETS accepted
CLOSED never
PROPRIETOR Camilla Balzarro

VENETO

VERONA

TORCOLO
~ TOWN HOTEL ~

Vicolo Listone 3, 37121 Verona
TEL 045 8007512 **FAX** 045 8004058
E-MAIL hoteltorcolo@virgilio.it **WEBSITE** www.hoteltorcolo.it

THE TORCOLO IS AN INEXPENSIVE hotel in an excellent location at the heart of lively Verona. 'Its most outstanding quality,' writes one recent guest, 'was the warmth and friendliness of our welcome and the consistent helpfulness of the staff.' A recent inspection confirmed this, and other positive comments continue to filter through.

Every room is individually decorated in varying styles – Italian 18th-century, art nouveau, modern – and all are fresher and have more charm than one normally finds at this price. Ours contained a complete set of Liberty-style bedroom furniture which had belonged to owner Silvia Pommari's parents when they first married. It was set off by white linen curtains and a colourful patchwork bedspread. Another has pretty painted Venetian-style furniture. Ceramic tiled bathrooms are somewhat cramped; the best have separate shower cubicles. Rooms are double-glazed against the considerable street sounds (people, not cars) but, despite air conditioning, they can get fuggy, especially in warm weather. Breakfast, including a jug of fresh orange juice, a good assortment of bread and croissants and yoghurt, can be taken in your room, which might be preferable to the rather cramped little breakfast room. In summer, it is served buffet-style in the small off-street courtyard.

~

NEARBY Arena; Via Mazzini, Piazza delle Erbe.
LOCATION just off Piazza Brà; garage parking
FOOD breakfast
PRICE €€
ROOMS 19; 13 double and twin, 4 single, 2 family, one with bath and 18 with shower; all rooms have phone, TV, air conditioning, minibar, safe, hairdrier; 10 rooms have minibar and safe **FACILITIES** sitting area, breakfast room, courtyard, lift
CREDIT CARDS AE, DC, MC, V
DISABLED access difficult **PETS** accepted
CLOSED late Jan to mid-Feb
PROPRIETORS Silvia Pommari and Diana Castellani

VENETO

VILLA MICHELANGELO
COUNTRY VILLA

Via Sacco 19, 36057 Arcugnano, Vicenza

TEL 0444 550300 **FAX** 0444 550490
E-MAIL reception@hotelvillamichel
angelo.com **WEBSITE**
www.hotelvillamichelangelo.com
FOOD breakfast, lunch, dinner
PRICE ©©© **CLOSED** never
MANAGER Alessandra Dalla Fontana

IN A PEACEFUL SETTING with wide views and a pool with a sliding glass roof overlooking the Berici hills, this severe-looking 18th-century villa was a Capuchin college before it became a hotel, and there is a simplicity about its decorative style even now. The dining room is elegant, with white walls, sparkling white Murano glass chandeliers suspended from a roughly beamed ceiling, a wall of glass doors leading to the terrace, and great vases of perfumed flowers. The food is fancy Italian, which doesn't always come off. Bedrooms are fairly uniform, comfortable enough but unmemorable. The bathrooms have large marble basins and proper towels. A tunnel connects the hotel with the conference centre, pool and piano bar.

DUSE
TOWN HOTEL

Via R. Browning 190, 31011 Asolo, Treviso

TEL 0423 55241 **FAX** 0423 950404
E-MAIL info@hotelduse.com
WEBSITE www.hotelduse.com
FOOD breakfast
PRICE ©©
CLOSED sometimes 2-3 weeks in Nov
PROPRIETOR Zavattiero Alessandro

THE NAME WAS INSPIRED by one of Asolo's best-known residents, the actress and mistress of Gabriele D'Annunzio, Eleanor Duse. This cosy little hotel is decked out almost entirely in blue and yellow, with a spiral staircase and a tiny first-floor breakfast room. Dark wood furniture, striped curtains, blue carpets and yellow bedspreads furnish all the bedrooms, with matching picture bows and fabric-covered lights, a little too twee for our taste, although the rooms were all being updated at the time of going to press. The best are the doubles at the front, which include somewhere to sit, but pack your earplugs to block out the nearby Duomo's early matins bell. There has been a change of ownership since our last visit; we welcome reports.

VENETO

CASTELFRANCO VENETO

AL MORETTO
TOWN HOTEL

Via San Pio X 10, 31033
Castelfranco Veneto, Treviso

TEL 0423 721313
FAX 0423 721066
E-MAIL albergo.al.moretto@apf.it
WEBSITE www.albergoalmoretto.it
FOOD breakfast
PRICE ⓔⓔ
CLOSED never
PROPRIETOR Signora Rigato

ADMIRERS OF THAT enigmatic artist, Giorgione, will not want to bypass Castelfranco Veneto, his birthplace. Within the moated Castello, its medieval core, you will find the Duomo and his Madonna and child – flawed and damaged, yet magical.

Al Moretto, despite its modern appearance, is the oldest hostelry in town, in the same ownership for generations. A few years ago, it was enlarged and refurbished, tastefully enough, but in a way that swaps character for streamlined comfort. You can be assured of a good night's rest in a well-equipped, softly coloured room, and a generous buffet breakfast.

CAVASO DEL TOMBA

LOCANDA ALLA POSTA
TOWN INN

Plaza XIII Martiri 13, 31034
Cavaso del Tomba, Treviso

TEL and **FAX** 0423 543112
FOOD breakfast, lunch, dinner
PRICE ⓔ
CLOSED first 2 weeks Jul;
restaurant Tue, Wed dinner
PROPRIETOR Remo Visentin

CAVASO DEL TOMBA IS A straggling village close to Possagno, birthplace of Canova and site of his moving Gipsoteca (gallery of plaster models) and his bizarre Temple. Alla Posta is a handsome building with something of the air of a Wild West saloon about it. There's a bar where locals congregate, and a simple restaurant in which surprisingly sophisticated food is served. Upstairs, wide, smartly decorated landings lead to the bedrooms, which are plain, but light, spacious and good value. Some are modern and functional, others – Nos 4 and 6 – have more interest, with matching Liberty furniture, and old-fashioned appeal.

VENETO

CORTINA D'AMPEZZO

MENARDI
TOWN HOTEL

Via Majon 110, 32043 Cortina d'Ampezzo, Belluno

TEL 0436 2400
FAX 0436 862183
E-MAIL info@hotelmenardi.it
WEBSITE www.hotelmenardi.it
FOOD breakfast, lunch, dinner
PRICE €€€ **CLOSED** Apr to mid-May, Oct to mid-Dec
PROPRIETORS Menardi family

THIS FAMILY-RUN HOTEL evolved from a coaching inn when its owners, the Menardi family, began hiring out horses. During the First World War, Luigi Menardi began to transform the rustic inn into a proper hotel. Today the long white building has proliferated carved green wood balconies and tumbling geraniums, plus extra rooms and a separate annexe behind, but the Menardi family can still justifiably proclaim: 'same house, same family, same relaxed atmosphere'. Inside, antiques, painted religious statues and old work tools are mixed with local custom-made furnishings which look somewhat dated, but which are nonetheless comfortable. The atmosphere is one of traditional warmth and service is polished.

COSTERMANO

LOCANDA SAN VEROLO
COUNTRY HOTEL

Località San Verolo, 37010 Costermano, Verona

TEL 045 7200930 **FAX** 045 6201166
E-MAIL info@sanverolo.it
WEBSITE www.sanverolo.it
FOOD breakfast, lunch, dinner
PRICE €€€€€
CLOSED early Nov to Feb/Mar
MANAGER Dagmar Gufler

AN 18TH-CENTURY FARM, 6 KM from Garda and once owned by the Counts of Pellegrini, is the setting for this smart younger and trendier sister of Locanda San Vigilio (see page 118), where guests can use the facilities. It was a simple *osteria* until four years ago when Count Guarienti decided to add rooms, and the restaurant is still highly regarded. Cosy, with deep pink walls, rush-seated chairs, a wood-burning stove and specialities chalked up on a blackboard, it buzzes every evening with outside diners as well as guests. Great attention to detail is obvious in the decoration: each bedroom (six in the main house, six in outbuildings) is a variation on a different-coloured theme. There is also a breakfast room, pool and dining terrace.

VENETO

MONTAGNANA

ALDO MORO
RESTAURANT-WITH-ROOMS

Via Marconi 27, 35044
Montagnana, Padova

TEL 0429 81351 **FAX** 0429 82842
E-MAIL info@hotelaldomoro.com
WEBSITE www.hotelaldomoro.com
FOOD breakfast, lunch, dinner
PRICE €€€
CLOSED 2 weeks Jan, 2 weeks Aug;
restaurant Mon
PROPRIETOR Sergio Moro

MONTAGNANA IS ONE OF THE MOST attractive towns in the Veneto, its arcaded streets enclosed by a superb rectangle of moated medieval walls. The Aldo Moro, opened in 1940 by the present owner's father (not the assassinated politician), makes the best base for an overnight stay. Typically bedrooms are a rather jarring mix of old and new, featuring glossy black headboards and wardrobes, and in each, a startlingly bright red armchair, though a few have attractive traditional wooden beds. Some bathrooms are large, with inviting showers properly enclosed. The restaurant rambles over several rooms, gleaming with polished glass and carefully folded napery.

PORTOBUFFOLE

VILLA GIUSTINIAN
COUNTRY VILLA

Via Giustiniani 11, 31019
Portobuffolé, Treviso

TEL 0422 850244 **FAX** 0422 850260
E-MAIL info@villagiustinian.it
WEBSITE www.villagiustinian.it
FOOD breakfast, lunch, dinner
PRICE €€€€ **CLOSED** 2 weeks
Jan **PROPRIETORS** Berto family

A RECTANGULAR WHITE PILE with two chimneys stuck on top like candles on a birthday cake, this villa is surrounded by a park of green lawns filled with statues and enclosed by a high hedge. Rooms are of awesome dimensions: hardly intimate, but certainly impressive. There are several public rooms with plaster moulding and frescoes, but nowhere cosy to sit; nevertheless, the atmosphere is pleasantly unstuffy. A balustraded stairway leads to an immense gallery, frescoed from floor to ceiling. There are eight suites in the main villa and simpler beamed rooms in the old stable block, where you will also find the restaurant, a stylish setting for excellent fish, and the *enoteca*, where you can sample fine wines and eat a snack.

VENETO

POZZOLO

VALLE VERDE
AZIENDA AGRITURISMO

*Via Fagnini 13, 36020 Pozzolo di
Villaga, Vicenza*

TEL 0444 868047/868242
E-MAIL agrivalverde@libero.it
WEBSITE www.agrituris-
movalverde.it

FOOD breakfast, lunch, dinner

PRICE €
CLOSED restaurant Mon
PROPRIETORS Donello family

IN A LUSH, PEACEFUL VALLEY, this cream-painted house offers five modest bedrooms with modern facilities, but its *raison d'être* is a bustling restaurant with a vast terrace for al fresco meals. There is no menu, but *mamma* – Evelina – does all the cooking herself, producing what she feels like and does best: pasta, roast meat – simple country fare. The restaurant is furnished with rush-seated chairs; immaculate linen covers the tables. Huge arched glass doors open on to the terrace, beyond which is a playground where children can slide and swing amidst the vines. This *agriturismo* is a cut above the norm, and is well placed for visiting Vicenza and the Palladian villas.

SAN BONIFACIO

RELAIS VILLABELLA
COUNTRY HOTEL

*Località Villabella, 37047 San
Bonifacio, Verona*

TEL 0456 101777 **FAX** 0456 101799
E-MAIL info@relaisvillabella.com
WEBSITE www.relaisvillabella.it
FOOD breakfast, lunch, dinner
PRICE €€€ **CLOSED** restaurant
Sun, Mon; piano bar Mon
MANAGER Francesco Puliese

DON'T BE PUT OFF BY the hideous sign set into the portico which spoils an otherwise handsome terracotta frontage. Inside, the Relais Villabella lives up to its name. Built as a humble rice mill and retaining its stone floors and timbered ceilings, it has been cleverly converted to a sophisticated hotel with numerous elegant public rooms and just ten equally elegant bedrooms. Two dining rooms testify to the importance placed on food. The emphasis of the excellent menu is on regional dishes – pasta, risotto, polenta. In a very different style, the piano bar has clusters of shiny black cane tables and chairs around a dance floor, where convention delegates and divas from the Verona opera may smooch the night away. Smart bedrooms are equipped with luxurious bathrooms.

VENICE, LAKES AND MOUNTAINS 129

VENETO

SOLIGHETTO

LOCANDA DA LINO
RESTAURANT-WITH-ROOMS

*Via Brandolini 31, 31050
Solighetto, Treviso*

TEL 0438 842377 **FAX** 0438 980577
E-MAIL dalino@tmn.it
WEBSITE www.locandadalino.it
FOOD breakfast, lunch, dinner
PRICE € **CLOSED** restaurant Mon,
Jul, Christmas Day
PROPRIETOR Marco Toffolin

THE CREATION OF AN inspired chef, Lino Toffolin, this country restaurant (tel 0438 82150) became an institution. Championed by the diva Toti Dal Monte, the young Lino was soon cooking for the glitterati and being patronized by stars such as Marcello Mastrioni. Although Lino died some years ago and now, to a certain extent, the place seems to be trading on his memory, it is still run by his family and continues to attract a faithful local following. One long room, with smaller rooms leading off it, can seat 400 for dinner at full stretch. The ceilings are hung idiosyncratically with hundreds of copper pots. The bedrooms are in annexes and range from comfortable doubles to extravagantly rococo suites. A one off.

TAI DI CADORE

VILLA MARINOTTI
CHALET GUESTHOUSE

*Via Manzago 21, 32040 Tai di
Cadore, Belluno*

TEL 0435 32231/33335
E-MAIL villa.marinotti@libero.it
WEBSITE www.villamarinotti.com
FOOD breakfast, dinner
PRICE €€ **CLOSED** never
PROPRIETORS Laura and Giorgio
Marinotti

TAI DI CADORE LIES JUST ALONG the road from Pieve di Cadore, birthplace of Titian and the main town in this mountainous and thickly wooded region, and Villa Marinotti has a typical backdrop of dark forest and rocky peaks. The owners of the modern stone, wood and white-painted chalet have created five spacious and comfortable suites, each one with its own little sitting room, sleeping up to four people, and most recently, two one-bedroomed chalets. There is a dining room serving good home cooking, and in the expansive grounds are a sauna and tennis court. The villa used to be closed in winter, but we are pleased to report that the Marinottis now keep it open throughout the year.

VENETO

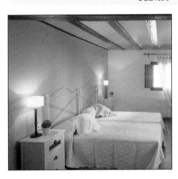

ALBERGO CAMPEOL
RESTAURANT-WITH-ROOMS

Piazza Ancilotto 10, 31100 Treviso

TEL and **FAX** 0422 56601
E-MAIL info@albergocampeol.it
WEBSITE www.albergocampeol.it
FOOD breakfast, lunch, dinner
PRICE € **CLOSED** restaurant Sun eve, Mon, Aug
PROPRIETOR Signor Campeol

T HE ROOMS ARE CONTAINED IN Albergo Campeol at the heart of old Treviso; the restaurant is Alle Beccherie (tel 0422 540871), an unpretentious family-run place across the street. 'Superb food without being overpriced,' says one visitor, while others praise the dignified, old-fashioned atmosphere of this fine old Venetian-style building. The owner's Albergo Campeol strikes a rather different chord: it has large, plain rooms with big beds and modern furnishings, including roomy wardrobes. Our bathroom had a huge shower and cruelly effective mirror lighting, and the spacious bedroom had a canal view. Be prepared for a gruff and peremptory welcome from the non-English-speaking *patron*.

VILLA PISANI
TOWN GUESTHOUSE

Via Roma 19, 35040 Vescovana, Padua

TEL 0425 920016 **FAX** 0425 450811
E-MAIL info@villapisani.it
WEBSITE www.villapisani.it
FOOD breakfast; lunch and dinner by arrangement
PRICE €€€
CLOSED never; 2-night and 2-room min stay in winter **PROPRIETOR** Mariella Bolognesi Scalabran

V ESCOVANA IS A SIMPLE PLACE, more of a village than a town, so what lies behind the walls at its centre is doubly impressive. Villa Pisani is a large, beautifully restored bishop's palace dating from the 16th century, in formal (but also charming) gardens. Inside, one room after another stuns you with frescoed walls, antiques, heirlooms and art collections. It is open to the public and, but for the warmth of your hostess, you might find it intimidating: there's an aristocratic ambience. There are eight bedrooms all, of course, are spacious and ornate. Not really suitable for children.

VENETO

VICENZA

ALBERGO SAN RAFFAELE

EDGE-OF-TOWN GUESTHOUSE

Viale X Giugno 10, Località Monte Berico, 36057 Vicenza

TEL 0444 545767 **FAX** 0444 542259
E-MAIL info@albergosanraffaele.it
WEBSITE www.albergosanraffaele.it
FOOD breakfast
PRICE €€ **CLOSED** never
PROPRIETORS Matiello family

THIS FAMILY-RUN HOTEL on the slopes of Monte Berico was recommended to us by a reader, who found it a breath of fresh air and remarkably inexpensive. Its location is one of the key advantages, with views over Vicenza whilst being only a kilometre from the centre, also within walking distance of two Palladian villas and a 40-minute drive from Verona. Public rooms are well-designed with comfortable seating, and bedrooms, though small, are charming, decorated in Tuscan style ('whitewashed walls, lovely dark oak furniture and good lighting'). Our reader also praised the 'excellent standard of housekeeping' and 'pleasant, friendly staff'. Her two caveats: a hard bed and occasional conferences. Try to avoid the latter.

LOMBARDIA

ALZATE BRIANZA

VILLA ODESCALCHI
~ COUNTRY VILLA ~

Via Anzani 12, 22040 Alzate Brianza, Como
TEL 031 630822 **FAX** 031 632079
E-MAIL info@villaodescalchi.it **WEBSITE** www.villaodescalchi.it

THE ODESCALCHI FAMILY built the splendid villa at the heart of this complex in Brianza at the beginning of the 17th century. Later Pope Innocent XI took such a fancy to its relaxing atmosphere – or perhaps to its private chapel – that he settled in himself. Set in 30 hectares of grounds, the fine formal gardens are now shared (like all the hotel's facilities) with 32 apartments. The villa, complete with a mezzanine gallery in its immense hall, has kept its period presence but has been extended to add all the usual features of a modern hotel: floodlit tennis courts, swimming pools indoors and out, gym, Jacuzzi and Turkish bath, conference rooms and most of the fairly standard bedrooms.

The attractive barrel-vaulted restaurant is housed in the original villa where it offers a competent mixture of international and local dishes. Highest marks here go to the presentation, excellent service and wine list. Breakfast includes a splendid assortment of cheeses and cold cuts, fruit and yoghurt. Como and Lecco are each 20 minutes away and it's a 40-minute drive to Milan.

~

NEARBY Lakes Como and Lecco; Milan (50 km).
LOCATION 10 km SE of Como; garage
FOOD breakfast, lunch, dinner
PRICE €€€
ROOMS 45; 39 double and twin, 6 single, 37 with bath, 7 with shower; all rooms have phone, TV, minibar, hairdrier; some rooms have air-conditioning, safe
FACILITIES restaurant, bar, conference rooms, gym, health centre, indoor and outdoor swimming pools, terrace, garden, tennis
CREDIT CARDS AE, DC, MC, V
DISABLED 2 specially adapted rooms
PETS small dogs accepted
CLOSED early Dec to mid-Jan
MANAGER Pierre Taillandier

LOMBARDIA

BELLAGIO

FLORENCE
~ LAKESIDE HOTEL ~

Piazza Mazzini, 22021 Bellagio, Como
TEL 031 950342 **FAX** 031 951722
E-MAIL hotflore@tin.it **WEBSITE** www.bellagio.co.nz

BELLAGIO IS THE PEARL OF LAKE COMO. It stands on a promontory at the point where the lake divides into two branches, and the views from its houses, villas and gardens are superb. The Florence is a handsome 18th-century building occupying a prime position at one end of the main *piazza*, overlooking the lake. A terrace under arcades, where drinks and snacks are served, provides a welcoming entry to the hotel and the interior is no less appealing. Whitewashed walls, high vaulted ceilings and beams create a cool, attractive foyer; to one side, elegant and slightly faded seats cluster round an old stone fireplace.

Bedrooms have the same old-fashioned charm as the public rooms, furnished with cherry-wood antiques and attractive fabrics; the most sought after, naturally, are those with balconies and views over the lake. Meals can be taken on a delightful terrace under shady trees across the street from the hotel, watching the various craft ply across the lake. The hotel has been in the same family for 150 years, and is now in the hands of brother and sister, Ronald and Roberta Ketzlar; they both speak good English, and have created a gourmet restaurant and two new suites. They've also introduced jazz performances in the bar every Sunday. A recent visitor was thoroughly enchanted.

~

NEARBY Villa Serbelloni; Madonna del Ghisallo (37 km).
LOCATION on main *piazza* overlooking lake; garage
FOOD breakfast, lunch, dinner
PRICE €€€
ROOMS 34; 32 double and twin, 2 suites, all with bath; all rooms have phone, TV, minibar, hairdrier, safe
FACILITIES dining room, bar, reading/TV room, lift, terrace **CREDIT CARDS** AE, MC, V
DISABLED not suitable **PETS** accepted
CLOSED late Oct to mid-Apr
PROPRIETORS Ketzlar family

LOMBARDIA

BELLAGIO

HOTEL DU LAC

~ LAKESIDE HOTEL ~

Piazza Mazzini 32, 22021 Bellagio, Como
TEL 031 950320 **FAX** 031 951624
E-MAIL dulac@tin.it **WEBSITE** www.bellagiohoteldulac.com

SMACK IN THE MIDDLE of Bellagio's waterfront, the Hotel du Lac's stunning view of Como is matched by the Leoni family's pretty faultless performance in all departments. If you want to be picky you might say that one or two of the rooms are on the small side, or that the decoration in some of the bathrooms is a little dated, but there your list would have to stop. The smart marble-floored reception hall runs off an arcade where the café's wicker chairs offer a comfy spot from which to keep an eye on Bellagio's pavement society. The bright and inviting bar is also on the ground floor but the staff will bring you a drink (they have an impressive selection of cocktails) anywhere in the hotel.

On the first floor the windows in the unfussy restaurant run the width of the building to make the most of the panoramic view and the inventive menu offers a broad choice of excellent dishes – with cheeses and wines to match. The impeccably maintained bedrooms are simply decorated, the beds comfortable and, it ought to go without saying, the best have views of the lake. The rooftop terrace offers another vantage point, with deckchairs for sunbathing and awnings for those who prefer some shade. Staff are friendly, professional and helpful.

~

NEARBY Villa Serbelloni; Madonna del Ghisallo (37 km).
LOCATION on main piazza overlooking lake; car parking
FOOD breakfast, lunch, dinner
PRICE €€€
ROOMS 47; 38 double and twin, 9 single, all with bath or shower; all rooms have phone, TV, air conditioning, minibar, hairdrier
FACILITIES sitting rooms, meeting rooms, restaurant, bar, terrace
CREDIT CARDS MC, V
DISABLED not suitable
PETS accepted
CLOSED Nov to late Mar; restaurant Tue
PROPRIETORS Leoni family

LOMBARDIA

BELLAGIO

LA PERGOLA
~ RESTAURANT WITH ROOMS ~

Piazza del Porto 4, 22021 Bellagio, Como
TEL 031 950263 **FAX** 031 950253
E-MAIL info@lapergolabellagio.it **WEBSITE** www.lapergolabellagio.it

L A PERGOLA IS RELAXED and informal, and very much a family affair. Don't come here looking for up-to-the-minute decoration, or even for clues on how they did it many years ago. But, set as it is on a little bay to the south-west of Bellagio, this simple hotel is away from the tourist bustle and there is a fishing village feel to the area. The hotel takes its name from the pergola that shelters diners at its enchanting lakeside restaurant, the focal point of the entire establishment. Really only a matter of centimetres from the water, this proximity is not just romantic: it is also reflected in the restaurant's enticing menu which features dishes based on fish from the lake, alongside a selection of non-fishy regional alternatives with wines to match. Some reports suggest that the cooking has gone downhill recently. Whilst we investigate, more feedback please.

A long passage, attractively flagged with black stone and housing a love-seat and a few pieces of furniture, connects the small reception with the restaurant's terrace. The bedrooms are reached by a large staircase which rises from the passage. The good sized rooms are simple and clean, and most have large windows with glorious views of the lake, and the best have balconies. There's no air conditioning, but each room has a serious-looking ceiling fan. Though it's only a few minutes walk to Bellagio, there are a great many steps to climb, so beware if you're not super fit.

NEARBY Villa Serbelloni; Madonna del Ghisallo (37 km).
LOCATION in village of Pescallo just SW of Bellagio, overlooking lake; public car parking
FOOD breakfast, lunch, dinner
PRICE €€
ROOMS 11; 5 double, 4 twin, 2 with bath, 7 with shower, 2 single with shower; all rooms have phone, TV, safe
FACILITIES restaurant, terrace **CREDIT CARDS** AE, DC, MC, V
DISABLED no special facilities **PETS** accepted **CLOSED** Nov to Mar
PROPRIETOR Mazzoni family

LOMBARDIA

BERGAMO

IL GOURMET

~ RESTAURANT WITH ROOMS ~

Via San Vigilio 1, 24100 Bergamo
TEL and **FAX** 035 4373004
E-MAIL il.gourmet@tiscali.it **WEBSITE** www.gourmet-bg.it

BERGAMO IS QUITE A FAVOURITE with the foodies and, given the pretty stiff competition downtown, it must have taken a certain amount of confidence to hang out a shingle in the High Town with 'gourmet' on it. Although the emphasis here is obviously on food, the rooms are not to be sniffed at. They are all of a good size, extremely well maintained and, although modern in decoration, there are plenty of wood fittings and pieces of furniture to soften them.

The entrance to Ristorante Gourmet is airy and spacious, with a pale tiled floor and a small seating area. This is not a seasonal business: there is as much dining space indoors as there is outside on the large (covered) but uncrowded terrace. The atmosphere is gently civilized and unforced, with pleasant staff taking their cue from the charming owner. The menu is a refined document, wide-ranging and creative with a broad selection of regional specialities, with an extensive wine list. The whole place is dotted with lush, well-cared-for plants, and guests have the use of a lovely private garden when they feel the need for some real peace and quiet. A reader tells us he enjoyed his stay: 'room large, airy and well appointed, though somewhat marred by the view of the felt roof below; dinner excellent, served by waiters who breathed the spirit of the Commedia dell Arte'.

~

NEARBY Brescia (48 km); Milan (50 km); Lakes Como, Lecco and Iseo.
LOCATION in Città Alta (High Town); car parking
FOOD breakfast, lunch, dinner; room service
PRICE ©©
ROOMS 11; 2 double, 7 twin, 3 with bath, 6 with shower, one single with shower, one suite with bath; all rooms have phone, TV, air conditioning, minibar, hairdrier
FACILITIES restaurant, bar, terrace, garden
CREDIT CARDS AE, DC, MC, V
DISABLED no special facilities **PETS** not accepted
CLOSED late Dec to early Jan
PROPRIETORS Aldo Battista Beretta and Giovanni Cornacchia

LOMBARDIA

CANNERO RIVIERA

CANNERO

~ LAKESIDE HOTEL ~

Lungo Lago 2, 28821 Cannero Riviera, Verbania
TEL 0323 788046/788113 (winter) **FAX** 0323 788048
E-MAIL info@hotelcannero.com **WEBSITE** www.hotelcannero.com

CANNERO IS ONE OF THE quietest resorts on Lake Maggiore and its most desirable hotels lie right on the shore. Only the ferry landing-stage and a dead-end road separate the Cannero from the waters of Maggiore.

The building was once a monastery, though only an old stone column, a couple of vaulted passageways, a quiet courtyard and a beautifully preserved 17th-century well suggest it is anything other than a modern hotel. The emphasis is on comfort and relaxation, and the atmosphere is very friendly, thanks largely to the attention of Signora Gallinotto and her family. Downstairs, big windows and terraces make the most of the setting. The restaurant focuses on the lake, with an outdoor terrace running alongside. Bedrooms are light and well cared for with adequate bathrooms, and the restoration of a next-door house provides an additional 15 rooms plus some new apartments. There are gorgeous views of lake and mountains from front rooms, all with balconies, though many guests are happy overlooking the pool at the back – which, if anything, is quieter. By day this provides a delightful spot to take a dip or hang out under the yellow parasols. Readers' plaudits are legion: 'please be sure to rate it A+++!'; 'clean as a whistle, exceptional value, wonderful'; 'family and staff the most friendly and helpful imaginable'.

~

NEARBY Borromean Islands; Ascona (21 km), Locarno (25 km).
LOCATION in resort, overlooking lake; car parking
FOOD breakfast, lunch, dinner; poolside snacks
PRICE €€€
ROOMS 55 double and twin and single, all with bath or shower; all rooms have phone, TV, air conditioning, hairdrier, safe; 10 self-catering apartments
FACILITIES sitting room, piano bar, dining room, library, meeting room, lift, 2 lakeside terraces, garden, swimming pool, tennis, rowing boat, bicycles **CREDIT CARDS** AE, DC, MC, V **DISABLED** 10 rooms accessible **PETS** accepted
CLOSED Nov to mid-Mar
PROPRIETORS Signora Gallinotto and sons

LOMBARDIA

CERVESINA

CASTELLO DI SAN GAUDENZIO

~ CONVERTED CASTLE ~

Loc. San Gaudenzio, 27050 Cervesina, Pavia
TEL 0383 3331 **FAX** 0383 333409
E-MAIL info@castellosangaudenzio.com **WEBSITE** www.castellosangaudenzio.com

SET IN FORMAL GARDENS less than 60 km from Milan, this spacious and elegant 15th-century *castello* has been owned over the years by a succession of smart Italian families and has the ivy, walls, towers, gateways, statuary and other embellishments to prove it. Times have changed: the horses are now gone from the stables and have been replaced by an indoor swimming pool and solarium, and a spectacular barrel vault has been turned into a conference room. Period furniture is watched over by ancestral portraits, and red and black marble fireplaces remind you that woodburning can be done in considerable style.

Most of the bedrooms are brand new, with handsome bathrooms to match, but their pale striped wallpapers and hangings, polished parquet or stone floors, panelled and frescoed ceilings and light, elegant furniture have successfully integrated them with the well-restored older portions of the castle. Almost all look out over the garden. There are three suites, the most baronial (and expensive) of which occupies two stories of a tower.

The restaurant offers Italian and international dishes and the wines on their list include some specially bottled for the *castello*. The staff are professional and helpful.

~

NEARBY Voghera (6 km); Pavia (25 km); Milan (56 km).
LOCATION 6 km NW of Voghera, exit Casei Gerola from the 'Autostrada dei Fiori'; car parking
FOOD breakfast, lunch, dinner
PRICE €€€
ROOMS 45; 35 double and twin, 7 single, 3 suites, all with bath or shower; all rooms have phone, TV, minibar, safe, hairdrier; some rooms have air conditioning
FACILITIES sitting rooms, dining room, conference rooms, bar, indoor swimming pool, solarium, lift, garden **CREDIT CARDS** AE, MC, V
DISABLED 2 specially adapted rooms **PETS** not accepted
CLOSED restaurant Tue
MANAGER Pierangelo Bergaglio

LOMBARDIA

ERBUSCO

L'ALBERETA

◇ COUNTRY VILLA ◇

Via Vittorio Emanuele 11, 25030 Erbusco, Brescia
TEL 030 7760550 **FAX** 030 7760573
E-MAIL albereta@albereta.it **WEBSITE** www.terramoretti.it

IN THE MIDDLE OF THE famous vineyards of Francioforta, L'Albereta is an ancient manor which has had a very elegant and upmarket new life breathed into it. Home of the Moretti family, who still own it, this (Relais & Châteaux) villa is so smart that, unless they have met you at the station or airport, you might just consider nipping through a car-wash before driving up to the front door. But you needn't bother, because the staff here are very professional though not in the least precious. You will also find muted marble, arches, parquet, wrought iron, chintz, beams, flowers and vineyards as far as the eye can see. Virtually everything has been put here to please you and this includes Gualtiero Marchesi's double-starred restaurant which is as much of a draw as the stunning modern bedrooms. His kitchen is a symphony of stainless steel, copper and starched white chefs' uniforms. If you feel an urgent need to work off the effects of a particularly good dinner, you can either play tennis or get your exercise flitting between the Jacuzzi, the sauna and the solarium. Last but not least, just in case you are thinking of arriving by helicopter, L'Albereta helpfully publishes its GPS co-ordinates so that your navigation system can deliver you with pinpoint precision.

◇

NEARBY Brescia (20 km); Bergamo (30 km).
LOCATION 3 km N of A4 Milan-Venice motorway (Rovato exit); car parking
FOOD breakfast, lunch, dinner; room service
PRICE €€€€€
ROOMS 41; 25 double, 10 twin, 32 with bath, 3 with shower, 3 single with shower, 3 suites with bath; all rooms have phone, TV, air conditioning, minibar, hairdrier, safe
FACILITIES sitting rooms, billiard room, restaurant, bars, meeting rooms, health and fitness centre, indoor swimming pool, garden, tennis, helipad
CREDIT CARDS AE, DC, MC, V
DISABLED not suitable **PETS** not accepted
CLOSED early Jan to mid-Feb; restaurant Sun dinner, Mon
PROPRIETORS Moretti family

LOMBARDIA

GARDONE RIVIERA

DIMORA BOLSONE
~ COUNTRY BED-AND-BREAKFAST ~

Via Panoramica 23, 25083 Gardone Riviera, Brescia
TEL 0365 21022 **FAX** 0365 63367
E-MAIL dimorabolsone@gardalake.it **WEBSITE** www.dimorabolsone.com

THIS UNUSUAL B&B MIGHT BE remote – at the end of a bumpy track, perched high above the town – but it is surprisingly sophisticated. Raffaele Bonaspetti, an elegant, spiritual man, bought the house (together with the hillside) as a 15th-century ruin some 20 years ago. With 'the spirit of the place' in mind, he transformed both property and land, replanting the garden with olives, cypresses and laurels to satisfy his passion for trees. Inside, every room is different, beautifully decorated and filled with exquisite things from polished mahogany antiques to a battered chest. One room has Alpine furniture, another remarkable painted lacquer beds. Raffaele inherited much of the furniture from his family, and, with an unerring eye, picked up the rest in antique shops and markets. But his heart lies in the garden, some 10 hectares of trees, shrubs, herbs, flowers and waterfalls, criss-crossed by paths and dedicated to the five senses. When we visited, he was trying to set up guided tours.

Though she speaks little English, Raffaele's wife Catia takes immense care of their guests. A wonderful housekeeper and cook, she prepares a delicious buffet breakfast of fruit, freshly squeezed orange juice, rolls and home-made jam, cold meats and cheese or, if you prefer, pancakes and eggs (from their own chickens). If it's not warm enough to eat on the covered terrace, from where the view is superb, it is served in an attractive yellow room with a crackling fire. (No children under 12 and no smoking.)

~

NEARBY Vittoriale degli Italiani; Brescia (40 km); Sirmione (35 km).
LOCATION up a steep hill, to the west of town; car parking
FOOD breakfast, dinner occasionally on request; drinks
PRICE €€€; 2 nights minimum
ROOMS 4 double and twin with bath
FACILITIES sitting room, breakfast room, terrace, garden **CREDIT CARDS** AE, DC, MC, V
DISABLED not suitable **PETS** not accepted
CLOSED Dec to Mar
PROPRIETORS Raffaele and Catia Bonaspetti

LOMBARDIA

GARDONE RIVIERA

VILLA FIORDALISO

~ LAKESIDE RESTAURANTS WITH ROOMS ~

Corso Zanardelli 132, 25083 Gardone Riviera, Brescia
TEL 0365 20158 **FAX** 0365 290011
E-MAIL info@villafiordaliso.it **WEBSITE** www.villafiordaliso.it

MICHELIN-STARRED VILLA FIORDALISO has been well known as one of the best restaurants in Northern Italy for some years, but it is also a chic and romantic small hotel. Built in 1902, the pale pink and white lakeside villa was home to Gabriele d'Annunzio, and later to Claretta Petacci, Mussolini's mistress. Inside, the intricately carved wood and marble work on walls, floors and doorways and the splendid gold and frescoed ceilings are the perfectly preserved remnants of another age. A magnificent Venetian-style marble staircase, with columns and delicate wrought iron-work leads from the reception hall at garden level to the intimate first-floor restaurant, the heart of the hotel, where the food is exquisite (the chef has a penchant for little glass pots filled with delectable things) and beautifully presented, and on up to the seven luxurious bedrooms. Three of these have been left with their original furniture and decoration. The Claretta suite, a room of impressive dimensions with terrace and lake view, has a stunning marble bathroom. Other rooms are lighter in style with fresh wallpapers and fabrics.

The shady garden, bordering the lake (and, unfortunately, the main road), is a wonderful setting for the elegant summer restaurant, immaculately decked out in a terracotta and white colour scheme.

~

NEARBY Brescia (40 km); Sirmione (32 km).
LOCATION on SS572, 3 km NE of Salò; ample car parking
FOOD breakfast, lunch, dinner
PRICE €€€€
ROOMS 7; 6 double, one suite, all with bath or shower; all rooms have phone, TV, air conditioning, minibar
FACILITIES sitting room, dining room, tower with bar, terraces, garden
CREDIT CARDS AE, DC, MC, V
DISABLED no special facilities **PETS** not accepted
CLOSED mid-Nov to Feb; restaurant Mon, Tues lunch
PROPRIETORS Tosetti family

LOMBARDIA

GARGNANO

BAIA D'ORO
⌁ LAKESIDE HOTEL ⌁

Via Gamberera 13, 25084 Gargnano, Brescia
TEL 0365 71171 **FAX** 0365 72568
E-MAIL hotel-baiadoro@gardalake.it **WEBSITE** www.gardalake.it/hotel-baiadoro

GIAMBATTISTA TERZI WAS BORN in one of a pair of neighbouring fishermen's cottages built on the edge of the lake in 1780, and his wife was the moving force behind turning them into a hotel in the 1960s. Since then the facilities have slowly been updated. To appreciate the fabulous setting, you should arrive by boat.

You can almost dip your hand in the lake from the romantic dining terrace, a splendid vantage point from which to watch night succeed day to the gentle lapping of the water. Boats dock at a little jetty also used by sunbathers. For cool nights, there's a pleasant dining room overlooking the terrace to the lake. Here the Terzis' son Gabriele is in charge, and the fine, short menu consists of saltwater and freshwater fish, served simply.

The Terzis have gradually redecorated the bedrooms in slightly dubious shades of pink and blue, with painted wooden furniture, shiny fabrics and mirrored glass bedheads. Not to everyone's taste, but they are comfortable with sparkling new bathrooms, and the doubles all have lake views.

The cosy, low-ceilinged sitting room has an open fire, and Giambattista's paintings of the area cover the walls.

⌁

NEARBY Gardone Riviera (12 km); Sirmione (44 km).
LOCATION on edge of town, on lake; car parking
FOOD breakfast, lunch, dinner
PRICE €€
ROOMS 14; 10 double and twin, 2 with bath, 8 with shower; 3 single with shower; one suite with bath; all rooms have phone, TV, minibar, hairdrier, safe
FACILITIES sitting room, dining room, bar, terrace, sun deck
CREDIT CARDS not accepted
DISABLED not suitable
PETS accepted
CLOSED Oct to Apr
PROPRIETORS Terzi family

LOMBARDIA

GARGNANO

VILLA FELTRINELLI
∾ LAKESIDE VILLA ∾

Via Rimembranza 38-40, 25084 Gargnano, Brescia
TEL 0365 798000 **FAX** 0365 798001
E-MAIL grandhotel@villafeltrinelli.com **WEBSITE** www.villafeltrinelli.com

THIS ASTONISHING HOTEL MAKES even the most spoilt guests feel lucky to be here, and the most jaded feel soothed, relaxed and completely at home. Built in 1892, the historic pink and white Liberty villa was the summer residence of Italy's wealthiest family, Feltrinelli, and later sheltered Mussolini during the war. With much of the original furniture intact, it has been fabulously restored by American hotelier Bob Burns, no expense spared, and now feels like the most arresting and luxurious private home you could hope to stay in.

The suites, whether in the villa itself or in houses dotted around the lakeside grounds, are eye-poppingly sumptuous. Seven have frescoed ceilings, painted by the Lieti brothers, and each is filled with objects such as silver-framed photographs, handmade Venetian glass lamps and hand-printed paper desk sets. The white embossed bedspreads come from Pratesi and the Frette sheets are of the finest Egyptian cotton. Technology hasn't been forgotten either, so you can listen to opera, jazz or rock music, piped throughout your suite on a high-fidelity sound system, and the vast, opulent bathrooms have heated marble floors.

Of the public rooms, the salon is perhaps most impressive with its frescoes, grand piano and dramatic antique mirrors reflecting the lake. The service is faultless and genuinely friendly. Expensive, but worth it.

∾

NEARBY Gardone Riviera (12 km); Salò (15 km); Sirmione (44 km).
LOCATION on northern edge of town, on lake; car parking
FOOD breakfast, lunch, dinner
PRICE €€€€€€; 2 nights minimum
ROOMS 20 suites with bath; all rooms have phone, TV, air conditioning, minibar, hairdrier, safe **FACILITIES** sitting rooms, 2 dining rooms, library, bar, terrace, garden, croquet, swimming pool, private boat **CREDIT CARDS** AE, DC, MC, V
DISABLED access possible **PETS** accepted
CLOSED mid-Nov to mid-Mar
MANAGER Markus Odermatt

LOMBARDIA

GARGNANO

VILLA GIULIA

~ LAKESIDE HOTEL ~

Viale Rimembranza 20, 25084 Gargnano, Lago di Garda, Brescia
TEL 0365 71022/71289 **FAX** 0365 72774
E-MAIL info@villagiulia.it **WEBSITE** www.villagiulia.it

ONCE A SIMPLE PENSIONE, Villa Giulia is a beautiful, spacious house, built over 100 years ago in Victorian style with Gothic touches. The Bombardelli family has been here for 50 years, and have gradually upgraded their hotel to become one of the most delightful places to stay on Lake Garda.

For a start, it has a wonderful location, with gardens and terraces running practically on the water's edge. Inside, light and airy rooms lead off handsome corridors – a beautiful dining room with Murano chandeliers, gold walls and elegant seats; a civilized sitting room with Victorian armchairs; and bedrooms which range from light and modern to large rooms with timbered ceilings, antiques and balconies overlooking the garden and lake. The rooms in the rear annexe are less appealing, lacking view and air conditioning; other rooms are in three garden chalets. At garden level a second, simpler dining room opens out on to a terrace with ample space and gorgeous views. At any time of day, it is a lovely spot to linger among the palm trees and watch the boats plying the blue waters of Garda. The beautiful swimming pool is an added bonus.

~

NEARBY ferry services to villages and towns around Lake Garda.
LOCATION 150 m from middle of resort, with garden and terrace down to lake; car parking
FOOD breakfast, lunch, dinner
PRICE €€€-€€€€
ROOMS 22 double and twin, one single, all with bath or shower; all rooms have phone, TV, minibar, safe, hairdrier; most have air conditioning
FACILITIES dining room, veranda taverna, sitting room, TV room, bar, terrace, beach, swimming pool, sauna
CREDIT CARDS AE, DC, MC, V
DISABLED access possible **PETS** accepted
CLOSED mid-Oct to Apr
PROPRIETORS Bombardelli family

LOMBARDIA

ISEO

I DUE ROCCOLI

~ MOUNTAIN INN ~

Via Silvio Bonomelli, 25049 Iseo, Brescia
TEL 030 9822977 **FAX** 030 9822980
E-MAIL relais@idueroccoli.com **WEBSITE** www.idueroccoli.com

LAKE ISEO IS IN THE MISTY, southernmost foothills of the Alps. Sixty miles one way would take you into Switzerland and it is not much further in another to reach Austria. The lake's principal island, Monteisola, is the largest on any European lake and home to about 2,000 people. Between the southern tip of the lake and the *autostrada* connecting Milan with Venice lies the Franciacorta, a region highly respected for the quality of its wines. Up a winding mountain road to the south-east of the lake, elegant and tranquil in its carefully tended park, lies I Due Roccoli. Built of stone, and beautifully decorated inside, here is a place to rest and recharge batteries. Simply to praise the views is selling the place short because even the swimming pool has one, and from the moment you spot the vases of fresh roses on each of the tables on the fabulous terrace you just know that you have come to the right place.

Fish from the lake, organically-grown produce from their own gardens and home-cured ham all feature on the short but well-balanced menu and you will dine by candlelight. The spacious and spotless rooms are decorated in modern style with fine prints hanging on the walls. The staff are every bit as charming as their hotel. Our readers concur: 'maybe the best view anywhere I have ever been'; 'an amazing bargain'; 'great food'.

~

NEARBY Brescia (20 km); Lakes Idro and Garda.
LOCATION 4 km SE of Iseo up a mountain road; car parking
FOOD breakfast, lunch, dinner
PRICE €€€
ROOMS 19; 15 double and twin, one single, 3 suites, all with bath; all rooms have phone, TV, minibar, hairdrier, safe
FACILITIES sitting room, bar, dining room, garden, swimming pool, tennis
CREDIT CARDS AE, DC, MC, V
DISABLED access possible **PETS** accepted
CLOSED Nov to mid-Mar
PROPRIETOR Guido Anessi

LOMBARDIA

ISOLA DEI PESCATORI

VERBANO

～ LAKESIDE GUESTHOUSE ～

Via Ugo Ara 2, Isola dei Pescatori, 28838 Stresa, Novara
TEL 0323 30408/32534 **FAX** 0323 33129
E-MAIL hotelverbano@tin.it **WEBSITE** www.hotelverbano.it

THE ISOLA DEI PESCATORI may not have the *palazzo* or gardens of neighbouring Isola Bella (unlike the other islands, it has never belonged to the wealthy Borromeo family), but it is just as charming in its own way. The cafés and the slightly shabby, painted fishermen's houses along the front are, perhaps, reminiscent of a Greek island – though not an undiscovered one.

The Verbano is a large russet-coloured villa occupying one end of the island, its garden and terraces looking across Lake Maggiore to Isola Bella. It does not pretend to be luxurious, but it does offer plenty of character and local colour. There are beautiful views from the bedrooms, and 11 of the 12 have balconies. Each room is named after a flower; most are prettily and appropriately furnished in old-fashioned style, with painted furniture; those which were a little tired-looking have been refurbished, and more refurbishment has been undertaken since a change of ownership. The quietest bedrooms are those away from the terrace.

But the emphasis is really on the restaurant, with home-made pastas a speciality. If weather prevents eating on the terrace, you can still enjoy the views through the big windows of the dining room. 'Excellent food, friendly staff,' says a visitor. Reports welcome.

～

NEARBY Isola Bella; Stresa; Pallanza; Baveno.
LOCATION on tiny island in Lake Maggiore; regular boats from Stresa, where there is ample car parking space
FOOD breakfast, lunch, dinner
PRICE €€
ROOMS 12 double and twin, 8 with bath, 4 with shower; all rooms have phone, hairdrier
FACILITIES sitting room, dining room, bar, terrace **CREDIT CARDS** AE, DC, MC, V
DISABLED no special facilities **PETS** accepted
CLOSED mid-Jan to mid-Feb
MANAGER Signor Gafforini

LOMBARDIA

LENNO

SAN GIORGIO
LAKESIDE HOTEL

Via Regina 81, Lenno, 22019 Tremezzo Como
TEL 0344 40415 **FAX** 0344 41591
E-MAIL sangiorgio.it@libero.it

THIS LARGE WHITE 1920s VILLA on the shores of Lake Como stands out against a backdrop of wooded hills and immaculate gardens running right down to the shore. A path lined with potted plants leads down through neatly tended lawns to the lakeside terrace and the low-lying stone wall which is all that divides the gardens from the pebble beach and the lake. There are palm trees, arbours and stone urns where geraniums flourish. For a trip on the lake the ferry landing-stage lies close by.

The interior is no disappointment. The public rooms are large and spacious, leading off handsome halls. There are antiques wherever you go, and attractive touches such as pretty ceramic pots and copper pots brimming with flowers. The restaurant is a lovely light room with breathtaking views and the salon is equally inviting, with its ornate mirrors, fireplace and slightly faded antiques. Even the ping-pong room has some interesting antique pieces. Bedrooms are large and pleasantly old-fashioned. Antiques and beautiful views are the main features, but there is nothing grand or luxurious about them – hence the reasonable prices. One of our reporters rates this his favourite hotel – 'sensational view, friendly reception, firm bed, great towels'.

NEARBY Tremezzo, Cadenabbia, Villa Carlotta (2-4 km); Bellagio.
LOCATION on lakefront; car parking and garage
FOOD breakfast, lunch, dinner
PRICE €€
ROOMS 29; 26 double, 20 with bath, 6 with shower, 3 single; all rooms have phone, hairdrier, safe
FACILITIES dining room, reading room, table tennis, terrace, tennis
CREDIT CARDS MC, V
DISABLED access difficult
PETS not accepted
CLOSED Oct to Apr
PROPRIETOR Margherita Cappelletti

LOMBARDIA

MALEO

SOLE

~ RESTAURANT WITH ROOMS ~

Via Trabattoni 22, 26847 Maleo, Milano
TEL 0377 58142 **FAX** 0377 458058
E-MAIL solemaleo@interfree.it **WEBSITE** www.ilsolemaleo.it

THE EXTERIOR OF THIS 15TH-CENTURY coaching inn is marked solely by a gilt wrought-iron sun. Inside, the walls are whitewashed, the ceilings timbered and the arched chambers carefully scattered with antique furniture, copper pots and ceramics. There are three dining areas: the old kitchen, with its long table, open fire and old gas hobs where on occasion dishes are finished in front of the guests; a smaller dining room, with individual tables; and the stone-arched portico which looks out on to the idyllic garden.

The late Franco Colombani had brought his own distinctive personality to the regional cuisine – dark, tasty stews, roast meats and fish, accompanied by vegetables from the kitchen garden and fine wines from the unfathomable cellars. Now his son and daughter are continuing with the tradition that has helped rate the Sole as among Italy's finest restaurants.

The three traditionally styled, air-conditioned bedrooms above the restaurant all have individual high points, and good bathrooms, and make great places in which to collapse after a delicious dinner.

~

NEARBY Piacenza; Cremona (22 km).
LOCATION behind church, off main piazza in village, 20 km NE of Piacenza; car parking
FOOD breakfast, lunch, dinner
PRICE €€
ROOMS 3; 2 double, one single with bath; all rooms have phone, TV, air conditioning, minibar; one apartment
FACILITIES sitting room, 3 dining rooms, garden
CREDIT CARDS MC, V
DISABLED no special facilities
PETS accepted
CLOSED Jan, Aug; restaurant Sun eve, Mon
PROPRIETORS Mario and Francesca Colombani

LOMBARDIA

MANTUA

SAN LORENZO

~ TOWN HOTEL ~

Piazza Concordia 14, 46100 Mantova
TEL 0376 220500 **FAX** 0376 327194
E-MAIL hotel@hotelsanlorenzo.it **WEBSITE** www.hotelsanlorenzo.it

SAN LORENZO IS SMART, CONSERVATIVE, technologically up-to-date and as central as it could possibly be. It is literally surrounded by pearls of Mantua's historic architecture. Even if you are only there for a satellite-connected conference, skip past the registration desk, go straight up to the roof terrace, look around you, and marvel at how easy it is to slip back a few centuries (some rooms have terraces overlooking the monuments).

Inside is a hotel where all the 'i's have been dotted and the 't's crossed. It is the sort of place where you just know, as you step across the threshold, that there are no spiders lurking behind the plentiful antiques. The public rooms are quiet and well dressed with fresh flowers, elegant furnishings and furniture, some fine paintings, porcelain and a fascinating collection of 16th-century brass offertory plates.

The staff are generally friendly and professional and can provide you with a potted history of Mantua and a suggested walking tour with some very helpful notes on the places and buildings along the way. The bedrooms are spacious and bright ('I hated the lighting in mine', comments our inspector) each with its own complement of things ancient and modern; and the individual bathrooms, at least the ones she saw, were immaculate. Overall, a well-run, brilliantly located, if slightly characterless base.

~

NEARBY Piazza dell'Erbe; Basilica di Sant'Andrea; Palazzo Ducale.
LOCATION in city centre; garage
FOOD breakfast
PRICE €€€
ROOMS 32; 23 double and twin, 9 suites, 25 with bath, 7 with shower; all rooms have phone, TV, air conditioning, minibar, hairdrier
FACILITIES sitting room, meeting rooms, bar, terrace
CREDIT CARDS AE, DC, MC, V
DISABLED 2 specially adapted rooms **PETS** not accepted
CLOSED never
PROPRIETORS Giuseppe and Ottorino Tosi

LOMBARDIA

MILAN

ANTICA LOCANDA LEONARDO

~ TOWN HOTEL ~

Corso Magenta 78, 20123 Milano
TEL 02 48014197 **FAX** 02 48019012
E-MAIL info@anticalocandaleonardo.com **WEBSITE** www.leoloc.com

A SCANT 30 SECONDS AWAY FROM the tourist-powered mayhem that radiates outwards from Santa Maria delle Grazie, home of Leonardo's Cenacolo, Antica Locanda Leonardo presents a rather drab and faintly inauspicious exterior to the outside world. But don't be dismayed: as you cross the threshold of the front door on the courtyard, you enter a different world. The light, bright entrance hall has a cool pale grey mosaic floor with an attractive stone staircase rising gently to the first floor. Beyond the hall is a pale yellow living room which in turn gives on to a small, peaceful and tree-shaded private terrace with a white-painted wrought-iron table, chairs and a love seat.

Upstairs are the small reception, the breakfast room and all the bedrooms. With the sensible exception of the corridor passing the bedrooms, all the floors are polished wood and the furniture and beds made of rose or cherry wood. The breakfast room manages to be cheerful and elegant at the same time, its two large windows flooding it with light. Breakfast itself is continental – including cereals, fruit and yoghurt – all very fresh and of high quality. The spotless bedrooms are of modest size, but not cramped. Some have little terraces looking over the internal courtyard. Bathrooms are modern, functional, immaculate and graced with good towels.

NEARBY Palazzo delle Stelline; Teatro alla Scala; duomo.
LOCATION in city centre, W of duomo; car parking outside
FOOD breakfast; room service
PRICE €€€
ROOMS 23 double and twin, 11 with bath, 12 with shower; all rooms have phone, TV, air conditioning, hairdrier, safe
FACILITIES sitting room, breakfast room, garden
CREDIT CARDS AE, DC, MC, V
DISABLED not suitable **PETS** not accepted
CLOSED 3 weeks in Aug, late Dec to early Jan
PROPRIETOR Mario Frefel

LOMBARDIA

MILAN

SPADARI AL DUOMO

~ TOWN HOTEL ~

Via Spadari 11, 20123 Milano
TEL 02 72002371 **FAX** 02 861184
E-MAIL reservation@spadarihotel.com **WEBSITE** www.spadarihotel.com

'**H**OTEL' MAY BE A SLIGHT MISNOMER for this chic, unusual establishment, just steps away from the Duomo. While it's true that you can stay here (very comfortably, too), you also share the space with the owners' family passion: contemporary art and design. This is not mere decoration but a substantial collection of works by both known and up-and-coming artists and sculptors. The blue-themed decoration has been chosen to show the pieces to their best advantage and even the design of the striking furniture was specially commissioned from Ugo La Pietra.

Downstairs the reception and sitting room, with the American Bar beyond it, introduce the collection. The focal point is the fireplace with a sculpture by Gio Pomodoro above it. Yet in the midst of all this elegant form there is also excellent function. Although the bedrooms are not large they are well laid out, fresh looking and in tip-top condition; each is recharged daily with fresh fruit and flowers. The top-quality carpets, curtains and bedspreads complement the pictures and eye-catching furniture, and the beautiful bathrooms, all done in blue and white, are immaculate. There is no restaurant but the friendly staff will whip you up a snack if your feet won't carry you another step that day.

~

NEARBY Galleria Vittorio Emanuele; *duomo.*
LOCATION in city centre, just SW of *duomo*; private garage
FOOD breakfast; snacks
PRICE €€€
ROOMS 39; 25 double, 10 twin, 3 single, 1 suite, 27 with bath, 12 with shower; all rooms have phone, TV, air conditioning, minibar, hairdrier, safe
FACILITIES sitting room, bar
CREDIT CARDS AE, DC, MC, V
DISABLED not suitable
PETS not accepted
CLOSED Christmas
PROPRIETOR Marida Martegani

LOMBARDIA

MONTICHIARI

VILLA SAN PIETRO
~ TOWN VILLA ~

Via San Pietro 25, 25018 Montichiari, Breschia
TEL 030 961232 **FAX** 030 9981098 **E-MAIL** villasanpietro@hotmail.com
WEBSITE art-with-attitude.com/villa/san_pietro.html

"WE'RE IN A BEAUTIFUL TOWN, very well placed for visiting the region, but few tourists have heard of it. We're not on the lake, or in the mountains, we're not in Verona or Venice, so we have to offer something extra at our bed and breakfast," says Anna Ducros with disarming honesty. That extra is unusual in Italy: to share her home with their guests, and make them part of the family.

Anna's family have lived at Villa San Pietro, an oasis in the heart of town with a large garden, since the 17th century. It's not grand, but it is full of character and personality, with massive oak beams, old brick floors and a long loggia full of loungers overlooking the courtyard garden. Family furniture, faded black and white photographs and many mementos add to the warmth and charm exuded by vivacious Anna, her French husband Jacques (ex-French Legion) and their son Alexander. If you take part in Anna's carefully prepared five course dinner you will get to know them (they both speak excellent English) and perhaps the story of how they met, which is a touching one. They call their venture 'bed and breakfast, Italian-style' but in fact their hands-on involvement is more usual in Britain than in Italy, and very hard work. They deserve every success.

~

NEARBY Lake Garda; Mantua (45 km); Verona (45 km); Breschia airport.
LOCATION in historic old town, in a street leading off the cathedral square; phone for directions; private car parking
FOOD breakfast, dinner on request
PRICE €
ROOMS 5 double or family, all with bath or shower; all rooms have tea and coffee facilities, hairdrier
FACILITIES sitting room, breakfast room, loggia, garden
CREDIT CARDS MC, V
DISABLED one room on ground floor **PETS** not accepted
CLOSED never
PROPRIETORS Anna and Jacques Ducros

LOMBARDIA

MONZA

HOTEL DE LA VILLE

~ TOWN HOTEL ~

Viale Regina Margherita 15, 20052 Monza, Milano
TEL 039 382581 **FAX** 039 367647
E-MAIL info@hoteldelaville.com **WEBSITE** www.hoteldelaville.com

WHEN YOU ARRIVE AT THE SLIGHTLY dreary exterior of this hotel (facing Villa Reale, the former summer house of Savoy's royal family) your first thought may be that you have made a ghastly mistake. Actually you have done the opposite, because you are in for a delightful surprise. The atmosphere inside is one of opulent but understated elegance: vases of fresh flowers highlight the superb decoration, and throughout the hotel there is a never-ending succession of rare objects collected by Tany Nardi, the owner, for whom perfection is obviously a passion. The corridors are dotted with things like silver trays of little crystal glasses or pieces of perfectly preserved antique luggage, as well as collections of porcelain, glass, clocks, walking sticks and more. Good Persian rugs, antique furniture, pots, plants, gilt-framed pictures and polished marble are lit subtly and gently to persuade you to leave the cares of the world at the front door.

The immaculate bedrooms are beautifully furnished, decorated and appointed, the bathrooms perfect. Here too is the elegant yet cosy wood-panelled restaurant where food is superb. Adjacent to this building is a further surprise: a turn-of-the-century villa superbly restored to create seven luxurious rooms and suites decorated with antiques, gorgeous fabrics and every possible modern gadget artfully hidden in various ways .

~

NEARBY Villa Reale; *duomo*; Milan (15 km).
LOCATION in city centre, in front of Villa Reale; car parking
FOOD breakfast, lunch, dinner
PRICE €€€€€
ROOMS 57; 16 double and twin, 8 with bath, 13 with shower; 39 single, 2 suites, all with shower; all rooms have phone, TV, air conditioning, minibar, hairdrier, safe
FACILITIES restaurant, bar, meeting rooms; billiards, sauna, gym (for annexe only)
CREDIT CARDS AE, DC, MC, V
DISABLED one specially adapted room **PETS** not accepted
CLOSED Aug, Christmas
PROPRIETORS Nardi family

LOMBARDIA

RANCO

SOLE

~ RESTAURANT WITH ROOMS ~

Piazza Venezia 5, 21020 Ranco, Varese
TEL 0331 976507 **FAX** 0331 976620
E-MAIL ivanett@tin.it **WEBSITE** www.ilsolediranco.it

A S YOU ENTER THE SOLE'S LIGHT AND AIRY FOYER, you can't be sure whether you'll be met by the fifth or the sixth generation of the Brovelli family: Carlo and his son Davide run the restaurant and Andrea, Davide's younger brother, now looks after the hotel in this long-lived family business overlooking Lake Maggiore. Either way you will instantly realize that they have avoided the demon of self-importance which so often follows in the trail of culinary honours (currently one Michelin star and accolades for the superb wine cellar). This is an inviting, friendly place where they have combined a superb restaurant, a splendid view of the lake and truly delightful rooms to stay in; and now, a new pool.

To add to the expectations aroused by the star (there used to be two, and may well be again) you should know that, despite the sophistication of their menu, the Brovellis are loyal to their region and feature many local delicacies. Except in poor weather, when tables retreat into the charming dining room, they are set on the lovely terrace beneath a pergola. The bedrooms, recently renovated, are a treat, decorated in sophisticated country style with ankle-deep pile carpets and colour co-ordinated curtains, bedspreads and paintwork. The bathrooms are sparkling white with big tubs, bigger towels and stacked with high-quality 'freebies'.

~

NEARBY Lakes Lugano and Como; Milan (67 km).
LOCATION on E side of Lake Maggiore, N of Angera; car parking
FOOD breakfast, lunch, dinner
PRICE €€€
ROOMS 15; 3 double, 4 junior suites, 8 suites, one single, all with bath; all rooms have phone, TV, air-conditioning, minibar, hairdrier, safe
FACILITIES restaurant, breakfast room, garden,
CREDIT CARDS AE, DC, MC, V
DISABLED one specially adapted room **PETS** small dogs accepted
CLOSED late Nov to late Jan; restaurant Mon and Tue Nov to Apr
PROPRIETORS Brovelli family

LOMBARDIA

SAN FEDELE D'INTELVI

VILLA SIMPLICITAS
∼ COUNTRY VILLA ∼

22010 San Fedele d'Intelvi, Como
TEL 031 831132 **FAX** 031 830455
E-MAIL info@villasimplicitas.it **WEBSITE** www.villasimplicitas.it

As you get further from the A9 two things happen: the roads get smaller and a delicious sense of peace begins to creep over you. The final 2 km to Simplicitas are up a roughish mountain road, but when you finally reach this utterly unpretentious 19th-century villa, just switch off your engine, open the door and listen to the glorious sound of absolutely nothing at all. This is a much-loved, lived-in house, oozing charm and character and filled with 19th-century antiques and objects (and a magnificent billiard table) and an air of rustic gentility. Meals, taken on the terrace in fine weather, usually feature produce from the surrounding 80-hectare farm. 'Very variable, with very limited choice amongst the five courses and the wines,' has been a negative comment; other recent visitors have been happier (one described the dinner as 'excellent').

The bedrooms (some small), most with lovely views, are like comfortable guest rooms in a private house, with a liberal scattering of knick-knacks. Shower rooms are simple. Six further rooms have recently been renovated and added, but overall, with the exception of electric lights, the 20th century hasn't made much impression on the villa. Standards of housekeeping have been criticized by a couple of readers. Once your energy levels are restored, you can walk, ride, play tennis or golf nearby. 'Gorgeous building in a wonderful setting' – so ends the latest report .
∼

NEARBY Lakes Como, Lugano and Maggiore; Como 20 km.
LOCATION 2 km up mountain from San Fedele d'Intelvi; car parking
FOOD breakfast, lunch, dinner
PRICE €€
ROOMS 16 double and twin, all with shower; all rooms have phone
FACILITIES dining room, sitting room, billiard room, garden, table tennis
CREDIT CARDS AE, DC, MC, V
DISABLED not suitable **PETS** accepted
CLOSED mid-Oct to Apr
PROPRIETOR Ulla Wagner

LOMBARDIA

SIRMIONE

GRIFONE

~ LAKESIDE RESTAURANT WITH ROOMS ~

Vicolo Bisse (Via Bocchio) 5, 25019 Sirmione, Brescia
TEL 030 916014 **FAX** 030 916548

ALTHOUGH THE GRIFONE IS ONE of the cheapest and simplest hotels in this guide, it also has one of the loveliest locations, and makes a great place to stay for a night or two. Essentially it is a restaurant specializing in fish ('the waiter removed the bone with the air of a man cleaning his spectacles, a routine gesture, performed with aplomb' writes a correspondent) with a mouth-watering selection of *antipasto* to start. It has an enticing tree-filled terrace overlooking both Lake Garda and the ramparts of Sirmione's castle; also a tiny sandy beach.

The entrance to the hotel is found off a narrow street just inside the city walls. A small sitting room equipped with television and cheerful bamboo furniture leads to a little patio where breakfast is served (though our reader was directed to the baker's shop to buy it himself) and, if the water beckons, on to the scrap of beach. Upstairs, rooms are simple, furniture is basic, the fans noisy, but everything is spotless. Some rooms look right over the castle walls, and the five balconies are full of flowers. Those on the top floor enjoy the best views: rooftops, mountains, and of course the lake. There is no traffic noise in this pedestrian zone, but you may be woken by church bells. The younger generation of the Marcolini family – brother and sister – who now run the Grifone are friendly and helpful.

~

NEARBY Lake Garda; Brescia (39 km); Verona (35 km).
LOCATION just inside city walls, next to castle, on lake; car parking (50 m)
FOOD breakfast, lunch, dinner
PRICE €
ROOMS 16; 12 double, twin and triple, 4 with bath, 8 with shower, 4 single with shower
FACILITIES sitting room, dining room, lift, terraces, tiny beach
CREDIT CARDS not accepted
DISABLED access difficult except to restaurant **PETS** not accepted
CLOSED Nov to Easter
PROPRIETORS Marcolini family

LOMBARDIA

SORGIVE

TENUTA LE SORGIVE
～ FARM AGRITURISMO ～

Località Sorgive, 46040 Solferino, Mantova
TEL 0376 854028 **FAX** 0376 855256
E-MAIL info@lesorgive.it **WEBSITE** www.lesorgive.it

IF THE GARDA CROWDS PUT YOU OFF staying on the lake itself, Le Sorgive has the advantage of being only 13-km south in rural countryside with a view of rolling hills reminiscent of Tuscany. Judo teacher turned organic farmer, Vittorio Serenelli has converted his grandfather's farm into a rather special eco-friendly *agriturismo*. Its riding school, stables, working farm, gymnasium and swimming pool make it ideal for energetic families and fresh-air fiends. Food for the unpretentious restaurant, Le Volpi (100 m away) is produced on the farm, including organic vegetables and a fine herd of Chianino cattle, bred for Fiorentina steak. And the farm's own trees provide fuel for the wood-burner that heats the buildings.

The main entrance leads into the original stable, a cavernous room with a magnificent curved brick ceiling, which now functions as a breakfast room. The bedrooms are in the building next-door and are simple and rustic, with white walls, beams, tiled floors and antique furniture acquired from local house sales; two have sleeping platforms for children. There are also a couple of apartments, each with two double bedrooms plus a sofa-bed and kitchenette in the living room. Great value for a family holiday: prices in high season only just nudge it up into the double-euro band.

～

NEARBY Lake Garda; Brescia (25 km); Verona (40 km).
LOCATION 7 km E of Castiglione delle Stivieret, left off road to Mantova (signed 'Azienda Agricola Le Volpi'; car parking
FOOD breakfast, dinner
PRICE ⓔⓔ
ROOMS 8 double and twin, triple, family, all with shower; 2 apartments; all rooms have phone, TV, hairdrier; second-floor rooms have air conditioning
FACILITIES breakfast room, meeting room, restaurant 'Le Volpi' (100 m away), gym, terrace, garden, swimming pool, riding school **CREDIT CARDS** AE, DC, MC, V
DISABLED access possible to 2 rooms **PETS** accepted
CLOSED never; restaurant Mon, Tue dinner, Jan
PROPRIETOR Vittorio Serenelli

LOMBARDIA

ARGEGNO

VILLA BELVEDERE
LAKESIDE VILLA

Via Milano 8, 22010 Argegno, Como

TEL 031 821116 **FAX** 031 821571
E-MAIL capp.family@tin.it
WEBSITE www.go.to/belvedere
FOOD breakfast
PRICE €€
CLOSED Nov to Apr
PROPRIETORS Cappelletti family

DEVOTEES RETURN YEAR AFTER YEAR to this friendly family-run B&B. Giorgio, the third generation of Cappellettis to own it since 1951, is in charge with Jane, his Scottish wife. Built in the 18th century and turned into a hotel in the early 20th, it has 16 rooms, but only 12 overlook the lake so you need to book early to secure one. And be sure to book the right hotel: there are four 'Belvederes' on Lake Como. On sunny days or balmy evenings, the terrace, smack on the water's edge, is the most entrancing place to sit. But, if the weather is chilly, you can relax inside by a spoiling log fire, beneath a stunning frescoed ceiling. You'll find modest but pristine bedrooms, splendid breakfasts and a fair choice of local restaurants.

CLUSANE SUL LAGO

RELAIS MIRABELLA
LAKESIDE VILLA

Via Mirabella 34, 25049 Clusane sul Lago, Brescia

TEL 030 9898051 **FAX** 030 9898052
E-MAIL mirabella@relaismirabella. it **WEBSITE** www.relaismirabella.it
FOOD breakfast, lunch, dinner
PRICE €€ **CLOSED** never
PROPRIETORS Anessi family

A HOTEL THAT OFFERS THE BEST of both worlds. Newly converted, it is smart and well-equipped (it belongs to the upmarket Romantik chain), but nature lovers will be enchanted with its situation in a village amid woods, and with lawns leading down to Lake Iseo. Each of the 29 airy rooms enjoys this glorious view. The villa is a handsome fortified house, painted yellow, and with a huge terrace that girdles most of the building. Inside, it is crammed with old paintings. The food is regional, and guests can choose between the refined hotel dining room and a charmingly rustic alternative, La Catilina, in a converted farmhouse, a short walk away through the woods. There's an inviting pool in a garden filled with flowers.

LOMBARDIA

GARDONE RIVIERA

VILLA DEL SOGNO
LAKESIDE VILLA

Via Zanardelli 107, 25083
Gardone Riviera, Brescia

TEL 0365 290181 **FAX** 0365 290230
E-MAIL info@villadelsogno.it
WEBSITE www.villadelsogno.it
FOOD breakfast, lunch,dinner
PRICE €€€€€
CLOSED mid-Oct to Apr
PROPRIETORS Calderan family

BUILT IN 1904 AS THE HOLIDAY HOME of an Austrian silk industrialist, this imposing villa became a hotel in 1938. Like so many of the Garda hotels, it has an amazing position, above the lake but near enough to feel part of the lakeside scene. It is approached by a winding drive and cradled in exotic gardens. An extension added in the 1980s contains some rather ordinary rooms, including the reception (disappointing when you first arrive). But go through to the wood-panelled hall and you'll find much more character. The huge wooden fireplace and painted ceramic tiles reveal its Austrian heritage, only slightly at odds with the stone arches, Grecian urns and neoclassical flourishes. Slickly run but prices are steep.

GARGNANO

HOTEL DU LAC

LAKESIDE HOTEL

Via P. Colletta 21, 25084 Villa di
Gargano, Brescia

TEL 0365 71107 **FAX** 0365 71055
E-MAIL info@hotel-dulac.it **WEBSITE** www.hotel-dulac.it
FOOD breakfast, lunch, dinner
PRICE €-€€
CLOSED early Nov to late Mar
PROPRIETORS Arioso family

THE ARIOSO FAMILY HAVE BEEN welcoming guests to their friendly lakeside hotel since 1959. Endearingly old-fashioned, it seems to have changed little since. Downstairs, Persian rugs warm mosaic or tiled floors, and pictures jostle for space on the walls. Reception rooms and bedrooms are furnished with substantial antiques, including a piano, high wooden beds and carved wardrobes. Try for one of the six rooms with a private terrace or balcony. Traditional Italian meals are accompanied by the sound of lapping water as the airy restaurant, with a terrace above, juts out into the lake. In summer you eat on the terrace, shaded by a huge kiwi fruit vine and lit by night with lanterns and candles. Excellent value for money.

LOMBARDIA

MILAN

ANTICA LOCANDA DEI MERCANTI
CITY HOTEL

Via San Tomaso 6, 20123 Milano

TEL 02 8054080 **FAX** 02 8054090
E-MAIL locanda@locanda.it
WEBSITE www.locanda.it
FOOD breakfast, snacks **PRICE**
€€€ **CLOSED** never
MANAGER Alessandro Basta

CENTRALLY LOCATED IN A SMALL SIDE STREET off Via Dante, this is a delightfully decorated hotel in a 17th century building, each room furnished in unique style, some with four-posters, some with wrought-iron bedsteads, with beautiful duvet covers and curtains. Some of the rooms are relieved by stencilled borders, others have details (like climbing roses) painted over the base colour. People either love this hotel or loathe it. Our inspector thoroughly enjoyed her most recent stay here, but we have received an angry complaint too: tiny, ill-equipped bathrooms, freezing rooms, problems with the booking and the bill, a missing breakfast-in-bed, and, worst of all, 'rude' service. Oh dear. Let us know your impressions.

MILAN

MILAN TOWN HOUSE 31
CITY HOTEL

Via Goldoni 31, 20129 Milano

TEL 02 701561 **FAX** 02 713167
E-MAIL
townhouse31@townhouse.it
WEBSITE www.designhotels.com
FOOD breakfast **PRICE** €€€€
CLOSED 3 weeks around
Christmas and New Year, Aug
MANAGER Ornella Borsato

A DESIGN HOTEL THAT MANAGES to be human as well as cool, the 17-room Town House opened in 2002 and occupies an elegant turn-of-the-century building in a residential area near Porta Venezia. The style is a relaxed, contemporary take on an 'Out of Africa' idea (reflecting the owner's preferred travel destinations) with neutral colours effectively off-setting some fine antiques, beautiful ethnic pieces, Moroccan throws and artful flower arrangements. The cocktail bar on the back terrace plays host to a sleek crowd at night.

This is a useful (albeit pricey) address for anyone wanting discreet style combined with easy-going personal service.

LOMBARDIA

POMPONESCO

IL LEONE

RESTAURANT-WITH-ROOMS

Piazza IV Martiri, 46030
Pomponesco, Mantova

TEL 0375 86077/86145
FAX 0375 86770
FOOD breakfast, dinner
PRICE €
CLOSED Jan; restaurant Sun
dinner, Mon
PROPRIETOR Signor Pasolini

POMPONESCO WAS ONCE a flourishing town under the Gonzaga family, and the old part still has faded charm. The Leone lies just off the main *piazza* – a peeling old building once the home of a 16th-century noble-man. It is primarily an eating place. There are only seven bedrooms, and by far the most attractive features are the dining areas – the main restaurant has a coffered 16th-century ceiling and frieze. Elsewhere, decoration is suitably elegant. The food is among the best in the region, with some unusual combinations of flavour. Beyond the restaurant a courtyard leads to the bedrooms, built around an inviting pool and garden area. They are starkly modern, but comfortable and well maintained.

SALO

LAURIN

EDGE-OF-TOWN HOTEL

Viale Landi 9, 25087 Salò,
Brescia

TEL 0365 22022 **FAX** 0365 22382
E-MAIL laurinbs@tin.it
WEBSITE www.laurinsalo.com
FOOD breakfast, lunch, dinner
PRICE € €
CLOSED Dec to Mar
PROPRIETORS Rossi family

A FEATURE OF LAKE GARDA IS the many Liberty-style villas built as holiday homes by wealthy Italians at the turn of the 20th century. The Romantik Hotel Laurin is one of the best preserved. A splendid painted and stone façade rises above immaculate manicured gardens, a terrace and swimming pool. Inside on the ground floor, it is even more impressive with every detail apparently still in place: Art Nouveau frescoes, polished tiled or creaky parquet floors, stained glass, huge Murano chandeliers, palms in pots, and *belle époque* furniture. After this, the bedrooms (the four-star norm, comfortable but dull) are rather disappointing. It is still owned by the family who converted it to a hotel in the 1960s.

LOMBARDIA

SOTTO IL MONTE

CASA CLELIA
AGRISTURISMO

Via Corna 1/3, 24039 Sotto il Monte, Bergamo

TEL 035 799133 **FAX** 035 791788
E-MAIL info@casaclelia.com
WEBSITE www.casaclelia.com
FOOD breakfast, lunch, dinner
PRICE €
CLOSED hotel never; restaurant Mon
PROPRIETOR Rosanna Minonzio

IN FINE COUNTRYSIDE NORTH-WEST of Bergamo, an 11th-century friary is the setting for a new eco-friendly *agristurismo*, beautifully converted with wood fittings, fireplaces, stripped doors, beams and stone walls throughout. But the elegant, natural look of the place is not merely 'rustic chic'; each bedroom is equipped with a device that reduces electro-magnetic fields, heating comes from a wood-burner inset with solar panels, and cork, jute and clay brick provide sound-proofing. Casa Clelia's own organic farm products account for 80 per cent of the food served in the restaurant, a barrel-vaulted room with cheerful checked tablecloths. The bedrooms are furnished with antiques, and some have large claw-foot bathtubs.

TRENTINO-ALTO ADIGE

BARBIANO

BAD DREIKIRCHEN

~ MOUNTAIN HOTEL ~

San Giacomo 6, 39040 Barbiano, Bolzano
TEL 0471 650055 **FAX** 0471 650044
E-MAIL info@baddreikirchen.it **WEBSITE** www.baddreikirchen.it

THE NAME OF THIS IDYLLICALLY situated hotel, a 14th-century chalet owned by the Wodenegg family for 200 years, derives from its vicinity to three small churches which date back to the Middle Ages. The fact that you can only reach the hotel by four-wheel-drive taxi makes for a perfect escape.

The large old building, with its shingled roof and dark wood balconies, has wonderful views and is surrounded by meadows, woods, mountains and quantities of fresh air. There's plenty of space for guests, both inside and out, and the atmosphere is comfortably rustic with an abundance of aromatic pine panelling and carved furniture. A cosy library provides a quiet corner for reading, and simple but satisfying meals are served in the pleasant dining room or on the adjacent veranda, from which the views are superb. Bedrooms in the original part of the house are particularly charming, being entirely wood-panelled.

To sum up, the words of a guest at Bad Dreikirchen in 1908 are still appropriate: 'I stayed for some days ... the weather was continually fine, the position magnificent, and the food good.' Recent guests warmly agree. 'I fell in love with the place. Delightfully relaxed atmosphere, charming young owners.'

NEARBY Bressanone (17 km); Val Gardena (10 km).
LOCATION 21 km NE of Bolzano, exit from Brennero Autostrada at Chiusa, head S through Barbiano (6 km); hotel car park on right (call and the hotel will send a jeep to collect you from car park)
FOOD breakfast, lunch, dinner
PRICE (€); half-board only
ROOMS 26; 16 double and twin, 2 family, 8 single, all with bath or shower
FACILITIES sitting rooms, bar, restaurant, games room, library, garden, terraces, swimming pool, table tennis, tennis court (1 km)
CREDIT CARDS MC, V **DISABLED** access difficult **PETS** accepted
CLOSED late Oct to late Apr
PROPRIETORS Wodenegg family

TRENTINO-ALTO ADIGE

BRESSANONE

DOMINIK
~ TOWN HOTEL ~

Via Terzo di Sotto 13, 39042 Bressanone, Bolsano
TEL 0472 830144 **FAX** 0472 836554
E-MAIL info@hoteldominik.com **WEBSITE** www.hoteldominik.com

THIS IS ONE OF THE MOST unstuffy and relaxing Relais et Châteaux hotels you will find, run with great charm by the Demetz family. The hotel, built in the 1970s, stands on the edge of the oldest part of Bressanone looking out on to the mountains, with the Rienza river running beneath it. Window boxes are filled with geraniums and there is a flowery terrace for dining outdoors. Surrounding the building is a garden of lawns and terraces; inside, it has an open-plan ground floor.

The sitting room has a large open hearth, comfy chairs and coffee tables piled high with magazines, and there are two dining rooms, one cosy and traditional in style, the other contemporary. Bedrooms are modern, very comfortable, and done in bright colours. Fresh flowers and fruit await your arrival; the towels are fluffy and generous in size, and bathrooms are capacious.

Our satisfied inspector reports excellent food, with local dishes given an imaginative twist, elegantly presented, and served by helpful, friendly staff. Readers' reports would be welcome.

~

NEARBY cathedral; Novacella monastery (3 km).
LOCATION on N side of town; with garage
FOOD breakfast, lunch, dinner
PRICE €€-€€€
ROOMS 36; 25 double and twin, 9 single, 2 suites, all with bath or shower; all rooms have phone, TV, minibar, hairdrier, safe
FACILITIES sitting room, dining room, bar, lift, indoor swimming pool, sauna, terrace
CREDIT CARDS AE, DC, MC, V
DISABLED access possible
PETS accepted
CLOSED 2 to 3 weeks Mar, mid-Nov to late Jan
PROPRIETORS Demetz family

TRENTINO-ALTO ADIGE

BRESSANONE

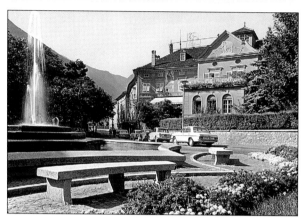

ELEPHANT

~ TOWN HOTEL ~

Via Rio Bianco 4, 39042 Bressanone, Bolzano
TEL 0472 832750 **FAX** 0472 836579
E-MAIL info@hotelelephant.com **WEBSITE** www.hotelelephant.com

BRESSANONE IS A PRETTY TOWN at the foot of the Brenner Pass, more Austrian than Italian in character. The same is true of the charming Elephant, named after a beast which was led over the Alps as a gift from King John of Portugal to Archduke Maximilian of Austria. The only stable big enough for the exhausted animal was next to the inn, so the innkeeper promptly changed its name to celebrate the event.

There is an air of solid, old-fashioned comfort throughout. Corridors decorated in sumptuous colours are lined with heavily carved and beautifully inlaid antiques. The public rooms are all on the first floor: an elegant 18th century-style sitting room, a large light breakfast room, and three dining rooms. The main one is panelled in dark wood with a vast green ceramic stove and stags' heads on the walls. The food is one of the highlights of a stay here. A reporter commented: 'We had a fabulous dinner; the cooking is imaginative but unfussy with lots of fresh herbs and local ingredients, beautifully presented and bountiful.' Bedrooms are large and comfortable, but disappointing compared with the more characterful public areas. Some have antiques, others have none.

~

NEARBY cathedral; Novacella monastery (3 km).
LOCATION at N end of town; in gardens with car parking and garages
FOOD breakfast, lunch, dinner
PRICE €€€
ROOMS 44; 28 double and twin, 27 with bath, one with shower; all rooms have phone, TV, minibar, hairdrier
FACILITIES breakfast room, sitting room, bar, dining rooms, lift, garden, swimming pool, tennis courts
CREDIT CARDS AE, DC, MC, V
DISABLED 2 ground floor rooms in annexe
PETS accepted
CLOSED Nov, Jan to Mar
PROPRIETORS Heiss family

TRENTINO-ALTO ADIGE

CALDARO

LEUCHTENBURG
~ COUNTRY GUESTHOUSE ~

Campo di Lago 100, 39052 Caldaro, Bolzano
TEL 0471 960093/960048 **FAX** 0471 960155 **E-MAIL** pensionleuchtenburg@
kalterersee.it **WEBSITE** www.kalterersee.com/pensionleuchtenburg

T HIS SOLID STONE-BUILT 16th-century hostel once housed the servants of
Leuchtenburg castle, an arduous hour's trek up the steep wooded
mountain behind. Today, guests in the *pension* are well cared for by the
friendly owners, while the castle lies in ruins. The setting is enviably tranquil, right on Lago di Caldaro, better known (at least to wine buffs) as
Kalterer See. Cross a road and you are at the water's edge, where a little
private beach is dotted with umbrellas and sunloungers.

Back in the *pension*, the Sparers provide solid breakfasts and three-
course dinners of regional cuisine in an unpretentious, homely atmosphere. White-painted low-arched dining rooms occupy the ground floor;
above is the reception, with a large table littered with magazines and surrounded by armchairs. There is another sitting area on the first floor, leading to the bedrooms. These have pretty painted furniture and tiled floors
(second floor rooms are plainer). Each one tells a story: for example, the
'old smoke room' was where food was smoked. All are large, and some
share the views enjoyed from the terrace across vineyards to the lake. The
Sparers have recently created seven new suites. Though not rock-bottom,
prices represent excellent value.

~

NEARBY swimming and fishing in lake.
LOCATION 5 km SE of Caldaro, on the edge of the lake; in courtyard with car parking
FOOD breakfast, dinner
PRICE €€
ROOMS 26; 15 double and twin, 2 single, 2 triple, 7 suites, all with bath or shower;
all rooms have phone, TV
FACILITIES sitting area, dining area, bar, terrace, beach
CREDIT CARDS MC, V
DISABLED not suitable
PETS accepted
CLOSED Nov to Easter
PROPRIETORS Sparer family

TRENTINO-ALTO ADIGE

FIÉ ALLO SCILIAR

TURM

~ MOUNTAIN VILLAGE HOTEL ~

Piazza della Chiesa 9, 39050 Fié allo Sciliar, Bolzano
TEL 0471 725014 **FAX** 0471 725474
E-MAIL info@hotelturm.it **WEBSITE** www.hotelturm.it

A SOLID FORMER COURTHOUSE dating from the 12th century, with views across pastures and mountains, Romantik Hotel Turm offers typical Tyrolean hospitality with style and warmth. Now run by dashing Stefan Pramstrahler, who is also the talented chef, the hotel has gained a hip edge in the last couple of years, as well as a wonderful new oriental-style 'wellness' suite and a new wing housing 14 luxurious rooms. Bedrooms are all different and vary considerably in size, but even the smallest has everything you could want for a comfortable stay, including traditional furniture and somewhere cosy to sit. The mini-apartments are excellent value: one, in a little stone tower, is done as a wood-panelled *stübe*, with spiral staircase to a double room and a children's room. The Pramstrahlers' fine collection of contemporary art is displayed everywhere, including the new bar/sitting room (with gorgeous sunny terrace) and spills out along the whitewashed corridor walls.

The main dining room is light and spacious, with low wood ceiling and windows overlooking the valley; or you can dine in a romantic little room at the base of the 11th-century tower. Either way, the elegant food is superb.

~

NEARBY Val Gardena; Bolzano (16 km); Castelrotto (10 km).
LOCATION in village, 16 km E of Bolzano; with garden and limited car parking
FOOD breakfast, lunch, dinner; room service
PRICE €€€-€€€€
ROOMS 35; 29 double and twin, one single; all with bath or shower; 5 apartments with kitchen, all rooms have phone, TV, minibar, hairdrier, safe
FACILITIES sitting room, dining rooms, bar, lift, garden, spa and beauty area, outdoor swimming pool, garage
CREDIT CARDS MC, V
DISABLED access possible
PETS accepted
CLOSED Nov to mid-Dec
PROPRIETORS Pramstrahler family

TRENTINO-ALTO ADIGE

LAGUNDO

DER PÜNTHOF

∼ COUNTRY HOTEL ∼

Via Steinach 25, 39022 Lagundo, Bolzano
TEL 0473 448553 **FAX** 0473 449919
E-MAIL www.puenthof.com **WEBSITE** info@puenthof.com

VIA CLAUDIO AUGUSTO, a Roman road to Germany, passed what is now the entrance to Der Pünthof, and the watchtower built to guard the road forms an integral part of the hotel. The main building was a medieval farmhouse and has been in the Wolf family since the 17th century. They opened it as a hotel 40 years ago, housing guests in the barn, but over the decades other buildings have been added. Although Lagundo is a rather dreary suburb of Merano, once inside the hotel's electronic barrier you could be miles from anywhere with only orchards, vineyards and stunning scenery in view.

The public rooms are in the old building: breakfast is served in a pale green *stube* with wooden floor, low ceiling, ceramic stove and traces of the original decoration on the panelled walls. Bedrooms in the barn are modern and comfortable, but uniform, though some have private terraces on to the garden. The most appealing are the rooms in the square tower. One has polished floorboards, a wood ceiling and antique bed. There are six well-equipped self-catering chalets, and six simpler cheaper rooms in another annexe.

∼

NEARBY Bolzano (28 km); Brennero (70 km); the Dolomites.
LOCATION 3 km NW of Merano, outside village; in own grounds with ample car parking
FOOD breakfast
PRICE ©© ; 3 days minimum
ROOMS 12 double and twin, 2 with bath, 10 with shower; 6 apartments with kitchenette; all rooms have phone, TV, minibar, safe
FACILITIES 2 breakfast rooms, sitting room, bar, restaurant, sauna, solarium, garden, tennis courts, swimming pool
CREDIT CARDS AE, DC, MC, V
DISABLED one room on ground floor **PETS** accepted
CLOSED early Nov to mid-Mar
PROPRIETORS Wolf family

TRENTINO-ALTO ADIGE

MARLENGO

OBERWIRT

~ MOUNTAIN RESORT HOTEL ~

Vicolo San Felice 2, Marlengo, 39020 Merano, Bolzano
TEL 0473 222020 **FAX** 0473 447130
E-MAIL info@oberwirt.com **WEBSITE** www.oberwirt.com

THE BUILDING IS TYPICAL of the area: solid, whitewashed, red-shuttered, with all sorts of arches and architectural ins and outs, and a crucifix and painted sundial on the front. Inside, public rooms are in traditional Tyrolean style with a profusion of wood panelling, carved furniture and knick-knacks; some bedrooms, however, lack character: comfortable, spacious, mostly with balcony or terrace, but few traditional touches.

Originally a simple inn, Oberwirt has been run by the Waldner family since 1749. Today, though (like so many hotels in the area) it has joined the Romantik chain, three generations work in the hotel: Signor Waldner's beaming mother, dressed in a *dirndl*, is at reception, while his daughter runs the restaurant. The hotel is often full, and though it has plenty to recommend it, character and intimacy are not strong features – the misty 'romantic' photo on the cover of the brochure somehow says it all.

The highlight is the food. Our reporter gushed: 'Local produce ... creative presentation ... melt in the mouth pan-fried duck liver, lamb cutlets in a herb crust ... and the best pudding I've ever tasted (well almost): marscapone and compote of bitter cherries between wafer thin layers of strudel pastry.'

~

NEARBY Passirio river and valley; Tirolo castle; Dolomites.
LOCATION in village, 4 km SW of Merano; parking in garage or car park
FOOD breakfast, lunch, dinner
PRICE €€
ROOMS 40; 34 double and twin, suites and junior suites, 6 single, all with bath or shower; all rooms have phone, TV, minibar, hairdrier, safe
FACILITIES sitting rooms, dining rooms, bar, meeting room, terrace, garden, indoor and outdoor swimming pools, sauna/solarium, tennis, riding, golf
CREDIT CARDS AE, DC, MC, V
DISABLED access to public rooms **PETS** accepted
CLOSED mid-Nov to mid-Mar
PROPRIETORS Joseph Waldner and family

TRENTINO-ALTO ADIGE

MERANO

CASTEL FRAGSBURG

~ CONVERTED CASTLE ~

Via Fragsburg 3, 39012 Merano, Bolzano
TEL 0473 244071 **FAX** 0473 244493
E-MAIL info@fragsburg.com **WEBSITE** www.fragsburg.com

A LOVELY DRIVE ALONG A NARROW COUNTRY LANE, through mixed woodland and past Alpine pastures brings you to the east of Merano where Castel Fragsburg – 300 years old and a hotel for more than 100 years – commands splendid views of the Texel massif.

Externally, Fragsburg still looks very much the hunting lodge, with carved wooden shutters and balconies. A terrace along the front of the house, covered with wistaria, is a wonderful place to eat or drink: you seem to be suspended over the mountainside. The adjoining dining room can be opened up in warm weather, and the food – a seven course dinner – is 'very good and carefully served' according to one visitor, with a huge breakfast buffet accompanied by Prosecco. In cooler weather you can choose from various Tyrolean-style sitting rooms and a congenial little library. Bathrooms, recently renovated, are modern and spotless and bedrooms all have balconies, carved pine furniture and colourful country fabrics. A wellness centre has now been added to the sauna and gym in the old cellars.

The wooded gardens provide plenty of space for lazing – as well as a wooden shelter reserved for all-over suntanning. Delightful owners.

~

NEARBY Promenades along the Passirio river in Merano; Passirio valley, Schloss Rametz; Dolomites.
LOCATION 6 km NE of Merano, in own gardens with ample parking
FOOD breakfast, lunch, dinner
PRICE €€€; half-board only
ROOMS 20; 6 double and twin, 12 suites, 2 single, all with bath; all rooms have phone, TV, minibar, hairdrier, safe
FACILITIES sitting rooms, library, smoking room, dining rooms, terrace, lift, sauna, gym, wellness spa, garden
CREDIT CARDS MC, V
DISABLED one specially adapted room
PETS accepted
CLOSED Nov to Easter
PROPRIETORS Ortner family

TRENTINO-ALTO ADIGE

MERANO

CASTELLO LABERS
~ CONVERTED CASTLE ~

Via Labers 25, 39012 Merano, Bolzano
TEL 0473 234484 **FAX** 0473 234146
WEBSITE www.labers.it

ON A HILLSIDE EAST OF MERANO, Castello (or Schloss) Labers is immersed in its own lush orchards and vineyards, with direct access to mountain walks through Alpine pastures. The hotel has been in the Neubert family since 1885, but the building itself dates back to the 11thC.

On a bad day, the Castello wouldn't look out of place in an Addams family film, but it has its charm, and the interior is welcoming with an impressive stone staircase with wrought-iron balustrades leading from the arched entrance hall up to the bedrooms. These vary enormously in size and standard: some elegantly proportioned with antique furniture, others rather too drab and basically furnished. The best rooms have balconies, particularly those on the corners; an attic room in the tower with a wood-panelled alcove is also charming.

The castle gardens are packed with trees and flowering shrubs, which can be admired from the conservatory restaurant; there are two other dining rooms, one baronial, with vaulted wooden ceiling. And what about the ambience? 'Elderly', writes a recent guest. 'Very pleasant, very quiet, but elderly.'

~

NEARBY Passirio river and valley; Tirolo Castle; Dolomites.
LOCATION 2.5 km E of Merano; with private grounds, garage and parking (locked at night)
FOOD breakfast, lunch, dinner
PRICE €€€
ROOMS 41; 22 double and twin, 20 with bath, 2 with shower; 9 single, 2 with bath, 7 with shower; 10 family with bath; all rooms have phone, TV, safe
FACILITIES 3 dining rooms, music/reading room, bar, billiard room, conference room, lift, tennis court, swimming pool, garden
CREDIT CARDS AE, DC, MC, V
DISABLED access difficult
PETS accepted
CLOSED Jan to Apr
PROPRIETORS Stapf-Neubert family

TRENTINO-ALTO ADIGE

MERANO

VILLA TIVOLI
~ EDGE-OF-TOWN HOTEL ~

Via Verde 72, 39012 Merano, Bolzano
TEL 0473 446282 **FAX** 0473 446849
E-MAIL info@villativoli.it **WEBSITE** www.villativoli.it

ALMOST IN COUNTRYSIDE, yet close to the town centre, standing in apple orchards, the pale yellow villa is surrounded by an 'exquisite' terraced garden filled with over 2,000 different plants. Inside all is cool and chic, spacious and light, yet not intimidating. The ground floor is open-plan, with a glass-walled dining room; over the bar an extraordinary contemporary fresco of many-breasted Artemis, a recurring theme in the hotel. Another corner holds a sitting area, elegantly furnished with antiques and there is a traditional wood-panelled Tyrolean *stübe*. Outside, a terrace with tables shaded by yellow umbrellas – as well as a new rock-lagoon surrounded by cypress and stone – and in the basement, a pool room with gaily painted walls. Bedrooms, named after Mediterranean flowers, are all different, all comfortable, with south-facing balconies. Some are huge, with separate sitting areas; some are furnished with antiques, others are very contemporary. Bathrooms are large, with double basins. Our reporter was hooked: 'Smart but relaxed; staff warm and welcoming, owners genuinely friendly and aiming to please; mountainous breakfast buffet, designed to see you through till evening, and a delicious dinner (half board includes five courses) with excellent local wines.'

~

NEARBY Passirio river promenades; Passirio valley; the Dolomites.
LOCATION on edge of town; in own grounds with ample car parking
FOOD breakfast, lunch, dinner
PRICE ©©
ROOMS 21; 16 double and twin, all with bath or shower, 5 suites with bath; all rooms have phone, TV, hairdrier, safe
FACILITIES sitting room, dining room, bar, library, indoor and outdoor swimming pools, sauna, lift, terrace, garden, bicycles
CREDIT CARDS AE, DC, MC, V
DISABLED access difficult **PETS** accepted
CLOSED mid-Dec to mid-Mar
PROPRIETORS Defranceschi family

TRENTINO-ALTO ADIGE

MISSIANO

SCHLOSS KORB

~ CONVERTED CASTLE ~

Missiano, 39050 San Paolo, Bolzano
TEL 0471 636000 **FAX** 0471 636033
E-MAIL info@schloss-hotel-korb.com **WEBSITE** www.schloss-hotel-korb.com

RISING UP ABOVE THE fertile vineyards and orchards that surround the outskirts of Bolzano is the 11th-century tower which forms the centre-piece of Schloss Korb.

The entrance to the hotel is a riot of colour – flowering shrubs and plants set against walls of golden stone and whitewash. Inside, furnishings and decorations are in traditional style, and antiques and fresh flowers abound. Reception is a cool, dark, tiled hall set about with a most eccentric collection of objects including carvings, golden angels on the walls, huge plants, busts, heavy mirrors, brass ornaments and armoury – the oldest part of the hotel. Surrounding the main restaurant is a terrace, hanging out over the valley and awash with plants, where breakfast and drinks can be enjoyed. The place feels relaxed, though not intimate.

The bedrooms in the castle are generous in size, with separate sitting areas and lovely views out over the vineyards. Best are those in the tower, or the traditional apartment with its carved furniture. Rooms in the annexe all have balconies, and here there is a lift and an indoor heated swimming pool.

~

NEARBY Bolzano (8 km); Merano (36 km); Dolomites.
LOCATION 8 km W of Bolzano, in gardens; ample parking
FOOD breakfast, lunch, dinner
PRICE €€-€€€; half-board only
ROOMS 62; 54 double and twin, 2 single, all with bath; 6 suites, 5 with bath, one with shower; all rooms have phone, TV; half the rooms have safe
FACILITIES sitting rooms, dining room, bar, sauna, beauty salon, conference rooms, terraces, garden, tennis courts, indoor and outdoor swimming pools
CREDIT CARDS not accepted
DISABLED access difficult
PETS accepted
CLOSED Nov to late Mar
PROPRIETORS Dellago family

TRENTINO-ALTO ADIGE

ORTISEI

UHRERHOF DEUR

~ MOUNTAIN CHALET ~

Bulla, 39046 Ortisei, Bolzano
TEL 0471 797335 **FAX** 0471 797457
E-MAIL info@uhrerhof.com **WEBSITE** www.uhrerhof.com

THE NAME MEANS 'HOUSE OF THE CLOCKS', and their ticking and chiming, along with birdsong, are very often the only sounds which break the silence at this traditional chalet set in a tucked-away hamlet 1,600 metres above sea level. Indeed, noise levels hardly rise above a whisper, and Signora Zemmer is at pains to point out that this is a place only for those seeking total peace and quiet. Outside, there is a grassy garden from which to enjoy the wide and wonderful view. Inside, all the rooms, including the balconied bedrooms, are bright, simple and beautifully kept, with plenty of homely details. The core of the chalet is 400 years old, and includes the all-wood *stübe* with working stove. The three adjoining dining rooms have wooden benches round the walls, Tyrolean fabrics for curtains and cushions, bright rugs on terracotta floors and pewter plates displayed in wall racks. Signor Zemmer is the chef, and his simple yet delicious food is elegantly presented on pewter plates.

Underneath the house is a surprisingly smart health complex, with huge picture windows so that you can relax in the open-plan Turkish bath and soak up the view. The hotel is strictly non-smoking.

~

NEARBY Val Gardena; Castelrotto (13 km); Bolzano (26 km).
LOCATION in mountainside hamlet, 13 km E of Castelrotto, off Castelrotto-Ortisei road; garage parking
FOOD breakfast, dinner
PRICE €€€
ROOMS 11; 8 double and twin, 4 with bath, 4 with shower; 3 single with shower; 2 apartments for 2-5 with kitchen; all rooms have phone, TV, hairdrier, safe
FACILITIES dining room, bar, sitting room,lift, health centre, garden, table tennis, play area
CREDIT CARDS MC, V
DISABLED suitable **PETS** not accepted
CLOSED Nov to mid-Dec, 2 weeks after Easter
PROPRIETORS Zemmer family

TRENTINO-ALTO ADIGE

PERGINE

CASTEL PERGINE

~ CONVERTED CASTLE ~

38057 Pergine, Valsugana, Trento
TEL 0461 531158 **FAX** 0461 531329
E-MAIL verena@castelpergine.it **WEBSITE** www.castelpergine.it

THIS MEDIEVAL HILLTOP FORTRESS is managed with enthusiasm by an energetic and cultured Swiss couple, Verena and Theo. Past and present coexist happily in a rather alternative atmosphere, and the castle has a truly lived-in feel despite its grand dimensions and impressive history. A recent visit confirmed that this is one of the most affordable and distinctive hotels in the region. Though it must be said that it's an aquired taste: one reader comments on the 'daunting approach, strange modern art, refectory-style dining room and Spartan comfort'.

The route from the car park to the hotel leads you under stone arches, up age-worn steps and through vaulted chambers to the airy, round reception hall where breakfast is also served. The two spacious dining rooms have wonderful views, and the cooking is light and innovative. As you would expect from their price, bedrooms are by no means luxurious, and some are very small, but all are furnished in simple good taste; the best have splendid, heavy, carved wooden furniture and wall panelling.

One of the most enchanting features of the castle is the walled garden. Spend an hour reading a book, or simply watching the mountains through the crumbling ramparts, and you may never want to leave.

~

NEARBY Trento (11 km); Lake Caldonazzo (3 km); Segonzano.
LOCATION off the SS47 Padua road, 2 km SE of Pergine; in own grounds with ample car parking
FOOD breakfast, dinner
PRICE €); half-board only
ROOMS 21; 13 double and twin, 8 with shower, 4 single, 3 with shower, 4 triple, 3 with shower; all rooms have phone
FACILITIES sitting room, dining rooms, bar, garden
CREDIT CARDS AE, MC, V
DISABLED access difficult **PETS** accepted
CLOSED Nov to Easter
PROPRIETORS Verena Neff and Theo Schneider

TRENTINO-ALTO ADIGE

RASUN DI SOPRA

ANSITZ HEUFLER

~ CONVERTED CASTLE ~

Rasun di Sopra 37, 39030 Rasun, Anterselva
TEL 0474 498582 **FAX** 0474 498046
E-MAIL info@ansitzheufler.com **WEBSITE** www.ansitzheufler.com

THE WORD 'ANSITZ' MEANS unfortified aristocratic residence and this one, dating from the 16th century, is a beautiful example. Although set rather incongruously on the edge of an unremarkable village, it is surrounded by stunning scenery.

Just before our inspector's last visit, the hotel changed hands and, though the alterations made by the new owners were subtle, they were not – to her mind – all beneficial. A profusion of beribboned candles, lace cushions and teddy bears in alcoves were too pretty-pretty for her taste. Now it's all change again since Thomas Steiner and his family took over. Unfortunately, we haven't been able to revisit the hotel yet, but we gather that the Steiners have introduced cleaner lines and less fussy decoration, allowing the character of this lovely hotel to reassert itself. Sadly, the superbly carved old *stübe* is still practically devoid of furniture and only used for receptions.

The food served in the three wood-panelled dining rooms has a strong Tyrolean bias. The bar is in the original smokery with blackened walls and vaulted ceiling. The bedrooms are all different, full of marvellous furniture and architectural features, but beware of hitting your head on low lintels. More reports please.

~

NEARBY Brunico (10 km).
LOCATION in village in wooded Anterselva valley, 10 km E of Brunico; car parking
FOOD breakfast, lunch, dinner
PRICE €€
ROOMS 8; 5 double and twin, 2 with bath, 3 with shower; 3 suites, 2 with bath, one with shower; all rooms have phone
FACILITIES sitting rooms and areas, dining rooms, bar, garden
CREDIT CARDS AE, DC, MC, V
DISABLED not suitable **PETS** not accepted
CLOSED late Dec to Mar
PROPRIETORS Steiner family

TRENTINO-ALTO ADIGE

REDAGNO DI SOPRA

ZIRMERHOF

~ MOUNTAIN HOTEL ~

39040 Redagno, Bolzano
TEL 0471 887215 **FAX** 0471 887225
E-MAIL info@zirmerhof.com **WEBSITE** www.zirmerhof.com

SITUATED JUST OUTSIDE the tiny hamlet of Redagno di Sopra, this 12th-century *mas* has been in the Perwanger family since 1890. Views are of mountains, green pastures and forests with few signs of civilization to mar the landscape. 'Idyllic', a contented guest tells us. The interior has been carefully restored. The dim, low-ceilinged hall with its intricate wood carving, ticking grandfather clock and old fireplace, immediately plunges you into the atmosphere of an old family home. There is a tiny cosy library, a sitting-cum-breakfast room with an open fire for winter days, and a rustic bar with a grassy terrace, from which to enjoy the superb views. The large wood-panelled dining room houses two elaborate ceramic stoves, and makes a fine setting in which to enjoy the local dishes and sophisticated wines on offer.

The comfortable bedrooms vary enormously in size, but all are attractive with traditional carved furniture (much of it made on the premises) and pretty fabrics; the largest rooms are on the top floor. For the energetic, there's plenty to do, particularly in winter, from skating and curling on the lake to cross-country and downhill skiing.

~

NEARBY Cavalese (15 km); skiing.
LOCATION 5 km N of Fontanefredde, off the SS48; car parking
FOOD breakfast, lunch, dinner
PRICE €-€€
ROOMS 33; 31 double and twin, single, 2 suites, all with bath or shower; rooms have TV on request
FACILITIES dining room, sitting room, bar, library, sauna, and steam room, garden, vineyard, riding
CREDIT CARDS MC, V
DISABLED ground-floor bedrooms available
PETS accepted
CLOSED early Nov to day after Christmas, early Jan to mid-May
PROPRIETOR Sepp Perwanger

TRENTINO-ALTO ADIGE

SAN OSVALDO

GASTHOF TSCHOTSCHERHOF
~ COUNTRY GUESTHOUSE ~

San Osvaldo 19, 39040 Siusi, Bolzano
TEL 0471 706013 **FAX** 0471 704801
E-MAIL info@tschoetscherhof.com **WEBSITE** www.tschoetscherhof.com

DON'T BE PUT OFF by the unpronounceable name; for lovers of simple, farmhouse accommodation in an unspoiled rural setting, this hostelry could be ideal.

The narrow road from Siusi winds through apple orchards, vineyards and open meadows, eventually arriving at the tiny hamlet of San Osvaldo and this typical 500-year-old farmhouse with its adjacent dark wood barn. The name, painted on the outside of the building, is almost hidden by the clambering vines, and the old wooden balconies are a colourful riot of cascading geraniums. The sun-drenched terrace is a perfect spot for relaxing and eating.

Inside, we were beguiled by smells from the kitchen at the end of the hall, and were drawn to the warmth of the low-ceilinged old *stübe* with gently ticking clock, rough wood floor and simple white ceramic stove.

A rustic stone stairway leads up to the modest but tidy bedrooms, some of which have balconies. They have no frills, but after a long day in glorious countryside, we were too tired to notice.

~

NEARBY Castelrotto (5 km); Bolzano (17 km); Sciliar Natural Park (10 km).
LOCATION in hamlet, 5 km W of Castelrotto; with parking
FOOD breakfast, lunch, dinner
PRICE ⓔⓔ
ROOMS 8; 7 double and twin, one single, all with shower
FACILITIES dining rooms, terrace
CREDIT CARDS not accepted
DISABLED access difficult
PETS accepted
CLOSED Dec to Mar
PROPRIETORS Jaider family

TRENTINO-ALTO ADIGE

SAN VALBURGA D'ULTIMO

EGGWIRT

~ MOUNTAIN GUESTHOUSE ~

39016 San Valburga d'Ultimo, Bolzano
TEL 0473 795319 **FAX** 0473 795471
E-MAIL eggwirt@rolmail.net **WEBSITE** www.eggwirt.it

THE QUIET AND UNSPOILT Val d'Ultima lies 30 kilometres south-west of Merano. An ideal setting for both summer and winter sports, the Gasthof Eggwirt has existed as a hostelry since the 14th century, and today the Schwienbacher family welcome guests as if to their own home. The hotel is on the edge of the village with a large terrace at the front and superb views all around. The long life of the house is best felt in the *stübe* which dates from 1611: entirely panelled in dark wood with an old ceramic stove in the corner and stags' heads on the walls, this room was a favourite haunt of Sir Herbert Dunhill (a regular guest), and his black and white photographs are on display. A larger room housing a little bar has a country feel to it, with a ticking clock and rough, bare floorboards (which are scrubbed daily).

Upstairs, the decoration is more modern, less personal. The bright bedrooms have lots of wood and cheerful duvet covers. Some of the larger ones are divided, and most have balconies with, of course, stunning views. We should mention that this inexpensive, relaxed and friendly family hotel offers some excellent ski deals for the children.

~

NEARBY Merano (35 km).
LOCATION 35 km SW of Merano, off SS238, in village; parking
FOOD breakfast, lunch, dinner; room service
PRICE €
ROOMS 20; 11 double and twin, 10 with shower, one with bath; 3 single with shower; 4 triple, 2 with bath, 2 with shower, 2 family with shower; all rooms have phone, TV on request, safe
FACILITIES restaurant, sitting room, bar, terraces
CREDIT CARDS not accepted
DISABLED not suitable
PETS accepted
CLOSED mid-Nov to late Dec
PROPRIETORS Schwienbacher family

TRENTINO-ALTO ADIGE

SIUSI ALLO SCILIAR

BAD RATZES

~ MOUNTAIN HOTEL ~

Bagnidi Razzes, 39040 Siusi allo Sciliar, Bolzano
TEL 0471 706131 **Fax** 0471 707199
E-MAIL info@badratzes.it **WEBSITE** www.badratzes.it

LEAVING THE SMALL TOWN OF SIUSI in search of Bad Ratzes, the road winds uphill past green meadows and into a dense forest where Hansel and Gretel would have felt at home. When at last you reach it in a clearing, the hotel, large and modern, looks disconcertingly grim, but the warmth and enthusiasm of the Scherlin sisters will put you immediately at ease. It is this warmth and enthusiasm, and the family-friendly atmosphere that keeps it in the pages of this guide, since, with the addition of 26 new bedrooms (designed especially for children) in August 2005, it is technically much too large to be featured here. Inside, the decoration is dull 1960s and 1970s, but comfortable. Public areas – including a formal sitting room with open fireplace, a children's playroom and two dining rooms – are extensive. All but four of the spotless bedrooms have balconies.

Food is important at Bad Ratzes: local dishes are carefully prepared and pasta is home made. One of the sisters bakes regularly, and her recipes are recorded in a little booklet. This is one of a group of family hotels in the area and there are many thoughtful child-orientated extras: pots of crayons and paper on the dining tables, a booklet of local bedtime stories, walks for children, a special menu and so on. Adults are not neglected; there is wonderful and varied walking in the neighbourhood and a free ski bus runs to the slopes in winter.

~

NEARBY Bolzano (22 km); Siusi National Park; skiing (10 km).
LOCATION 22 km NE of Bolzano, 3 km SE of Siusi; car parking
FOOD breakfast, lunch, dinner
PRICE €; full-board only
ROOMS 78 double and twin, single, family, all with bath; all rooms have phone, TV, hairdrier, safe; 26 rooms have minibar **FACILITIES** dining rooms, sitting rooms, bar, playroom, indoor swimming pool, sauna, lift, garden **CREDIT CARDS** not accepted
DISABLED not suitable **PETS** accepted
CLOSED Sun after Easter to late May, early Oct to mid-Dec
PROPRIETORS Scherlin family

TRENTINO-ALTO ADIGE

ALBERE DI TENNA

MARGHERITA
COUNTRY HOTEL

*Località Pineta Alberé 2, 38050
Tenna, Trento*

TEL 0461 706445
FAX 0461 707854
E-MAIL info@hotelmargherita.it
WEBSITE www.hotelmargherita.it
FOOD breakfast, lunch, dinner
PRICE €
CLOSED Nov to late Apr
PROPRIETOR Lino Angeli

IN A PINE FOREST on a mountainside, this family-run hotel could hardly have a more peaceful setting. Although peace is of the essence (a sign requests you to avoid 'unnecessary noise'), families are positively encouraged. One swimming pool is specifically for children, with a playground reassuringly close to the sun-loungers, and two spacious apartments are ideal for families. A modern chalet, it has a lovely big terrace at the front, but uninspired decoration inside. Public rooms are airy but characterless. The original 1950s bedrooms tend to be small and dreary, so ask for one of the larger new rooms.

CASTELROTTO

CAVALLINO D'ORO
TOWN HOTEL

*Piazza Kraus, 39040 Castelrotto,
Bolzano*

TEL 0471 706337
FAX 0471 707172
E-MAIL cavallino@cavallino.it
WEBSITE www.cavallino.it
FOOD breakfast, lunch, dinner
PRICE €€ **CLOSED** last 3 weeks
Nov **PROPRIETOR** Stefan Urthaler

RECORDS OF THIS FORMER coaching inn date back to 1393. Located on the central square of postcard-pretty Castelrotto, the hotel has a pleasant, professional and energetic host in Stefan Urthaler, whose family has been in charge for three generations. Parts are ancient and charming, particularly two of the dining rooms and the bar, popular with schnapps-swilling locals. Other public areas lack character, and the bedrooms facing the church walls are gloomy, with banal lighting. Ask for one of the much preferable wood-panelled rooms with Tyrolean furniture and mountain views. The old wine cellar has been converted into a small health centre.

TRENTINO-ALTO ADIGE

COGNOLA DI TRENTO

VILLA MADRUZZO
COUNTRY HOTEL

Via Ponte Alto 26, 38050 Cognola di Trento, Trento

TEL 0461 986220
FAX 0461 986361
E-MAIL info@villamadruzzo.it
WEBSITE www.villamadruzzo.it
FOOD breakfast, lunch, dinner
PRICE €-€€ **CLOSED** restaurant Sun **PROPRIETOR** Signor Polonioli

THIS IS AN IMPOSING red and yellow villa, built in neoclassical style, well placed for visiting Trento and set in lovely gardens – it is a shame that traffic noise from the nearby main road permeates the peace. Public rooms are pleasant, particularly the three dining roms, which are decorated along elegant, classical lines with Venetian chandeliers and a few well-placed antique sideboards and portraits. The spacious terrace running along two sides of the house provides plenty of room for outdoor eating. Bedrooms in the main villa have more character than those in the rather banal extension and are only fractionally more expensive.

COLFOSCO

CAPPELLA
MOUNTAIN CHALET

39030 Colfosco, Bolzano

TEL 0471 836183
FAX 0471 836561
E-MAIL info@hotelcappella.com
WEBSITE www.hotelcappella.com
FOOD breakfast, lunch, dinner
PRICE €€€€-€€€€€€
CLOSED Apr to mid-Jun, Oct to mid-Dec **PROPRIETORS** Pizzinini family

THE PRESENT OWNERS are the fourth generation to manage the hotel, which was rebuilt in classic chalet style in the 1960s. Renata Pizzinini's grandfather, a famous guide who collected walkers from Brunico by horse, pioneered tourism in the area. The hotel is comfortable and welcoming, but a trifle cluttered and fabrics are over-patterned. Tables are packed into the dining room, and myriad burnished metal lights are suspended from the ornate panelled ceiling. You can enjoy an indoor pool, skiing or walking from the door and spectacular views. As well as the 47 bedrooms in the main building, there are 17 in the Tyrolean-style Residence next door. All rooms are non-smoking.

TRENTINO-ALTO ADIGE

CORVARA

LA PERLA
RESORT HOTEL

Via Centro 44, 39033 Corvara in Badia, Bolzano

TEL 0471 836133
FAX 0471 836568
E-MAIL laperla@altabadia.it
WEBSITE www.romantiklaperla.it
FOOD breakfast, lunch, dinner
PRICE €€€€€€
CLOSED Jul to Sep, mid-Dec to mid-Apr
PROPRIETORS Costa family

WE INCLUDE THE FOUR-STAR La Perla (which belongs to the Romantik chain) for those who are looking for a touch of luxury and plenty of facilities in their Dolomite hotel without losing too much character. Situated in the centre of Corvara, in the heart of the lovely Alpine region of Alta Badia, the hotel is extremely comfortable in 'sophisticated rustic' style and has an indoor spa with heated pool, whirlpool, turkish bath, sauna, solarium and massage, as well as an outdoor heated pool for summer. The restaurant, La Stuä de Michil, serves elegant dishes. The modern bedrooms lack the character of the many public rooms, but are well equipped and handsomely furnished.

FIE ALLO SCILIAR

MOARHOF
COUNTRY APARTMENTS

39050 Fié allo Sciliar, Bolzano

TEL and **FAX** 0471 725095
FOOD none
PRICE €
CLOSED never
PROPRIETORS Kompatscher family

THIS IS AN AREA WHERE it is easy to find simple accommodation: every other house offers rooms or apartments for rent. This 12th-century farmhouse building with a sundial painted on the front caught our eye as being special. Situated just above the village of Fié, there are eight apartments for between two and five people, and all are decorated in rustic Tyrolean farmhouse style. Several have their original wood panelling and ceramic stoves; most have separate sitting and bedrooms, and well-equipped kitchen areas (with washing machine and dishwasher). There are two with balconies.

TRENTINO-ALTO ADIGE

MADONNA DI CAMPIGLIO

CHALET HERMITAGE
MOUNTAIN HOTEL

*Via Castelletto Inferiore 63, 38084
Madonna di Campiglio, Trentino*

TEL 0465 441558
FAX 0465 441618
E-MAIL info@chalethermitage.com
WEB www.chalethermitage.com
FOOD breakfast, lunch, dinner
PRICE €€€ **CLOSED** Sep to Dec
PROPRIETORS Maffei family

WE WERE ALERTED TO this modern 'bio' hotel it was refurbished in 1999 using only natural materials such as solid wood floors and pure wool carpets, ecological water and electricity supply and so on) by an enthusiastic guest who praised everything, but most of all the relaxed 'at home' family atmosphere and the 'superb' food (home-made pumpkin pasta with black truffle, wild rabbit *alla cacciatore*, sweet chestnut mousse). Also: well-equipped rooms ('fantastic mattresses'); a parkland setting; shuttle to the town centre and ski slopes; sun terrace; indoor pool; sauna. 'I'm going back', says our correspondent, 'this time for the alpine flowers'.

MERANO

CASTEL RUNDEGG
MEDIEVAL MANOR

*Via Scena 2, 39012 Merano,
Bolzano*

TEL 0473 234100
FAX 0473 237200
E-MAIL info@rundegg.com
WEBSITE www.rundegg.com
FOOD breakfast, lunch, dinner
PRICE €€€€ **CLOSED** never
MANAGER Peter Castelforte

OUR MOST RECENT REPORTER wrote about this hotel, '... a lovely old building, but it's a pity it doesn't enjoy a more rural setting. It's on quite a busy road with other buildings close by.' She found Castel Rundegg, 'a bit too slick and very beauty farm orientated'. The health and beauty complex is certainly impressive, and guests can submit themselves to all the latest treatments. The restaurant has a gothic stone-vaulted ceiling and alcove rooms. Bedrooms are well-appointed with luxurious bathrooms and special features. One of the most sought-after, the turret room, commands a 360-degree view.

TRENTINO-ALTO ADIGE

PINZOLO

CHALET MASO DOSS
MOUNTAIN CHALET

*San Antonio di Mavignola 72,
38086 Pinzolo, Trento*

TEL 0465 502758 **FAX** 0465 502311
E-MAIL info@masodoss.com
WEBSITE www.masodoss.com
FOOD breakfast, dinner; lunch on
request **PRICE** €€€; weekly
rates available **CLOSED** never
PROPRIETORS Caola family

HERE'S THE REAL THING: a simple, heart-warming 17th-century chalet in the Brenta Valley, set amidst the spectacular landscape of the Adamello-Dolomiti di Brenta National Park. In winter you can explore on cross-country skis, in summer on mountain bikes provided by the chalet, taking a packed lunch if you wish. On your return: wood panelling and simple furniture, check tablecloths and lace curtains, a warm fire, an excellent dinner, a Finnish sauna, and one of six cosy bedrooms with warm duvets and hand-embroidered sheets. Guests gather for a drink before dinner, and the atmosphere is very much that of a welcoming private house.

SAN CIPRIANO

PENSION STEFANER
MOUNTAIN GUESTHOUSE

*San Cipriano, 39050 Tires,
Bolzano*

TEL 0471 642175 **FAX** 0471 642302
E-MAIL info@stefaner.com
WEBSITE www.stefaner.com
FOOD breakfast, dinner
PRICE €€ **CLOSED** 3 weeks Jan,
early Nov to late Dec
PROPRIETORS Villgrattner family

HIGH UP IN THE BEAUTIFUL Tires valley, this is a newish Tyrolean chalet whose wooden balconies are a riot of colour in summer (unfortunately views from the front are interrupted by a row of lofty trees). Inside, furnishings are modern and uniform, and the carpet is busily patterned, but warm colours and a roaring fire in cold weather lend a cosy atmosphere. The simply-furnished rooms all have balconies and, though some are small, are spotless. The young Villgrattners are warm hosts, and Georg is an excellent and creative cook – dinner is served each evening on the stroke of seven. This pension has always been great value for money: it's only 10 euros on the cost of a double room that nudge it up into our second price band.

TRENTINO-ALTO ADIGE

SAN FLORIANO

OBEREGGEN
MOUNTAIN GUESTHOUSE

Via Obereggen 8, San Floriano,
39050 Nova Ponente, Bolzano

TEL 0471 615722
FAX 0471 615889
E-MAIL info@hotel-obereggen.it
WEBSITE www.hotel-obereggen.it
FOOD breakfast, dinner
PRICE €€€ **CLOSED** after
Easter to Jun, mid-Oct to Dec
PROPRIETORS Pichler family

THE SETTING FOR THIS modest chalet is ideal for skiers. At the top of a gorgeous Dolomite valley, 1,550 metres above sea level, it is only a few metres from the Latemar ski centre and lifts which give access to 40 kilometres of piste (one in use during summer). From the sunny terrace you can watch nearby sporting activity or the sun setting behind craggy peaks across the valley. The focal point of the hotel is the cosy bar with its ceramic stove, stags' heads and hunting trophies. The bedrooms are simple but clean with plump duvets adding a touch of comfort. About half have balconies, and those at the top enjoy fabulous views.

Charming hostess; good food.

SELVA

SPORTHOTEL GRANVARA
MOUNTAIN CHALET

39048 Selva Gardena, Bolzano

TEL 0471 795250
FAX 0471 794336
E-MAIL info@granvara.com
WEBSITE www.granvara.com
FOOD breakfast, lunch, dinner
PRICE €€€ **CLOSED** late Apr
to mid-Jun, mid-Oct to early Dec
PROPRIETORS Senoner family

THE NAME SAYS IT ALL. Facilities include a squash court, gym and indoor pool. For ski enthusiasts, it offers direct access to the Sella Ronda and the Dolomite superski area via the Ciampinoi cable car, and at the end of the day, you can ski back to the door. If you need advice, the owner and his son are both instructors. Like many hotels in the area, it is a chalet, surrounded by pastures and glorious scenery, its wooden balconies brimming with geraniums in summer. Inside, the large comfortable Tyrolean-style public rooms are particularly inviting after a hard day on the slopes. Bedrooms are relatively anonymous.

TRENTINO-ALTO ADIGE

SESTO

BERGHOTEL TIROL

MOUNTAIN HOTEL

Moso, 39030 Sesto, Bolzano

TEL 0474 710386
FAX 0474 710455
FOOD breakfast, lunch, dinner
E-MAIL info@berghotel.com
WEBSITE www.berghotel.com
PRICE ©©© **CLOSED** Easter to
mid-May, Oct to Christmas
PROPRIETORS Holzer family

THE LITTLE TOWN OF SESTO (or Sexten) is one of the prettiest in the region, and the surrounding area must be one of the most beautiful parts of the Dolomites. The Berghotel Tirol is a recently constructed chalet, with dark wood balconies overlooking classic alpine scenery: a gentle valley dotted with chalets, a church spire in the foreground, and in the distance, the jagged peaks which are so characteristic of the area. In summer, there are walking trails; in winter you can ski. The comfortable, pine-furnished hotel is run with great hospitality and efficiency by the Holzer family. It has 45 plain bedrooms with white walls and modern wood fittings, or, for self-caterers, there is an apartment-house next door.

TIROLO

SCHLOSS THURNSTEIN

CASTLE RESTAURANT-WITH-
ROOMS

Tirolo, 39019 Merano, Bolzano

TEL 0473 220255 **FAX** 0473 220558
E-MAIL thurnstein@dnet.it
WEBSITE www.thurnstein.it
FOOD breakfast, lunch, dinner
PRICE © **CLOSED** mid-Nov to Mar;
restaurant Thu
PROPRIETORS Bauer family

YOU MUST NEGOTIATE 4 kilometres of tortuous hairpin bends to reach this grey stone edifice built on the mountainside in 1200 as a defence tower for nearby Castel Tirolo. The reputation of the restaurant is well-established, and chef Toni Bauer is a larger-than-life figure, passionate about unpretentious cooking using the freshest of ingredients. Activity revolves around the series of dining rooms, and the two terraces (one on each side of the building – ideal for juggling sun and shade) have spectacular views. The comfortable bedrooms are in a nearby annexe; some have separate sitting areas.

TRENTINO-ALTO ADIGE

TRENTO

ACCADEMIA
TOWN HOTEL

Vicolo Colico 4-6, 38100 Trento

TEL 0461 233600
FAX 0461 230174
E-MAIL info@accademiahotel.it
WEBSITE www.accademiahotel.it
FOOD breakfast, lunch, dinner
PRICE €€
CLOSED Christmas to early Jan;
restaurant Mon
PROPRIETORS Fambri family

THIS UPMARKET HOTEL OCCUPIES an attractive medieval house in the old town, with quaint wooden shutters and geranium-filled window boxes. Inside, elements of the original architecture are also visible: a stone stairway, doorways and vaulted ceilings. The building's clean white lines are enlivened by vibrant rugs, parquet floors and the occasional antique. But after a negative report, we have decided to downgrade it from a long to a short entry. Our readers' biggest disappointment was with their bedroom: 'It had new low modern furniture with few pictures and nothing to relieve the bland uniformity. It could have been a chain hotel.' There is a well-regarded restaurant and a homely *enoteca*. Staff are friendly and helpful.

LA VILLA

LA VILLA
MOUNTAIN HOTEL

La Villa, 39030 Alta Badia, Bolzano

TEL 0471 847035
FAX 0471 847393
E-MAIL info@hotel-lavilla.it
WEBSITE www.hotel-lavilla.it
FOOD breakfast, lunch, dinner
PRICE €€€ **CLOSED** mid-Apr to
mid-Jun, mid-Sep to Dec
OWNER Rezidenza la Villa srl.

IF YOU WANT TO STAY IN THE lovely Alta Badia region of the Dolomites, here is a simpler alternative to La Perla in Corvara (see page 183). Although we haven't yet had a chance to inspect this hotel, we include it on the strength of a very positive letter of recommendation, which praises its beautiful and peaceful setting on the slope of a hillside with wide views across the valley. Our reader sums it up: 'An old mountain building completely renovated, with a garden full of flowers in summer. Inside the hotel is fresh and neat, with lots of white walls, natural fabrics and modern pine furniture.' Corvara is less than 5 kilometres away, and a ski bus is laid on in winter to transport guests to and from the slopes. New management took over in May 2005.

TRENTINO-ALTO ADIGE

VILLANDRO

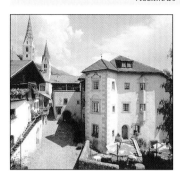

ANSITZ ZUM STEINBOCK

RESTAURANT-WITH-ROOMS

San Stefano 38, 39040 Villandro, Bolzano

TEL 0472 843111 **FAX** 0472 843468
E-MAIL steinbock@dnet.it
WEB www.ansitzsteinbock.com
FOOD breakfast, lunch, dinner
PRICE ⓔ **CLOSED** mid-Jan to mid-Mar; restaurant Mon **PROPRIETORS**
Rabensteiner family

VILLANDRO IS A PRETTY MOUNTAIN village, and Ansitz Zum Steinbock stands at its centre. An imposing 18th-century building, it looks rather forbidding from the outside, but the jolly terrace (where you can eat in warm weather) is a clue to the welcoming, typically Tyrolean interior – fresh and simple, with pine-clad or white-painted walls, pretty fabrics for curtains and tablecloths and rustic furniture and artefacts here and there. You will eat well: the restaurant is highly regarded locally for its regional cooking. Bedrooms are beamed, with modern pine beds and plump white duvets. The Rabensteiner family took over from the Kirchbaumers three years ago.

FRIULI-VENEZIA GIULIA

BANNIA DI FIUME VENETO

L'ULTIMO MULINO
∼ CONVERTED MILL ∼

Via Molino 45, 33080 Bannia di Fiume Veneto, Pordenone
TEL 0434 957911 **FAX** 0434 958483
E-MAIL info@ultimomulino.com **WEBSITE** www.ultimomulino.com

A S THE NAME SUGGESTS, this 17th-century building is one of the very last functioning mills in the area. In use until the 1970s, the three old wooden wheels are still in working condition; indeed, they are set in motion in the evenings for the benefit of guests. The lovely stone house and garden are set in gentle farmland and surrounded by three rivers; the soothing sounds of water are everywhere.

Opened as a hotel in 1994, restoration work has been carried out with great taste and flair, preserving as much as possible of the original character of the house. The long, open-plan sitting room and bar area have even incorporated the hefty innards of the mill machinery. Throughout, attractive fabrics are teamed with handsome antique furniture, rustic stone and woodwork, and soft, elegant lighting. The comfortable and stylish bedrooms, while different in layout, are all along similar lines with wooden fittings and pale green and cream country fabrics. Those on the second floor have attic ceilings and some have squashy sofas. Bathrooms are in pale grey marble. New owners have recently taken over, and have opened the restaurant for lunch as well as dinner, with fish a speciality.

∼

NEARBY Pordenone (10 km); Venice (80 km); Trieste (80 km).
LOCATION 10 km SE of Pordenone, exit from A28 at Azzano Decimo; in own garden with parking
FOOD breakfast, lunch, dinner
PRICE €€€
ROOMS 8 double and twin, 4 with bath, 4 with shower; all rooms have phone, TV, air conditioning, minibar, hairdrier
FACILITIES breakfast room, sitting rooms, dining rooms, bar, music/conference room, garden, terrace
CREDIT CARDS AE, DC, MC, V
DISABLED no special facilities **PETS** accepted
CLOSED 10 days Jan, Aug; restaurant closed Sun eve, Mon
PROPRIETORS Mattarello family

FRIULI-VENEZIA GIULIA

RIVAROTTA

VILLA LUPPIS

~ COUNTRY VILLA ~

Via San Martino 34, 33087 Rivarotta, Pordenone
TEL 0434 626969 **FAX** 0434 626228
E-MAIL hotel@villaluppis.it **WEBSITE** www.villaluppis.it

THIS RAMBLING AND MELLOW L-shaped building, acquired by the Luppis family in the 1800s, was once a monastery. Set in gentle countryside, there is not much sign of Spartan living today; it is now a comfortable and elegant yet relaxed hotel run by Giorgio Luppis and his wife. One side of the 'L' is a long room incorporating reception hall, sitting room and bar, bright and welcoming with low, timbered ceiling and central columns. At the front of the house is the equally long main restaurant – a dreamy room with pale pink and white table linen, period furniture, antique silver and fresh flowers. There is (rather incongruously) also a piano bar with dance floor. Long corridors, softly lit and thickly carpeted, lead to the luxurious bedrooms which are furnished with period pieces, and have superior king-size beds. Fine fabrics – Regency stripes or fresh chintzes – are co-ordinated with soft carpeting, and the suites have separate sitting areas.

The villa's extensive park with its venerable old trees and green lawns has a pleasant pool and a fitness centre. A minibus service runs to and from Venice – Piazzale Roma – (only 40 minutes away) every day.

~

NEARBY Pordenone (15 km); Treviso (35 km); Venice (50 km).
LOCATION 15 km S of Pordenone; exit A4 at Cessalto, and take road for Motta di Livenza; in extensive grounds with ample parking
FOOD breakfast, lunch, dinner
PRICE €€€
ROOMS 21; 18 double and twin, 3 suites, all with bath; all rooms have phone, TV, air-conditioning, hairdrier
FACILITIES sitting room, dining room, bar, meeting room, lift, pool tennis court, gym
CREDIT CARDS AE, DC, MC, V
DISABLED access possible
PETS accepted
CLOSED never
PROPRIETORS Giorgio and Stefania Luppis

FRIULI-VENEZIA GIULIA

SAN FLORIANO DEL COLLIO

GOLF HOTEL CASTELLO FORMENTINI

~ CONVERTED CASTLE ~

Via Oslavia 2, 34070 San Floriano del Collio, Gorizia
TEL 0481 884051 **FAX** 0481 884052
E-MAIL isabellaformentini@tiscalinet.it **WEBSITE** www.golfhotelcastelloformentini.it

WE ASKED FOR FEEDBACK ON THIS HOTEL in our last edition, and we've had plenty. Most speak very positively, praising the 'lovely' rooms ('we lit the little candles in our big modern bathroom'), the 'lavish' breakfast and the 'very reasonable' prices. One, however, criticized the housekeeping: ('the cookie under the nightstand encased in cobwebs was a little scary').

The hotel's name, referring to its nine-hole golf course (closed Mon), gives the impression of something modern, but it is in fact two ancient renovated houses just outside the walls of Castello Formentini, which has belonged to the Formentini family since the 16th century. The present owner, Contessa Isabella Formentini, has filled the rooms of the tiny hotel with family furniture and pictures. Each beautifully decorated and spacious bedroom is named after a prestigious wine, emphasizing the vinous interest of the Formentini family. Three of them are within the castle walls, but all guests are at liberty to use the castle grounds and its swimming pool. The family's restaurant, called Castello Formentini, is open only for groups (minimum 8-10 people) but guests are directed to another excellent, cosy restaurant nearby. This is a charming spot, with gentle, wooded countryside spread out around the hilltop castle.

~

NEARBY Gorizia (4 km); Trieste (47 km).
LOCATION in town, just outside castle walls; private grounds; car parking
FOOD breakfast, all day cold buffet
PRICE €€€€
ROOMS 15; 12 double and twin, 2 single, 1 suite in tower, all with bath or shower; all rooms have TV, minibar; 12 rooms have phone; 3 rooms have no phone but air conditioning
FACILITIES sitting room, breakfast room, garden, swimming pool, tennis court, nine-hole golf course
CREDIT CARDS AE, DC, MC, V
DISABLED not suitable **PETS** accepted
CLOSED Jan
PROPRIETOR Contessa Isabella Formentini

FRIULI-VENEZIA GIULIA

TRIESTE

GRAND HOTEL DUCHI D'AOSTA

~ TOWN HOTEL ~

Piazza Unita d'Italia 2. 34121 Trieste
TEL 040 7600011 **FAX** 040 366092
E-MAIL info@grandhotelduchidaosta**WEBSITE** www.grandhotelduchidaosta.com

A T THE POINT WHERE THE LATIN AND BALKAN worlds meet, close to Italy's borders with Slovenia, Croatia and Austria, Trieste is a town with a fascinating history. Not only did it belong to Austria, but was its principal port until 1918, and although its importance has faded, it still bears the architectural legacy of its years as part of the Hapsburg Empire. The old town boasts a clutch of gracious palazzi; one dating from 1873 is now home to the aptly named Grand Hotel Duchi d'Aosta. Behind a splendid pale porticoed facade, a series of large, lavishly furnished salons and a fleet of polite, attentive staff recall the grandeur of a bygone era. Bedrooms share the traditional elegance of the public rooms, but with modern amenities and bathrooms. And the restaurant, specializing in local seafood, has an excellent reputation.

Most of the sights are within walking distance of the hotel, convenient-ly located at the heart of the old town, although there is one that must not be missed on a promontory 5 km to the west. It is the glorious white Castello di Miramare, where the Hapsburg Archduke Maximilian lived and which is now the setting for a *son et lumière* between June and September.

~

NEARBY Roman theatre; cathedral; port; Castello di Miramare.
LOCATION in the old part of town near the fort; garage parking
FOOD breakfast, lunch, dinner
PRICE €€€
ROOMS 50; 48 double and twin, 2 suites, all with bath or shower; all rooms have phone, TV, air-conditioning, minibar, hairdrier
FACILITIES sitting room, restaurant
CREDIT CARDS AE, DC, MC, V
DISABLED one specially adapted room
PETS not accepted
CLOSED never
MANAGER Hedy Benvenuti

FRIULI-VENEZIA GIULIA

UDINE

ASTORIA HOTEL ITALIA

~ TOWN HOTEL ~

Piazza XX Settembre 24, 33100 Udine
TEL 0432 505091 **FAX** 0432 509070
E-MAIL astoria@hotelastoria.udine.it **WEBSITE** www.hotelastoria.udine.it

UDINE IS FRIULI-VENEZIA GIULIA'S CAPITAL. Though a busy centre of commerce, it has buildings of interest at its historic core, and we can just about recommend this, its premier hotel, which retains a certain grandeur and sense of its past (it has been a hotel since the 1850s), despite its main function as a business stopover. In the dining room you will be served probably the best food in the city, by friendly, helpful waiters. The hotel's bedrooms are uniform (in pink or blue), comfortable, and mostly spacious. Best are those overlooking the piazza. While staying here, don't miss the lovely 19th-century interiors of the adjacent palazzo – now used for exhibitions and conferences. They were designed by Japelli, famous for his Caffè Pedrocchi in Padua.

On our latest inspection trip for this guide, we made a concerted effort to find more hotels in this far north-eastern corner of Italy. One hopeful contender did elude us, Pa'Krhaizar at Sauris di Sopra: though it was late April, our road was blocked by snow and we were forced to turn back. So our best offering in this area, sadly short of interesting places to stay, remains this town hotel in Udine.

~

NEARBY Duomo; Piazza Matteotti; Museo Civico.
LOCATION in city centre; parking
FOOD breakfast, lunch, dinner
PRICE €€€
ROOMS 75; 39 double, 33 single, 3 suites, all with bath; all rooms have phone, TV, minibar, air-conditioning, hairdrier, safe
FACILITIES dining room, bar, lounge, courtyard, lift
CREDIT CARDS AE, DC, MC, V
DISABLED access possible
PETS accepted
CLOSED never
PROPRIETOR Signor Mocchiutti

INTRODUCTION

Readers appreciated it when we introduced a restaurant section to this guide's companion title, *Charming Small Hotels and Restaurants* **Paris**, so now we have done the same for Venice.

True to the *Charming Small Hotel Guide* philosophy, the selection of eating places we feature here is special, different to anything you could find in another guide or website. Of course, some of the names crop up in other guides; but just as many don't, and in these you will find refreshing opportunities to eat among locals, to be a traveller rather than a tourist, and to experience food and ambience that are relatively unpolished, but real.

Michela Scibilia, author of an excellent guide to eating in Venice,* has put together her very personal selection for this book, echoing the qualities we search out in our hotels. As a Venetian, she understands better than most that charming doesn't have to be expensive, although sometimes it is. Like us she is unimpressed by style – whether hip, cool or just smart – unless it has integrity.

As a result, the selection of restaurants in these pages is probably more eclectic and interesting than you'll find anywhere. There is every type of eating place, from the stand-up *rosticceria* serving one or two dishes, to the expensive cult restaurant. The territory in between is especially interesting in Venice, where so many bars and indeed wine shops serve a superior range of snacks or light dishes (*cicheti*), and these are especially well represented here. Sometimes, you eat *cicheti* at the bar; but often enough, such places also have a dining area where you can sit and eat in comfort. In many of these places it is acceptable just to have a glass of wine at the bar, passing on to eat elsewhere, and this we note in the text.

Glossary
All the Italian names of ingredients or dishes are translated into English in the Menu decoder on page 219.

'Favourites'
All of these places are favourites, but Michela can't help liking some more than others; these we note these in the text.

Opening and closing
For bar-eateries, we give both opening and closing times.

Credit cards
Please note that most entries accept payment cards and that under this heading we refer to credit cards not debit cards.

Prices
Instead of price bands we give figures (accurate at time of printing) for the average price of a meal including antipasto, primo, secondo, side dish, dessert, table charge and service, but excluding wine or other drinks. In Venice, a city of outrageous prices, an accurate fix on price is important; also, given the wide range of places featured here, price comparisons are especially useful.

* *Venice Osterie & Dintorni: A guide to the eateries of Venice*; published in English; on sale locally.

VENICE RESTAURANTS

R

E

S

T

A

U

R

A

N

T

S

CAVATAPPI

Campo della Guerra, San Marco 525
Tel 041 2960252

Marco and Francesca recently opened this bar-with-a kitchen and their enthusiasm is still fresh. The bar caters for snack attacks with well-made *panini* and *tramezzini*. In the evening, you'll find locals gathered for a before- or after-dinner drink; at midday, the tables are filled with neighbourhood shopkeepers, who appreciate the simple menu of rice and pasta dishes (E7), or the light but tasty main courses (E10). On Thursdays, the pasta is freshly made. Desserts are all created on the premises. Every two months, there are wine tastings with as many as 30 wines, accompanied by cheeses and cold meats from various regions of Italy. Tables indoors and out.

PRICE snacks for E10 or less
OPEN 9 am-12 pm
CLOSED Sun eve, Mon
CREDIT CARDS DC, M, V

ROSTICCERIA SAN BARTOLOMEO

Calle della Bissa, San Marco
No bookings by phone

From the Campo San Bartolomeo you see nothing of this place except an obvious illuminated sign with the word Rosticceria. We recommend it for its excellent, informal stand-up lunch bar, full of middle-class Venetians enjoying dishes such as roast veal or fish risotto. First-class sandwiches, too. Given the fact that you can have lunch for less than E5, it's busy.

PRICE E5-10
CLOSED Sun
CREDIT CARDS not accepted

VENICE RESTAURANTS

SAN POLO

ANTICHE CARAMPANE

Rio Terà de le Carampane, San Polo 1911
Tel 041 5240165

If you're a visitor, get directions from the restaurant before venturing into the maze of long, narrow *calli*, dark *sottoporteghi*, courtyards and *rio terà* that characterize the city's former red light district. Your effort will be well rewarded, not least by the welcome that awaits you at this calm oasis. The ambience is elegant and the fish is the freshest, masterfully cooked. Try the monkfish *al cartoccio*, which comes with a crust of parmesan cheese; or the wonderfully delicate mixed fried fish and spring vegetables.

Tables indoors and out. Value for money. One of our favourites.

Price E47
Closed Sun, Mon
Credit cards AE, DC, MC, V

SAN POLO

AL BANCOGIRO

Campo San Giacometto, San Polo 122
Tel 041 5231061

This wine shop with a kitchen, under the porticos of the 16th-century Fabbriche Vecchie, stands on the site of one of Venice's earliest 'retail' banks, from which it gets its name. There are two entrances, one from the market and church of San Giacometto, the other (with tables outside) facing the Grand Canal. Sip a glass of wine at the bar (Andrea offers a fresh choice most days) or sit in the small, no-smoking dining room upstairs. You'll need to wait patiently: the dishes, remarkable value at E11 to 14, are cooked to order from ingredients bought fresh from the nearby market: prawns with *castraure*, *carpaccio* of bass garnished with mixed, aromatic herbs, *sarde incinte* ('pregnant' sardines stuffed with raisins, pine nuts, garlic, parsley and orange juice); creamed dentex; steamed fish salads or smoked American beef. There's also a limited range of cold meats and cheeses. Interesting wine list.

PRICE E14
OPEN 10.30am to 3 pm and 6.30 pm to 12 pm
CLOSED Sun, Mon
CREDIT CARDS not accepted

VENICE RESTAURANTS

SAN POLO

ALLA MADONNA

Calle de la Madonna, San Polo 594
Tel 041 5223824

A trusted, well-loved restaurant right by the Rialto Bridge. It's spacious, but usually crowded, catering for large numbers of diners with fast but attentive service. The food is reliably good and because of the high turn-over it offers a great range of fish and meat dishes at prices not matched elsewhere.

Among our many favourites on the wide-ranging menu are: *sarde in saor*, *granseola*, *folpeti*, fish soup, *schie*, eels, fried squid, cuttlefish, grilled red mullet and lobster with mayonnaise, lasagne *pasticcio*, tripe, Venetian style liver, roast chicken, breaded veal cutlets, and fried veal chops, all with seasonal vegetables. A perfect spot for a large family gathering.

PRICE E44
CLOSED Wed
CREDIT CARDS AE, MC, V

SAN POLO

OSTERIA AL GANGHELO

Calle dei Boteri, San Polo 1571
No bookings by telephone

Sit at the counter, and eat as the local market traders do. Our reporter had a wonderful plate of warm vegetables, beans (made fresh twice a day in a piquant tomato sauce with rosemary), good *polpette* and a delicious almond cream pudding – chilled, but with hot Amaretto in the middle. Draught wines. Between the Rialto Bridge and San Cassiano. For a market trader's lunch place, rather sophisticated.

PRICE dishes E7 to 11
CLOSED Sun
CREDIT CARDS not accepted

VENICE RESTAURANTS

SANTA CROCE

AL NONO RISORTO

Sottoportego de la Siora Bettina, Santa Croce 2338
Tel 041 5241169

Young, friendly owners, a spacious dining area, fair prices and late closing make this trattoria the choice of many a Venetian thirtysomething, especially in summer. Nono Risorto means 'resurrected grandad', by the way. The large, gravelled, wistaria-shaded garden has attractive, heavy oak tables. Pizzas at E5 to 8; salads; and a Venetian menu. Tables indoors and out. Especially suitable for adults dining with children.

PRICE E36 euros
CLOSED Wed, Thur mornings
CREDIT CARDS not accepted

SANTA CROCE

AL PROSECCO

San Giacomo dall'Orio, Santa Croce 1503
Tel 041 5240222

In a city full of enchanting places in which to sit and watch the world go by, Campo di San Giacomo dall'Orio is still one of the most delightful. The outdoor tables of al Prosecco, right on the Campo, offer just the necessary comfort and shade from which to view the antics of the children, and dogs, while you sip – what else – a glass of Prosecco. The hard-working young owners attract customers from all over Venice. They offer a fair selection of cheeses and cold meats, crostini, seven or eight wines by the glass and plenty of bottles. On Saturdays, there are oysters and raw fish. The room inside is a pleasant refuge on wet days.

PRICE E10-20, plate of snacks for two
Open 8 am to 10.30 pm
CLOSED Sun
CREDIT CARDS not accepted

VENICE RESTAURANTS

SANTA CROCE

ALLA ZUCCA

Ponte del Megio, Santa Croce 1762
Tel 041 5241570

A classic. The quiet, well-lit dining area opens on to a few outside tables at the foot of the Ponte del Megio. Service is pleasingly informal and the cooking is imaginative without being pretentious. The menu offers an interesting range of vegetable (or vegetable-oriented) dishes, some with a hint of the East: try asparagus and potato soup; penne pasta with aubergine and Greek feta cheese; roast lamb with fennel and pecorino cheese; mustard-baked rabbit with polenta; pumpkin flan with mature ricotta, grilled breast of chicken with garlic and mint-flavoured tzatziki sauce; or shin of veal on the bone with leeks and parmesan cheese. Among the desserts we enjoyed yoghurt ice cream with bilberries and strawberries in Prosecco. The wine list is brief, but, like the food, imaginative. Value for money.

PRICE E35
CLOSED Sun
CREDIT CARDS AE, DC, MC, V

CASTELLO

BANDIERETTE

Barbaria de le Tole, Castello 6671
Tel 041 5220619

This is a typical local *trattoria*, plain and anonymous on the outside; inside, it is somewhat harshly lit, perhaps even with a slightly cold atmosphere. But we recommend it because of its integrity: no pretensions here, and it passes the acid test of being a firm favourite with local residents. The prices are more than fair and the cooking is home-style, with a touch of imagination. The fish-oriented menu is straightforward, offering baked scallops, fried sardines, monkfish or grilled bass. The tasty pastas include *tagliatelle* with scampi and spinach, *spaghetti* with *canoce* or prawns with asparagus. Tables indoors and out.

PRICE E28
CLOSED Mon eve, Tues
CREDIT CARDS AE, DC, MC, V

VENICE RESTAURANTS

CASTELLO

CORTE SCONTA

Calle del Pestrin, Castello 3886
Tel 041 5227024

A cult *osteria*, partly because of its position and partly for its name, which reminds us how wonderfully full is Venice of *sconto* (hidden) corners. The friendly owners serve expertly made, traditional Venetian lagoon dishes. The list of starters is almost endless: marinated anchovies, *granseola* pate, *schie* with polenta, *latti di sepia*, *garusoli*, *sarde in saor*, *canoce* and more. A special 'tasting menu' allows you to taste them all. *Primi* include *gnocchetti* with baby squid; *tagliolini* (all fresh pasta is made on the premises) with scallops and artichokes; and *bigoli in salsa*. *Secundi* are equally impressive: grilled or fried fish, herb-baked baby red mullet, dory in sweet and sour sauce. Finish with genuine *zabaion* and kosher biscuits. There are 100 wines on the list and a fine selection of grappas. Tables indoors and out. One of our favourites.

PRICE E52
CLOSED Sun, Mon
CREDIT CARDS AE, DC, MC, V

CASTELLO

AL COVO

Campiello della Pescaria, Castello 3068
Tel 041 5223812

This small restaurant behind the Riva degli Schiavoni is a magnet for gourmets, local and from far afield. The menu is based on fresh, never farmed, fish, cooked in ways that bring out the freshness and fragrance of the raw material. Whether you go for the fish and shellfish crudités with vegetables, the fish soups, the gnocchi with fillets of *gò*, the steamed eel or the fried or grilled fish, it's all superb. The desserts are memorable, and sublime is the only word for the chocolate cake with its dark chocolate sauce. No fewer than 300 choices on the wine list, not to mention 40 spirits and ten olive oils. Tables inside and out.

PRICE E75
CLOSED Wed, Thur
CREDIT CARDS not accepted

VENICE RESTAURANTS

CASTELLO

ALLA MASCARETA

Calle Lunga Santa Maria Formosa, Castello 5183
Tel 041 5230744

One of Venice's oldest *enoteche* (wine shops). In addition to the bar area there's a peaceful, warm room with attractive tables and old sideboards. Here the genial female *osti* will welcome you and advise on what to drink, then leave you to drink in peace. You can order by the glass or by the bottle, and proper tasting glasses are provided. With your wine you can order simple dishes such as a plate of cold meats, some cheeses or *crostini*. Afterwards, you could change to sweet white wine and petits fours. A great place to get know the wines of Veneto, and then buy a bottle or two to take home.

Try the delicately aromatic Bianco di Custoza; a young Soave; an up-front Cabernet from Pramagiorre; a richly scented Sauvignon from the Colli Euganei; or a sweet Recioto.

PRICE less than E10
OPEN 7pm to 2am
CLOSED Wed, Thur
CREDIT CARDS not accepted

CASTELLO

AL PORTEGO

Calle de la Malvasia, Castello 6015
Tel 041 5229038

In a quiet upper-floor room of a house between San Lio and Santa Marina, this small, cosy *osteria* has wood everywhere you look – ceiling, walls, bar, tables and barrels. The windows are prettily curtained and there is a separate, peaceful dining area for those who want to be a little removed from the main buzz. The *cicheti* include meat and tuna balls, fried vegetables, *folpeti* and *crostini*. If you want something hot, there's *bigoli in salsa*, fish risottos, *pasta e fasioi*, Venetian-style liver or *museto* with polenta. OK just to have a glass of wine. One of our favourites.

PRICE E25
OPEN 10 am-3 pm and 6 pm-10 pm
CLOSED Sun
CREDIT CARDS not accepted

VENICE RESTAURANTS

CASTELLO

SANTA MARINA

Campo Santa Marina, Castello 5911
041 5285239

Two couples joined forces to launch this upmarket venture: Agostino, Betty and Caterina run the kitchen and Danilo the front of house. After a shaky start, they have earned the respect of many local foodies for their extravagantly named, beautifully presented dishes. Try scampi in leek and ginger *saor*, *folpeti* with Tropea onion, orange peel and balsamic vinegar; raw lobster and mignonette pie, cream of borlotti beans with spicy tuna morsels, or grilled skewers of fish and shellfish with smoked lard. To follow go for the rightly popular chocolate pie or the apple pie with cinnamon ice cream; or maybe basil sorbet with wild berries. There's an interesting wine list. Tables inside and out. Although the prices are highish, they remain value for money.

PRICE E59
CLOSED Sun, Mon midday
CREDIT CARDS MC, V

CASTELLO

ALLE TESTIERE

Calle del Mondo Buovo, Castello 5801
Tel 041 5227220

This tiny restaurant with a handful of tables, in the *calle* between Salizada di San Lio and Santa Maria Formosa, is consistently popular. Its secret is the skill and enthusiasm which Bruno and Luca bring to bear on every detail. In the kitchen, Bruno insists on quality ingredients to create dishes such as tiny gnocchi with baby squid in cinnamon; *caparossoli* sautéed with a hint of ginger; linguine with slivers of monkfish; tepid *granseola*; and filet of dory with aromatic herbs in orange and lemon sauce. The same attention to detail is also lavished on the desserts: pear, ricotta and chocolate pie, or the crema rosada, a rediscovery from the past. Luca is the wine man, responsible for a small but thoughtful list, and he supervises the cheese board, which includes Escarun Cuneese, Verde di Montegalda Vicentina and Buccia di Rospo, a rare Tuscan pecorino. Enough? Book well in advance. OK just to have a drink at the bar.

PRICE E53
OPEN 12 am to 3 pm and 7 pm to 11pm
CLOSED Sun, Mon
CREDIT CARDS AE, DC, MC, V

VENICE RESTAURANTS

DORSODURO

AGLI ALBORETTI

Rio Terà Antonio Foscarini, Dorsoduro 882
Tel 041 5230058

This place was once an artists' haunt, but today the retro elegance, impeccable service and an enviable kitchen attract people who know their food. The quality and freshness of the raw materials are beyond doubt, and special attention is paid to balancing textures and flavours, then enhancing them with sauces and spices. Try the *baccalà mantecato* with a timbale of crispy potatoes on a bed of stewed *radicchio trevigiano*; pumpkin risotto with diamonds of tarragon-flavoured cuttlefish; or baked sea bream with spiced bread and brandy-baked mussels. The cheese trolley will satisfy even the pickiest and there's an especially interesting wine list, with an emphasis on *vini da meditazione* and grappas. Excellent value for money. Tables indoors and out.

PRICE E55
CLOSED Wed, Thur morning
CREDIT CARDS AE, MC, V

DORSODURO

LA BITTA

Calle Lunga San Barnaba, Dorsoduro 27531
Tel 041 5230531

An *osteria*-cum-restaurant with a limited menu of vegetable and meat dishes. It's plainly decorated, with white walls and dark, waist-high panelling, but that doesn't signify much because the atmosphere is friendly. You might find *grana* cheese salad; *penne* pasta with smoked speck ham and pumpkin; or Irish fillet steak. The wine list is interesting and there are tasty *cicheti* at the bar. OK if you just want a drink at the bar.

PRICE E40
Open 6 pm to 2 am
CLOSED Sun
CREDIT CARDS AE, MC, V

VENICE RESTAURANTS

CANNAREGIO

DA ALBERTO

Calle Larga Giacinto Gallina, Cannaregio 5401
Tel 041 5238153

Located between Campo Santi Giovanni e Paolo and the beautiful Miracoli church, this *trattoria* offers and comfort and refreshment to locals, and to tourists. Served straight from the bar come fried sardines and *baccalà*; excellent meatballs; shrimps and boiled *latti di sepia*. You will find *nerveti* with onion or *museto* in winter, and *castraure* in spring. If you take a table, the menu offers a range of pastas and risottos, fish or shellfish and vegetables, mixed seafood fries, grilled fish, steamed cuttlefish and *baccalà* with polenta. OK just to have a drink at the bar.

PRICE E32
OPEN 10 am to 3 pm, 6 pm to 11pm
CLOSED Sun
CREDIT CARDS MC, V

CANNAREGIO

L'ANGOLO DI TANIT

Calle dell'Aseo, Cannaregio 1885
Tel 041 720504

At last, a genuine Sicilian eatery in Venice. This friendly restaurant-cum-osteria was opened recently in a quiet *calle* by Signor Battista who is, of course, from Sicily. It offers a limited but daily-changing menu: you might find *caponata* (aubergine, celery, tomatoes, onions, capers and olives sautéed in oil and served with a sweet and sour dressing); *spaghetti* with *pesto trapanese* (made with fresh tomatoes, garlic, basil, almonds and olive oil); a fish couscous; tuna with capers and olives; and to finish, *cannoli*. Friendly atmosphere. Short list of Sicilian wines. OK just to have a drink at the bar.

PRICE E44
CLOSED Sun, Tues
CREDIT CARDS not accepted

VENICE RESTAURANTS

CANNAREGIO

ANICE STELLATO

Fondamenta della Sensa, Cannaregio 3272
Tel 041 720744

The name says it all. *Anice stellato* is a star anise, and the theme here is spices and aromatic herbs. They will perfume your *carpaccio* of tuna or swordfish; your fresh salmon or the sea bream; the steamed *barboni*; the *tagliatelle* with scampi; the courgette flowers; or the fish risotto.

Careful preparation, creative cooking and effort hunting out the best ingredients have, in few years, turned this small out-of-the-way place into a successful enterprise. Run by a well-organized family team, the place also has a reputation for value for money. Book well in advance. Between meals, the bar is open for *ombre* and *cicheti*. Tables indoors and out. A favourite.

PRICE E34
OPEN 10 am to 2 pm and 7 pm to 10pm
CLOSED Mon, Tues
CREDIT CARDS AE, DC, MC, V

CANNAREGIO

DA BEPI – GIÀ 54

Campo Santi Apostoli, Cannaregio 4550
Tel 041 5285031

A This is strategically placed at the intersection of three major Venetian thoroughfares: one from Strada Nuove and the station; one from Rialto and one from Fondamente Nuove. It's a favoured spot with Venetians, who sit at the tables outside, watch the world go by and chat with the young *oste*. The menu has classic Venetian fish dishes, for example *canoce*, *caparossoli*, seafood risotto and cuttlefish with polenta. More workaday dishes include *pasta e fasioi*, gnocchi with tomato or grilled steak.

PRICE E39
CLOSED Thurs
CREDIT CARDS MC, V

VENICE RESTAURANTS

CANNAREGIO

DA BES – TRE SPIEDI

Salizada San Cancian, Cannaregio 5906
Tel 041 5208035

This is an old-fashioned *trattoria* run by two brothers who are married to two sisters. They make a friendly, unpretentious family team and attract a faithful clientele of locals as well as plenty of *foresti* who happen to be in the know. (*Foresti* translates as foreigner, but to Venetians it has a particular meaning - anyone who lives *al di là ponte* – 'beyond the bridge' – i.e. on the mainland.) Mixed fish starters, such as *latti di sepia* and *foleti*; the traditional *saor*; *spaghetti* with *caparossoli*; fish risottos and, of course, *baccalà*. To round it off, have a *sgropin*. First come, first served: bookings not accepted.

PRICE E39
CLOSED Sun evening, Mon
CREDIT CARDS AE, MC, V

CANNAREGIO

BOCCADORO

Campiello Widman, or dei Biri, Cannaregio 5405a
Tel 041 5211021

A bright new restaurant in the broad *campo* on the way from the Miraoli church to the Fondamente Nuove ferry for the northern lagoon islands. The chef, Davide, is young but professional. He specializes in the freshest of fish – so fresh that it's almost a shame to cook it. In fact, some things on the menu are indeed raw: try the oysters or raw swordfish and tuna. The shrimps and fan shell scallops are excellent, too. Or you could have grilled *canestre*; *gnocchetti* with mussels; or dory with *castraure*. Plenty of Sardinian cheeses, and Sardinian wines are offered - no prizes for guessing where the proprietors come from. Tables indoors and out. OK just to have a drink at the bar.

PRICE E50
CLOSED Mon
CREDIT CARDS AE, MC, V

VENICE RESTAURANTS

CA' D'ORO – ALLA VEDOVA

Ramo Ca' d'Oro, Cannaregio 3912
Tel 041 5285324

A The best-known of Cannaregio's historic *osterie* and a mandatory stop on any *giro di ombre* in Strada Nuova. *Giro di ombre* means a pre-dinner stroll, taking in a glass of wine and *cicheti*. Bags of atmosphere: people stand around waiting for tables, eating meat balls from napkins and drinking wine from jugs. A wide range of *cicheti*, covering almost the entire range of traditional Venetian cuisine – predictable, but excellent. You'll find whitebait; meatballs; *folepti consi*; grilled, boiled and stuffed vegetables; *castraure baccalà*; skewered shrimps; *sepe roste* (grilled cuttlefish) and much more. The choice of draught wines is a bonus. If you want more than a snack at the bar, book a table well in advance. However, we recommend Ca' d'Oro mainly for its *cicheti*. 'Very friendly, very local, very nice' writes George Pownall, guest contributor to the hotels section of the guide.

PRICE E32
OPEN 11.30 am to 2.30 pm and 6.30pm to 10.30pm
CLOSED Sun morning, Thurs
CREDIT CARDS not accepted

LA CANTINA

Campo San Felice, Cannaregio 3689
Tel 041 5228258

A wonderful place for people watching: the tables outside give you a grandstand view of the passers-by hurrying along Strada Nuova as you sip a Prosecco, a draught beer or perhaps a bottle suggested by Andrea. At the same time, savour a mouthwatering small *pannini*; or a *bruschetta* with roast pork, smoked beef, gorgonzola, anchovies, baby artichokes, olive pate, or sun-dried tomatoes; or with quail's eggs and grilled asparagus, burrata cheese and *aringa sciocca* (unsalted herring), pears with parmesan and horseradish *mostarda*. Sometimes there are fresh *tartufi di mare* (*Venus verrucosa* shellfish) gathered by hand. Regulars enjoying perching on the stools at the bar, swapping tales with Francesco and watching him prepare his irresistible *crostini*.

PRICE all dishes cost a few euros
Open 10 am to 10 pm
CLOSED Sun
CREDIT CARDS not accepted

VENICE RESTAURANTS

DA FIORE

Salizada San Giovanni Grisostomo, Cannaregio 5719
Tel 041 5285281

If you want to impress someone special, bring them here. The decoration and ambience is understated but elegant and classic Venetian meat and fish dishes, prepared from the finest ingredients, are offered on a balanced menu that changes with the seasons. Our reporter goes back again and again for the mixed fry of monkfish, squid, soft-shell crab and cuttlefish; and for Mariuccia's sweet trolley, with its honey and hazelnut parfait in a chocolate timbale, or the pears in flaky pastry with fruit sauce. Albino proudly runs the cellar, offering a choice of 900 wines. Tables inside and out.

PRICE E50 to 60
CLOSED Mon morning, Tues
CREDIT CARDS AE, DC, MC, V

CANNAREGIO

DALLA MARISA

Fondamenta San Giobbe, Cannaregio 652b
Tel 041 720211

This place used to be simply a no-nonsense *trattoria* for residents of San Giobbe and one or two adventurous diners from the other side of the Cannaregio *fondamenta*. Today, it has been discovered by outsiders and features in many a travel guide. Fame has not changed it, however, and Marisa continues to do what she knows best. She comes from a family of butchers (*becheri*) and offers a meat-based menu. It features huge plates of *tagliatelle* with duck sauce; risotto with *secoe*; *squassetti alla bechera* (beef in gravy); mixed boiled meats; tripe; and succulent ragouts of venison with seasonal vegetables. Everything is fresh and cooked to order. Tables are much in demand, so book well in advance. At the end, you'll be given a 'doggy bag' with your leftovers. Tables inside and out. One of our favourites.

PRICE E27
CLOSED Sun, Mon and Wed evening
CREDIT CARDS not accepted

VENICE RESTAURANTS

CANNAREGIO

VINI DA GIGIO

Fondamenta San Felice, Cannaregio 3628a
Tel 041 5285140

Just off Strada Nuova, by the church of San Felice, is one of the best-value restaurants in Venice. Plenty of people know this, so book well in advance. The comfortable dining rooms and small tables are ideal for small groups – say four or five. Despite it being busy, you can eat well, without being hurried. The service is exceptionally courteous, and you won't feel pushed.

Specialities include the raw fish antipasto, *baccalà* croquettes, beef *carpaccio*, *penne* pasta with *granseola* or gorgonzola and pistachios, grilled eel, fried fish, *masorino alla buranella* (Burano-style duck) and *fegato alla veneziana*. There's an impressive list of Italian and international wines (likewise grappas from the Veneto and Friuli), and the waiters will give honest advice on what to choose to go with your food. Don't miss the puddings, including the fruit *crostata*. One of our favourites.

PRICE E44
CLOSED Mon
CREDIT CARDS MC, V

LAGOON ISLANDS - GIUDECCA

MISTRÀ

Giudecca 212a
Tel 041 5220743

Disembark at the Redentore, turn your back on the city, and head down a narrow alley that will take you to the far side of Giudecca with its magical outlook on to the south lagoon. On the first floor of an abandoned industrial building (with great views from the outside staircase) you will find a well-lit restaurant offering a blend of Ligurian and Venetian cuisine. The midday menu is short and inexpensive, for the benefit of local dock workers – staples are pasta with *bolognese* sauce and steak. In the evening, you'll be offered, in addition: well-prepared fish; octopus and potato salad; *trofie* pasta with pesto; *spaghetti al cartoccio* and fish baked or grilled in salt.

PRICE E28/43
CLOSED Mon evening, Tues
CREDIT CARDS AE, DC, MC, V

Hotel & Restaurant names

In this index hotels and restaurants are arranged in order of the most distinctive part of their name: very common prefixes such as 'il' and 'la' are placed after their name, but more descriptive words such as 'Castello', 'Locanda' and 'Villa' are included in the name. *Restaurants are shown in italics.*

HOTEL & RESTAURANT NAMES

Hotel & Restaurant names

Hotel & Restaurant names

Hotel & Restaurant locations

A
Alberé di Tenna, Margherita 181
Alzate Brianza, Villa Odescalchi 132
Arcugnano, Villa Michelangelo 124
Argegno, Villa Belvedere 158
Asolo, Al Sole 102
Asolo, Duse 124
Asolo, Villa Cipriani 103

B
Bannia di Fiume Veneto, Ultimo Mulino, l' 190
Barbarano, Castello, il 104
Barbiano, Bad Dreikirchen 163
Bellagio, Florence 133
Bellagio, Hotel du Lac 134
Bellagio, Pergola, la 135
Bergamo, Gourmet, il 136
Bressanone, Dominik 164
Bressanone, Elephant 165

C
Caldaro, Leuchtenburg 166
Cannero Riviera, Cannero 137
Castelfranco Veneto, Al Moretto 135
Castelrotto, Cavallino d'Oro 181
Cavaso del Tomba, Locanda alla Posta 125
Cervesina, Castello di San Gaudenzio 138
Clusane-sul-Lago, Relais Mirabella 158
Cognola di Trento, Villa Madruzzo 182
Colfosco, Cappella 182
Cortina d'Ampezzo, Menardi 126
Corvara, Perla, la 183
Costermano, Locanda San Verolo 126

E
Erbusco, Albereta, l' 139

F
Fié allo Sciliar, Moarhof 183
Fié allo Sciliar, Turm 167
Follina, Hotel dei Chiostri 106
Follina, Villa Abazzia 105

G
Garda, San Vigilio 118
Gardone Riviera, Dimora Bolsone 140
Gardone Riviera, Villa Fiordaliso 141
Gardone Riviera, Villa del Sogno 159
Gargagnago, Foresteria Serègo Alighieri 107
Gargnano, Baia d'Oro 142
Gargnano, Hotel du Lac 159
Gargnano, Villa Feltrinelli 143
Gargnano, Villa Giulia 144

I
Iseo, I due Roccoli 145
Isola de Pescatori, Verbano 146

L
Lagundo, Der Pünthof 168
La Villa, Villa, la 188
Lazise, Alla Grotta 108
Lenno, San Giorgio 147
Levada, Gargan 109
Località Monte-Berico, Albergo San Raffaele 131
Località Sorgive, Tenuta le Sorgive 157

M
Madonna di Campiglio, Chalet Hermitage 184
Malcesine, Bellevue San Lorenzo 110
Maleo, Sole 148

Hotel & Restaurant locations

HOTEL & RESTAURANT LOCATIONS

HOTEL & RESTAURANT LOCATIONS

MENU DECODER

A selection of the words and phrases that visitors find hardest to understand on Venice menus. Plurals are shown in brackets:

Aciughèta (aciughète)	anchovy
al Cartòccio	baked in sealed paper or foil parcel
Anguèla (anguèle)	sand smelt, common small lagoon fish
Antipàsto (antipàsti)	starter
Àmolo (àmoli)	damson
Ànara (ànare)	duck
Arancìno (arancìni)	fried breaded rice ball with meat/cheese
Armelìn (armelìni)	apricot
Articiòco (articiòci)	artichoke
Asià	spiny dogfish
Baccalà	dried cod
Baccalà alla vincentìna	dried cod cooked in tomatoes and olives
Baccalà mantecato	dried cod blended with oil, garlic, parsley
Bàcaro (bàcari)	*see* Osterìa
Bagìgi	peanuts
Baìcoli	dry Venetian biscuits
Baìcolo	young sea bass
Barbòn (barbòni)	red mullet
Barbunsàl	cooked calfs chin eaten cold with vinegar
Bechèr (bechèri)	butcher
Bevaràssa (bevaràsse)	cockle or clam
Biancomangiàre	milk pudding with cinnamon, lemon, nuts
Bìgoli	coarse spaghetti
Bìgoli in salsa	as above with onions and anchovies
Birìn	smallest measure of beer (about 10cl)
Birèta (birète)	small glass of beer (about 20cl)
Bisàto	adult eel
Bisi	peas
Bògio	boiling
Bòsega	grey mullet
Bovoléti	snails with garlic and parsley
Bòvolo (bòvoli)	circular venetian bread roll
Branzìno	sea bass
Bruscàndoli	wild hop buds used in risottos
Bruschétta (bruschétte)	toasted bread rubbed with garlic and oil
Bussolài buranèi	ring shaped biscuits made with egg
Bussolài ciosòti	savoury ring shaped biscuit
Butìro	butter
Canarìn	digestive drink of lemon in hot water
Canestrèlo (canestrèli)	queen scallop
Canòce	mantis prawn
Caparòssolo	cross-cut carpet shell
Capatònda/margaròta	bivalve mollusc from the lagoon
Capelònghe/càpe da dèo	razor shell
Capesante	fan shell scallop
Caragòl	a variety of winkle-like molluscs
Carlèti	bladder campion, leaves used in cooking
Carpàccio	thin slices of raw meat or fish
Castradìna	castrated ram meat, served with cabbage
Castraùre	small spring artichokes, fried or battered
Cichèto (cichèti)	Venetian tapas
Clintòn	an illegal wine from an American grape
Cògoma (cògome)	coffee pot
Cotolétta alla Milanése	breaded veal cutlet

MENU DECODER

Cochetìno	pork sausage, served boiled
Cràf	doughnut
Crèma frìta	breaded, fried egg custard
Crostàta (crostàte)	uncovered sweet pastry tart
Crostìno (crostìni)	toasted bread with savoury topping
Curasàn	Venetian pronunciation of croissant
Dìndio	turkey
Durèlo (durèli)	chicken gizzard
Enotèca (enotèche)	wine shop, may serve wine by the glass
Fasiòl (fasiòi)	kidney beans
Fenòcio (fenòci)	fennel
Figà	liver
Figà a la Veneziana	thin slices of liver cooked with onions
Fiorentìna	t-bone steak
Folpèto/moscardìno	octopus with one row of suckers
Folpèto (folpèti)	baby octopus
Folpèti cònsi	as above boiled with carrots and celery
Fòlpo (fòlpi)	common octopus
Fragolìn	wine made from American grapes
Frègola (frègole)	crumb
Fritoìn	fried fish stall
Frìtola (frìtole)	raisin and pine nut fritter
Fugàssa (fugàsse)	flat bread; focàccia (focàcce)
Galàni	sweet pastry rolled thin and fried
Garùsolo (garùsoli)	sea snail
Gnocchéti	small gnòcchi
Gnòcchi	potato dumplings
Gò	goby
Gransèola (gransèole)	edible crab
Grànso	common shore crab
Latte (latti) di seppia	contents of cuttlefish egg or sperm sac
Lièvaro (lièvari)	hare
Lugànega (lugàneghe)	long thin sausage
Maneghèto (managhèti)	beer served in a jug (about 20 cl)
Masanèta (masanète)	female common shore crab
Mazzancòlla (mazzancòlle)	shallow water prawn
Misticànza	mixed baby greens salad
Moèca (moèche)	male common shore crab
Mostàrda	mixed fruit chutney
Mozzarèlla in Carròzza	mozzarella and anchovy sandwich, fried
Musèto (musèti)	similar to cochetino, served with lentils
Munèghéte	Venetian popcorn
Mùsso (mùssi)	donkey
Narànsa (narànse	orange
Nervèti	boiled veal cartilage with onion, parsley
Nicolòta	stale bread and milk, flour, raisins, fennel
Novellàme	young sea fish
Oràda (oràde)	gilthead or sea bream
Òste (òsti)	owner or manager of an Osterìa
Osterìa (òsterie)	wine bar with snacks or simple food
Òmbra/ombréta	red or white wine drunk at the bar
Osèi Scampài	skewered beef, veal or pork
Ossocòlo	pressed collar of pork
Panàda Venexiàna or Pan bògio all'ògio	bread soup with garlic, oil, bay leaf and parmesan
Pancétta	fatty pork belly

MENU DECODER

Panìno (panìni)	filled roll
Panòcia (panòce)	corn on the cob
Parsèmolo	parsley
Parsùto	ham (Prosciutto)
Passarìn (passarìni)	small plaice
Pàsta e fasiòi	thick pasta and bean soup
Pastìccio (pastìcci)	leftovers mixed with polenta and baked
Peòchio (peòci)	mussels
Persegàda	quince jam
Pesse novèllo	*see* Novellame
Perveràda	bread, stock, spices and cheese sauce
Piadìna (piadìne)	flat round unleavened bread
Pìnsa	cake made at Epiphany
Piròn (piròni)	fork
Polènta	coarsely ground cornflour
Pòmo (pòmi)	apple
Polàstro (polàstri)	chicken
Porcìno (porcìni)	cep or penny bun mushroom
Prìmo (prìmi)	first course
Prosciùtto crùdo	air cured ham
Puìna	ricotta cheese
Radìcchio trevigiàno/di Trevìso	red leaf chicory, a speciality of Treviso
Rìsi e bìsi	rice soup with peas
Rosàda	custard
Rumegàl	calfs gullet
Saltimbócca	sauteed chicken or veal escalope
Sanguèto	black pudding
Saòr	marinade
Sarde in saòr	sardines with onion, pine nuts, raisins
Sarèsa (sarèse)	cherry
Schìla (schìe)	small grey shrimp, from the lagooon
S'ciòso (s'ciòsi)	snail
Scugèr (scugèri)	spoon
Sècoe	meat used in risottos
Secóndo (secóndi)	second course
Sèpe nère	cuttlefish, often cooked in their ink
Sègola (sègole)	onion
Sfògio (sfògi)	sole
Sgropìn (sgropìni)	lemon, vodka and Prosecco sorbet
Sòpa coàda	bread and roast pigeon soup
Soprèssa	country style pork salami
Spàreso (spàresi)	asparagus
Spiènsa	spleen
Sprìtz	white wine with Amaro and soda
Spumìlia (spumìlie)	meringue
Stracaganàse	dried chestnuts (literally 'jaw strainers')
Stròpolo	bottle top or cork
Sùca	pumpkin
Sùgoli	dessert made with American grapes
Sùpa	soup
Tècia	pan or frying pan
Tegolìne	French beans
Tetìna	cow's udder
Tirimesù/tiramisù	dessert with coffee, marscapone, biscuits
Tochèto (tochèti)	small piece
Tòcio	sauce

Menu decoder

Tòla	table
Torbolìn	young, still cloudy wine
Tramezzìno (tramezzìni)	white bread sandwich with no crust
Vedèlo (vedèli)	calf
Vìno (vini) da meditazióne	complex medium sweet to sweet wine
Vóngola veràce (vóngole veràce)	*see* Caparòssolo
Vòvo (vòvi)	egg; mèso vòvo is a popular bar snack of half a boiled egg
Zabaiòn	custard with cinnamon and fortified wine
Zalèto (zalèti)	yellow biscuit with raisins

SPECIAL OFFERS

Buy your *Charming Small Hotel Guide* by post directly
from the publisher and you'll get a worthwhile discount. *

Titles available:	Retail price	Discount price
Austria	£10.99	£9.50
Britain	£12.99	£10.50
France	£13.99	£11.50
Germany	£11.99	£8.50
Greece	£10.99	£9.50
Italy	£11.99	£10.50
Mallorca, Menorca & Ibiza	£9.99	£8.50
Southern France	£10.99	£9.50
Spain	£11.99	£9.50
Switzerland	£9.99	£8.50
USA: New England	£10.99	£9.50

Please send your order to:

Book Sales,
Duncan Petersen Publishing Ltd,
31 Ceylon Road, London W14 0PY

enclosing: 1) the title you require and number of copies
2) your name and address
3) your cheque made out to:
Duncan Petersen Publishing Ltd

*Offer applies to this edition and to UK only.

Visit charmingsmallhotels.co.uk
Our website has expanded enormously since
its launch and continues to grow. It's the
best research tool on the web for our kind of
hotel.

Exchange rates
As we went to press, $1 bought 0.82 euros
and £1 bought 1.45 euros